Feminism and Deconstruction

Ms. en abyme

Diane Elam

London and New York

First published 1994
by Routledge
11 New Fetter Lane London EC4P 4EE

Simultaneously published in the USA and Canada
by Routledge
29 West 35th Street, New York NY 10001

© 1994 Diane Elam

Phototypeset in Times by Intype, London
Printed and bound in Great Britain by
TJ Press (Padstow) Ltd, Padstow, Cornwall

British Library Cataloguing in Publication Data
A catalogue record for this book is available from the
British Library.

Library of Congress Cataloging in Publication Data

Elam, Diane
   Feminism and deconstruction / Diane Elam.
      p.   cm.
   Includes bibliographical references and index.
   1. Feminist theory.   2. Deconstruction.   I. Title.
HQ1190.E4   1994
305.42'01--dc20   93–37369
                                                                          CIP

ISBN 0–415–09165–9   0–415–09166–7 (pbk)

9.99

FE~~MINISM AND DECONSTRUCTION~~

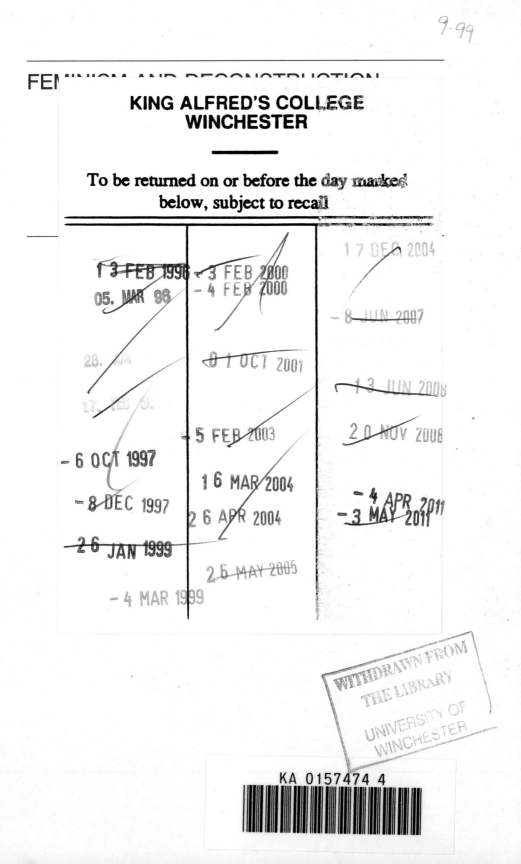

QUESTION: I guess I'm asking you to explain how woman as man's "random drift" is different from woman as man's "truth."

RESPONSE: This is an abyssal question, for there is a certain determination of truth which permits one to answer that woman as truth is that which stops the drift, that which interrupts and assures truth. But there is a way of thinking about truth which is more adventurous, risky. And at that point, truth, which is without end, abyssal, is the very movement of the drift. There is a way of thinking about truth which is not reassuring, which is not in general what we think of truth. That would bring us into a discourse about the truth of truth, and Heidegger who says that truth is non-truth; the field is open. As is the case with women's studies and any discipline, at a certain moment one can no longer improvise or hurry. You have to go slowly, look at things in detail. At a certain point it is necessary to stop; one cannot improvise on a question of truth. It would not be surprising, considering all the fields of research in women's studies, that one day, in a program of Women's Studies, there will be the question of truth, and that someone will spend three or four years researching "truth."[1]

1 "Women in the Beehive: A Seminar with Jacques Derrida," *Men in Feminism*, ed. Alice Jardine and Paul Smith (New York and London: Methuen, 1987), 203.

For WJR

Contents

Acknowledgments   xi

1 Unnecessary introductions   1
Introductions   1
Definitions   4
Theories   6
Movements   8
Philosophies   9
Crossdisciplines   11
And   13
Estrangement   15
Tool-boxes and pedagogics   19
The abyss   24
Obligations   25

2 Questions of women   27
Undetermined or determined?   27
Her-story or his-story?   35
Gender or sex?   42
Linguistic or material girl?   58

3 Towards a groundless solidarity   67
Political differences   67
Subject to change: identity politics   69
To be negotiated: the politics of the undecidable   81

INSTITUTIONAL INTERRUPTIONS   89
1: Institutions?   89
2: Academic?   91
3: Disciplines?   95
4: Philosophy?   98
5: Women's studies?   100
6: The future of disciplinarity?   103

4 Groundless solidarity   105
Ethical activism   105
Turning away from subjective agency   106
Taking a distance from pragmatism   111
Approaching an impossible justice   115

Notes   121
Index   151

Acknowledgments

Almost every book is written to be read, but this one had the special help of a number of readers who graciously read it as it was being written. Sabina Sawhney, Robyn Wiegman, and Steve Watt unselfishly read the entire manuscript and gave me invaluable revision suggestions at every step of the way. Judith Butler and Drucilla Cornell offered timely words of encouragement over the past few years. Talia Rodgers, Sue Roe, Jane Mayger, and Fiona Parker have lent their crucial support at Routledge.

I also could not have written this book without my students. The women of Bryn Mawr helped me to understand why I needed to write it, and I continue to owe a special debt to those who attended my seminar on deconstruction. I'm also grateful for the input from my graduate seminar on feminism and deconstruction at Indiana University. They first heard many of the ideas in this book and improved it immeasurably with their questions. Here I especially would like to thank Donya Samara and Yung-Hsing Wu, as well as Elizabeth Kuhlmann who prepared the index and offered invaluable research assistance.

Indiana University provided summer faculty research funds and grants-in-aid, while Steve Watt and Jim Naremore graciously wrote more recommendation letters in support of this project than they probably care to remember. Portions of this book appear in altered form in "Ms. en abyme: Deconstruction and Feminism," *Social Epistemology* 4, 3 (1990), and in "Doing Justice to Feminism," *Surfaces* II, 9 (1992).

Finally, my biggest debt is to Bill Readings, who lived with this project from beginning to end. He has read every word more than once, and his contribution is greater than I can describe.

Montréal 1993

Chapter 1

Unnecessary introductions

INTRODUCTIONS ✓

How do feminism and deconstruction go together, if at all? Does deconstruction need to be feminized? Or does feminism need to be deconstructed? In either case, it would be possible to be seduced by a narrative of initial mistrust and final reconciliation. However, I am not going to tell the kind of story in which feminism learns to love the hand that corrects the error of her ways, learns to appreciate proper theoretical rigor. Nor am I going to propose that what we need is either a kinder and gentler deconstruction or a deconstruction that can be put back in touch with real problems by the mediating action of women. Thus, rather than introducing feminism and deconstruction to each other or tracing the story of their partnership, I want to argue that there is an interest in setting these two ways of thinking (which do not make a pair) alongside each other, and that this interest does not simply reside in the question of what either one may usefully learn from a partnership with the other.

So, not "how do they go together?" but "how are they beside each other?". Initially, the two seem to have little in common. Feminism seems to be a political project, whereas deconstruction appears more philosophical or literary. By this account, their mutual interests do not converge. Such an argument does indeed have some merit in so far as *convergence* is *not* the right way to characterize the interaction between feminism and deconstruction. Instead, I will argue that feminism and deconstruction are beside one another in that they share a parallel *divergence* from (or dislocation of) politics and philosophy. On the one hand, feminism shifts the ground of the political, interrogating the opposition between the public and the private spheres. On the other hand, deconstruction displaces our understanding of how theory relates to practice by rethinking the opposition of philosophical reflection to political action. To draw this distinction out a bit further, it would be fair to say that feminism necessarily upsets the way we think about politics because its activist political movement is inseparable from a critique of the history of representation.

And it's inseparable because of a notion of solidarity. Deconstruction upsets the way we think about philosophy because its analysis of the philosophical tradition is inseparable from an attention to the performative effects of the discourse of analysis itself. This is what distinguishes deconstruction from ideology critique. In short, then, these double displacements undo the map of intellectual and social space inherited from the Enlightenment, and this book will argue that such untying is of crucial contemporary relevance.

The contemporary relevance of setting feminism and deconstruction beside one another may not, however, be immediately transparent. Feminism's academic success has been accompanied by an anti-feminist backlash in contemporary North America, and the high academism by which deconstruction is often characterized would hardly seem to be just what the doctor ordered. My sense that it is worthwhile to consider deconstruction and feminism together *now* takes issue with this view on two points. First, I am suspicious of distinctions between academic and practical feminism: in contemporary Western society, being a woman is just as much a philosophical as it is a practical problem. Secondly, I do not believe that deconstruction is as merely academic as it is often made out to be: deconstruction helps one to think about the schizophrenic complexity of contemporary experiences of time and representation.

But is this really saying anything very new? After all, I am hardly the first to take up the possible relationship between feminism and deconstruction, so in a sense the answer is "no."[1] The book does not have a title like "A New Theory of Woman," because I think one needs to have a healthy disregard for the static prescriptions embedded in modernist manifestos of that sort. I hope, instead, to have approached my topic with a different sort of logic. The introductory chapter will be concerned with the various ways that feminism and deconstruction have been paired – as theories, as movements, as philosophies, and as disciplines. What follows, however, is not a mere summary of positions that have already been mapped out in advance of their exposition. What will be different about this book is not its content (there are other discussions of deconstruction and feminism), but rather the kind of metonymic links or *enchaînements* it makes possible *between* and *within* elements.[2] The emphasis, then, is not so much on sorting out answers as it is on posing questions and examining their ethico-political effects.

With that in mind, it is worth saying a few words about the organization of this book. My argument could have moved in any number of directions after it sorted through the general concerns which arise when deconstruction and feminism are placed beside one other. I have chosen to focus on areas which strike me as particularly important. Chapter 2 takes up a series of questions which have been central to feminism: What are women and what can they do? Can gender be distinguished from sex? Where does an emphasis on representation leave the materiality of women's bodies and the reality of women's experiences? Chapter 3 considers how feminism and deconstruction allow us to rethink the political and explore the possibility that there is indeed life after identity politics. The concluding chapter considers how feminism and deconstruction give rise to an ethics best understood as groundless solidarity and ethical activism.

However, even the arguments these chapters contain are not meant to be exhaustive. I have tried to offer a series of notes which indicate some of the other areas that could be explored and the other approaches that could be taken. These notes outline previous work and ongoing debates on a variety of issues, and should be used in parallel to my own argument. At one point, this structure, which is designed to preserve the flow of discussion, actually takes on a life of its own. The "Institutional Interruptions" that intervene between Chapter 3 and Chapter 4 should best be understood as a long footnote, which itself tries to reflect upon the problem of situating the debate between feminism and deconstruction.

In this respect, the unfinished nature of the book is constitutive rather than accidental. I have no pretensions that I have told the entire story of feminism and deconstruction, or even that there is an entire story to tell. Likewise, I have no investment in the belief that the final chapter must contain the obligatory happy ending of conjugal bliss. So while my argument wants to imagine the multiple interactions, the variety of intersections of feminism and deconstruction in the hopes of a possibility of social justice, I am steering clear of the heterosexual paradigm that has frequently been unjustly offered up for the couple's theoretical presentation, just as I hope to avoid any suggestion of producing the final word on "feminism and deconstruction." This book promises neither "resolution nor revolution," as Robyn Wiegman would put it, although it may offer interminable analysis.[3]

For this reason, if there is a structuring principle behind my argument it is the insistence on the formulation of questions rather than the search for conclusive answers. And these questions, as I hope I have indicated, include those which interrogate the book's own organizing principles, political effects, and ethical implications. That is to say, I am arguing that the real work of the juxtaposition of feminism and deconstruction is the possibility it creates for certain questions to be asked – questions with political-ethical implications, including the epistemological question of who knows more, the one who asks, or the one who replies? Here both feminism and deconstruction share a refusal to privilege the answer over the question in thinking.

The question of privilege also relates to the status accorded to the two protagonists of my title. I think that feminism can do as much for deconstruction as deconstruction can do for feminism; however, it would be an error to think that this implies that we can reach an ideal balance or harmony between the two. As I have said, there is no conjugal happy ending. So I have tried to make this book function like a Rorschach ink blot test, in which what the reader finds will depend on where she or he reads from. Those primarily interested in deconstruction may find an argument for thinking seriously about feminism, while those who have learnt to think in feminism may find themselves moved to take deconstruction more seriously. There exists no neutral reader, and other possibilities will no doubt arise (although those who come to this book with a burning interest in landscape gardening are likely to find little to stimulate them). In short, what I am trying to suggest is that feminism and deconstruction are not mirror images of one another, and it would thus be impossible to treat them in symmetrical ways.

DEFINITIONS ✓

Given that supplying answers is not the only task of thinking and that there will be several ways to read this book, I want to turn to the problems which accompany the attempt to understand the terms of my discussion. The reader may be entitled to expect some answers, for example, to the questions "what is feminism?" and "what is deconstruction?" The answer to both these questions is the same: "it is not, in any simple way, one thing."

To understand why this is so, it is important to recall that definitions work on the basis of consensus, on general agreement as to what words or phrases mean.[4] Limits must necessarily be imposed in order to fix the definition in either synchronic or diachronic terms. However necessary this process is for everyday communication, the danger of thinking you know it all is at no time greater than when it comes to grasping hold of definitions. Definitions threaten to function like final answers which erase the fact that there were ever any questions asked in the first place; their status becomes unshakable, almost natural, and rarely if ever interrogated.

Thus, I think it would be a mistake to offer up easy definitions of either feminism or deconstruction. In this regard, Alice Jardine seems to me to be on the right track when she hints that we will not solve our problems by reaching a consensus about what "feminism" is or exactly who is or is not a "feminist."[5] The same could be said of "deconstruction" and "deconstructionist." In each instance, not only will "we" fail to solve our problems, we may not even recognize that we have any in the first place if we spend too much time trying to find the right way down the lexicographical road. I would even go so far as to argue that not only is the search for a universally agreed upon definition of "feminism" and "deconstruction" a waste of time, it is also highly undesirable. For once you think you know what "feminism" and "deconstruction" are, then their political and ethical work is done. As I have already hinted, short hand definitions, while practical at times, can easily lead to caricature, dismissal, and unnecessary limits placed on thought and political action.

Still, the argument can be made that what I am doing here is simply taking a longer route to the same defining end. That is to say, the "isness" (*Dasein*) of "feminism" and "deconstruction" will inevitably emerge over the course of the book, finally establishing limits which are unavoidable if not permanently necessary. I will concede that such is the problem of any writing, but however correct that may prove, I nonetheless want to postpone establishing my limits for as long as possible. This book, therefore, will neither begin with definitions nor openly establish them at any point; rather it will let such definitions emerge only as the limits of writing necessarily impose them after the fact. As much as possible, I want to keep the act of naming and defining as a site of contestation, for the question that should continually be posed is: who gets to name what?

As a way to postpone establishing unnecessary limits, as a way to keep open the question "who names?" I want to deploy the terms of my argument in such a way as to embrace a plurality of changing definitions, encourage the thinking of feminisms and deconstructions in the plural.[6] To put it simply, there is no single feminism or deconstruction to define, only feminisms and deconstructions. This is not to insist, however, that there need be a different feminism for every different deconstruction, or vice versa.[7] I want to abandon an easy symmetry between the terms and concede that at times "feminism" becomes dislodged from "deconstruction." One of the problems this book faces is taking into account the plurality within and between feminism and deconstruction, while at the same time acknowledging that these terms do determine realms, categories, or spaces with a certain coherence or rigor.

In putting it this way, I have, of course, raised the possibility that feminism and deconstruction are theories – although not exactly in the scientific or philosophical sense. Feminism and deconstruction would be theories insofar as they are said to describe observable practices and experiences from a meta-discursive position and, as such, proffer knowledge on the basis of which further practices can be elaborated. "Theory" would also be appropriate in the sense that the term, in departments of literature, serves as a kind of catch-all category for certain interdisciplinary work. As Jonathan Culler describes it, "theory" is a genre of works that "exceed the disciplinary framework within which they would normally be evaluated and which would help to identify their solid contributions to knowledge."[8] Significantly, Culler also explains a popular objection to theory's disciplinary challenge:

> Works claimed by the genre [of theory] are studied outside the proper disciplinary matrix: students of theory read Freud without enquiring whether later psychological research may have disputed his formu-

lations; they read Derrida without having mastered the philosophical tradition; they read Marx without studying alternative descriptions of political and economic situations.[9]

In short, theory's skeptics see a sort of willed ignorance at work, a disregard for the knowledge derived from disciplinary contexts. Feminism, of course, provides a challenge – what is its original disciplinary context? What discipline is feminism removed from in the first place? These questions will form part of the focus for my discussion of crossdisciplinarity in "Institutional Interruptions." But without taking up these questions now, it would be possible to say much more simply that referring to deconstruction and feminism as theories possibly provides a way to acknowledge their plurality and connectedness, at the same time that it marks both feminism and deconstruction as excessive in the ways Culler maintains.

And yet another danger of thinking of feminism and deconstruction as theories is that of lapsing into a rigid distinction between theory and practice, the distinction in terms of which deconstructive theory has so often been opposed to feminist practice. For this reason, "theory" is perhaps a bad name for the work Culler describes, an all too easy way to contain political practice. I will take up feminism's and deconstruction's joint engagement with the political in Chapter 3; at this point it is still worth mentioning that feminism and deconstruction are political practices that do not proceed from theories in any simple way. The threat of theory is that it allows us to forget the interaction with praxis. And in light of the seriousness of this memory lapse, I think it is worthwhile to pause and consider in more detail what happens when we begin to think of feminism and deconstruction as theories. In short, I want to point out what we would swallow if we were to take the theoretical bait.

THEORIES ✓

Whether it is used in the name of academic innovation or political revolution, theory takes its toll. Understood as a set of interpretative generalizations which explain particular texts or justify political actions, theory can actually function as a methodology that contracts rather than expands the field of knowledge and the possibilities for political action. In the case of "deconstruction turned theoretical method of literary analysis," a sort of party game atmosphere takes over from serious intellectual work: undermine-the-binary-opposition replaces pin-the-tail-on-the-donkey as favorite pastime. Which is not to slight the value of the latter; sometimes it's hard to tell which, through sheer repetitive methodology, is the more ridiculous exercise. In a different light, or perhaps just at a more sophisticated party, deconstruction too often becomes "deconstructionism" – yet another delicate reading of a poem or novel, yet another girls' and boys' club on the academic theoretical scene.[10] In this instance, we're back to the problem Jardine posed, where too much time and energy is expended on trying to figure out who's in and who's out, who's allowed to wear the official badge "deconstructor."

To say this is not simply to bash deconstruction. There is altogether too much of that in the popular press and in academic essays whose authors rarely bother with a serious engagement with the issues. This is the danger when Derrida's insistence on deconstruction as neither a system nor a methodology has been ignored in favor of theoretical business as usual.[11] The ethical obligations of which deconstruction should remind us are abandoned in favor of institutional recognizability.

Likewise, feminism verges on the possibility of turning into yet another form of thematic criticism appropriated by the academy. The most widespread form of this is an endless series of readings, whose theoretical operations could be described as: 1. find the women in the text; 2. women are oppressed in ——; or 3. women find their voice in ——. While there was certainly a great deal of political force behind the readings which first broached these topics so as to connect readings of representations of women to social and cultural positions of women, how many times must these readings be repeated? Is there another kind of injustice committed when all discussions must revolve around "the problem of women" in history, science, literature, society, etc.? Feminism as thematic criticism (although I would not want to dismiss its legitimacy altogether) tends to forget the variety of inflections of feminism. For some, feminism means equal pay, abortion rights, and a partnership in a law firm. For others, feminism means a celebration of women as separate and distinct from men. To others still, feminism is a subversive ideology used to undermine authority and create alternative power structures. There is no thematic identity to "woman" in these various arguments, which doesn't mean that feminism ought not to support them all in different contexts.

The problem with thematic criticism is that notions of "women's issues," "women's interests," and so on cannot help but imply that there is an identity to "woman," which would legitimate the determination of what the correct interests, attitudes, and concerns of any particular woman or of all women are. What this boils down to is a problem that feminism, especially in her academic gown, shares with deconstruction: the main concern becomes a question of: who's a good feminist and who's a bad daughter? What is correct feminist theory and political action? In this (dis)guise, feminism also threatens to become an old girls' (and sometimes boys') club, organized around the same power structure of the patriarchy that it set out to displace. That is to say, in the strongest version of this theoretical pitfall, feminism takes on the power structure in which hierarchical mothers make certain that their daughters remain dutiful in the name of feminism, or more precisely in the name of *the* theory of feminism.

Again, I think it's worth stating that my remarks about the restrictions potentially imposed in the name of feminism as a theory are not meant to join the chorus of backlash anti-feminists or "post-feminists." I neither simply oppose feminism nor write from a historical moment in which I believe that feminism is over, has done all the work she can do, or has been killed off by the patriarchy that she set out to fight. What I am trying to say is that when feminism fixes its theoretical gaze it is neither immune to appropriation designed to make it lose its political effectiveness nor exempt from committing the same kind of injustices it seeks to oppose.[12]

Trinh Minh-ha compellingly articulates this serious predicament when she argues that:

> Theory no longer is theoretical when it loses sight of its own conditional nature, takes no risks in speculation, and circulates as a form of administrative inquisition. Theory oppresses, when it wills or perpetuates existing power relations, when it presents itself as a means to exert authority – the Voice of Knowledge.[13]

Univocal theoretical methodology threatens to cripple any attempt by feminism and deconstruction to redefine the political or consider ethical obligations. However, it seems to me that salvation does not lie in purifying theory (keeping theory theoretical), as Trinh's remarks imply, but in the refusal of theoretical purity, the refusal to believe that action happens elsewhere. To illustrate this, I would like to return to the important nexus of theory/practice and thus imagine a critical space for feminism and deconstruction which is not simply a theoretical one.

MOVEMENTS

If feminism and deconstruction are neither terms available for definition, nor theories, we may perhaps consider them as "movements." The term already has considerable currency in the feminist context. While "movement" does lend a sense of political coherence around which to negotiate, I would argue that it also can too readily associate itself with common cause identity politics, with political groups composed of leaders with identifiable followers (who "identify" with one another). That a feminism and a deconstruction would want to challenge the foundationalism of identity politics is an important concern that I will take up in Chapter 3; the challenge actually could be said to begin earlier in Chapter 2 with the recognition that there is also no small problem with the deployment of the word "women" – a problem exacerbated in this context by those who seek to oppose the women's movement with the deconstruction movement.

And yet for all these difficulties, "movement" is still not without merit here, for it suggests that feminism and deconstruction, as political movements of sorts, have a historical development in a political context. There is a great deal of political strength to be gained from this description in the appeal to a kind of structural coherence which exerts a political force. In light of these remarks, if I were to describe the focus of this book as being on the feminist and deconstructive movements, such phrasing would suggest that I am tracing the development of their political effectiveness over time. And to a certain extent this book will do that, although it does not really need the term "movement" to make its engagement with historical and political questions clear. In some instances, "movement" even hinders more than it helps in highlighting the way in which this book is a historical project or feminism and deconstruction are political. For just as my argument hopes to challenge commonly held understandings of "the political," it also attempts to rethink its own will to historicity. The book will contain an interrogation of what it would mean to tell a historical story of the relationship between feminism and deconstruction, insofar as history, in the wake of feminism and deconstruction, does not remain the same – either in force or narrative structure. Deconstruction and feminism change what it means to understand the past, to recognize the force of and our obligation to past events. Thus, they cannot best be understood as movements, as the incarnation of modernist projects that seek to erase our obligation to the past in favor of our obligation to the future. The feminist movement has been condemned to a succession of generational tensions over the past eighty years or so, as each daughter claims to be a "new woman," the first to affirm her identity, and each mother complains that the daughter is ignoring an existing struggle – losing her identity, going too far. One important feature of the encounter between feminism and deconstruction is that it allows us to rethink the temporality of feminism's movement, perhaps as something closer to the dance than to Mao's long march.

PHILOSOPHIES

If "movement" proves a less than satisfactory alternative for all occasions, other ready-to-hand choices certainly are available. Since philosophy has traditionally been charged with establishing the relations between disciplines, it would seem the most convenient and obvious choice of a disciplinary ground for the encounter of feminism and deconstruction. Nevertheless, philosophy does not supply an untroubled disciplinary ground upon which to judge the relationship between the two.

The fact that feminism and deconstruction have met at best with chilly receptions in most philosophy departments in the United States speaks to an initial difficulty: there is certainly some territory to be negotiated here. One of the problems is that some philosophers do not consider either feminism or deconstruction to be philosophy, properly speaking. Likewise, some feminists have sought to discard the Western philosophical tradition as irrevocably patriarchal. Deconstruction has evinced a similar uncertainty about its relation to philosophy. While Derrida insists that he has never done anything but philosophy, some epigones have identified deconstruction as the triumph of writing (or literature) over philosophy.[14] Historically speaking, philosophy in the West has emphasized a notion of universal or absolute truth, of which deconstructors have been suspicious and of which women (among others) have been the victims.

But these are not the only problems in considering deconstruction and feminism both as philosophies. It would be unfair not to mention the increasing disciplinary divide between analytic or ordinary language philosophy, logic, and speculative philosophy – and each camp would certainly want to carve up feminism and deconstruction in their own ways, some dismissing them altogether from the realm of serious philosophy. If that is not enough, it would also be possible to say that there no longer is any such thing as philosophy in which deconstruction and feminism could participate. Such is the argument in Heidegger's late writing, where he claims that "philosophy is ending in the present age" because "it has found its place in the scientific attitude of socially active humanity."[15]

Leaving aside for the moment Heidegger's complaint and discarding an interest in whether philosophy has a disciplinary method of its own which would thus determine feminism's and deconstruction's status, I think the most significant obstacle or resistance to the wholesale appropriation of the term "philosophy" is that feminism and deconstruction can be considered philosophies, can "belong" to the discipline of philosophy, only if we rethink what it is we mean by "philosophy" and what it might mean to belong to its discipline.[16] The issue here is not one of "add gender and stir," or deconstructive party games invading the serious halls of wisdom. Rather, the double bind is that feminist philosophy turns into feminist readings of philosophy, deconstructive philosophy depends upon the deconstruction of philosophy. That is to say, there is no use in trying to fit feminism and deconstruction into the pre-existing disciplinary boundaries of "philosophy" if those disciplinary borders cannot be renegotiated as deconstruction and feminism insist they must. While I will hold open the possibility that these borders can and have been renegotiated, that deconstruction and feminism are philosophy in a certain sense, I do not think that it is particularly useful to listen to the conversation between feminism and deconstruction solely positioned in the philosopher's seat. Although philosophy will have a certain status in my argument, it will not reign supreme throughout the entire book, not the least because there is always that rhetorical problem, as Derrida well understands, where "philosophy, as a theory of metaphor, first will have been a metaphor of theory."[17]

CROSSDISCIPLINES

Having thus far found fault with the wholesale appropriation of either "theory," "movement," or "philosophy" for the purposes of my argument, I do not mean to give the impression that I am trying to restrict my discussion by insisting on some third term that will establish a common ground which feminism and deconstruction must always share. I am not searching for some common or neutral ground so much as I am hoping to put into play terminology which acknowledges that the work of deconstruction and feminism takes place in a number of spaces, both outside and inside the academy. Thus, I am trying to avoid framing my argument in ways that would automatically align deconstruction and feminism with any particular discipline, movement, or theoretical predisposition.

However, one of the practical effects of feminism has been the development of multi-disciplinary programs in women's studies, which may suggest that one thing deconstruction and feminism share is a disciplinary uncertainty or ambiguity. For this reason, I want to make the case for thinking of them as "crossdisciplines," or in more deconstructive graphics: "disciplines." This process is what Derrida, after Heidegger, has called "putting under erasure." The crossing through is a mark of questioning (a cross-examination), which does not completely obliterate or erase the original term. Rather, the effect of "crossing" or "putting under erasure" is one which is meant to *radicalize* the term in question.[18] By using the term "crossdiscipline," I am deliberately avoiding the term "interdisciplinary," because in my mind it leaves too much of a sense that old disciplinary boundaries still hold up, even if special interdisciplinarians are allowed to traverse them. So, for instance, with an interdisciplinary model in place, feminism may be spotted in philosophy, biology, sociology, and literature, but no radical change need occur within each of these separate disciplines simply because they have allowed for a little interdisciplinarity. To put this another way, interdisciplinary studies can merely amount to the formal presentation of two or more separate but equal disciplines – a sort of "on the one hand, on the other hand" approach, if one could imagine a rhetorical octopus with enough hands to go around. To pursue this analogy, even if the hands "shake," this friendly gesture is usually at the prompting of a will to develop a new disciplinary *model* (based, of course, on "interdisciplinarity"), which still fits comfortably within existing institutional structures. Rather than shaking the disciplinary paradigm, such interdisciplinary work often confirms the territorial boundaries that it is supposed to breach. To think mainly in terms of disciplines and interdisciplines presupposes that the work being done is entirely academic and institutional, something that would be very difficult for feminism, for one, to accept.

By contrast, crossdisciplines, as a way of calling into question the very boundaries of disciplines, can potentially expose the impossibility of containing thought/action within the walls of the ivory tower. I will develop this in more detail in the "Institutional Interruptions," arguing that women's studies potentially is not just another interdisciplinary handshake. But even in this introductory space I think the term "crossdiscipline" best allows for the sense in which deconstruction and feminism do "not aim at *praxis* or theoretical practice but [live] in the persistent crisis or unease of the moment of *techne* or crafting."[19] I borrow Gayatri Spivak's words on deconstruction here, but in this context I think they also apply to feminism, perhaps more so than the Heideggerian echo might make clear. The term "crossdiscipline," I would argue, insists on the crisis or unease of what I would rephrase as the *event* (rather than moment) of *techne* or crafting, in order to get away from the implications of either the singularity or instantaneous act.

In making this substitution, I am borrowing from yet another source, this time Derrida's remarks in "Letter to a Japanese Friend." In his attempt to sort out the problems which surround the problem of translating "deconstruction," Derrida emphasizes – and this would be in line with my earlier discussion of theory – that "in spite of appearances, deconstruction is neither an *analysis* nor a *critique*" nor a *method*.[20] Continuing his negations, Derrida also insists that deconstruction is "not even an *act* or an *operation*," not an idiom or a signature. But Derrida will allow – and this is the point which is most crucial to my own argument – that:

> Deconstruction takes place, it is an *event* that does not await the deliberation, consciousness, or organization of a subject, or even of modernity. *It deconstructs itself. It can be deconstructed* [*Ça se déconstruit*].[21]

Derrida's remarks do not so much apply to feminism as call attention to what is already deconstructive about feminism: the taking place as event without subjective agency or defining historical epoch (which does not mean that deconstruction is inactive or ahistorical).

"Crossdiscipline," then, would be that name for the force of the events of deconstruction and feminism and would go a distance in pulling away from my own storyline. To return to Spivak, it is important to make clear that neither deconstruction nor feminism is merely a narrative, a series of linked events which can be ordered into one coherent storyline, as it were.[22] But nonetheless, and this is why I continue to phrase my argument in terms of telling a story, there is a need to recognize the way in which feminism and deconstruction employ narrative and also have narrative deployed against them. As I will argue throughout this book, their political effectiveness, their ethical force as events, has most readily been understood (and misunderstood) through narration, through the possibility of linking events.

AND

If feminism and deconstruction are each to be thought of as crossdisciplines, I have yet to settle the problem of exactly how the link is to be forged *between* feminism and deconstruction. If neither feminism nor deconstruction is easily defined, perhaps we may make something of the third word in my title. In the way that I have thus far referred to each of them, I have relied on (or at least hinted at) some kind of separation: feminism on one side, deconstruction on the other. The bar that has kept them apart is that little word "and" – that innocuous conjunction, place saver, link, chain, go-between. Yet despite this break, as my stress on events and narration suggests, linking – *enchaînement* between and within elements – is a central concern of this book. The "and" not only breaks but also joins, as is indicated by the classic suffragette gesture: chaining oneself to railings, performing a *disruptive linkage*.

To begin with, a word needs to be said about why the "and" is necessary at all. Why not simply collapse the terms into deconstructive feminism or feminist deconstruction? This proves unsatisfactory on a couple of counts. First, it introduces the problem of deciding whether feminism and deconstruction are nouns or adjectives. Any negotiation of the grammatical arrangement still subordinates one term to the other, making one the descriptive term for the correct noun. Even more worrisome is the way in which these phrases lose the sense of feminism and deconstruction as verbs, as actions. In short, noun phrases merely send us back into a theoretical tail spin.[23]

Second, the grammatical shift to adjective and noun risks collapsing feminism and deconstruction into a single event, by ignoring the ways in which they don't "relate." That is to say, the force of the construction "feminism and deconstruction" is that it marks the way in which this relationship also depends on non-relation, on the potential for feminism and deconstruction *not* being the same thing.[24]

However, if the "and" marks a potential difference, it also threatens to perform a similar collapse of terms. Despite any insistence on my part that deconstruction and feminism are always plural, always are deconstructions and feminisms, that plurality is limited by the necessity of reducing the two (deconstruction and feminism) into one: *a* couple, *a* pair, *a* relationship. While I cannot completely avoid this grammatical reduction, I certainly want to insist as much as possible that this relationship is not static, is more of a fluid than a solid, to use Luce Irigaray's distinction.[25]

Simply remarking on the fluidity of this relationship still does not fully avoid the problems which go along with the way in which "and," as a coordinate conjunction, insists upon equivalence but also subordination. On the one hand, "and" functions to put "deconstruction" and "feminism" on equal terms, on the same crossdisciplinary footing, as it were. Both sides of the "and" share equivalent status. But on the other hand, inevitably one term must come first, suggesting that the first term subordinates the second.[26] Yet must order always connote hierarchy? Must some one or some thing always be "on top" and thus in a position of mastery? How would it be possible to justify what comes first, the point of departure? On these counts, I think Derrida's remarks in *Of Grammatology* are important:

> We must begin *wherever we are* and the thought of the trace ... has already taught us that it was impossible to justify a point of departure absolutely. *Wherever we are*: in a text where we already believe ourselves to be.[27]

This is not mere absolution from responsibility; Derrida admits that the point of departure, the origin, the common ground, is not recoverable as such. Nonetheless, were I to begin my justification with the title of this book, with my belief in "wherever we are," I would want to say that I place feminism first to suggest that feminism is not subordinated to deconstruction, should not in any way be considered a handmaiden to a more powerful, almighty deconstruction. However, my lack of consistency on this score throughout the book – deconstruction sometimes precedes feminism – is meant to stress that deconstruction is also not a tool that feminism picks up with an "and." All along, my question will be whether it's possible to think of a relationship – and to think difference – without a hierarchy. And if so, whether it's even desirable. Admittedly, this is a deconstructive move, but it is also, and perhaps first of all, a feminist one.[28]

The point I am trying to suggest here is that feminism and deconstruction do not work in isolation. When we speak of feminism or deconstruction, we can only speak of feminism and..., or deconstruction and.... Neither deconstruction nor feminism works nor acts by itself, independent of other considerations, which might even include yet to be named categories of difference. However, the dependence of feminism is not subordination, another version of the dutiful daughter syndrome, nor is deconstruction's reliance best understood as the friendly domestication of an otherwise unruly monster. That deconstruction and feminism should not pretend to be autonomous is not a weakness but rather a strength which moves beyond the modernist myth of the importance of self-reliance.

Perhaps, then, one of the advantages of speaking of "feminism and deconstruction" (or "deconstruction and feminism") is the possibility of recognizing the limitations of the relationship – recognizing what feminism and deconstruction cannot do either separately or together. This inadequacy – and I think it's fair to call it that – cannot be redressed by the discovery of a more complete feminism or a more total deconstruction. Nor do I believe that deconstruction and feminism join together to create a bigger horizon of Being. Rather, what I hope for is the acknowledgment of the injustice which would result from thinking that one can act only in the name of feminism and/or deconstruction – that either feminism or deconstruction is the name for Justice.

But in saying this, I'm getting ahead of myself. Before I continue my discussion of justice and ethics (which will get its fullest treatment in Chapter 4), it is worth slowing down here in order to catalogue some of the directions that the relationship between deconstruction and feminism has taken. Since I have initiated a conversation which addresses the link between the "and" in the middle of feminism *and* deconstruction, one way to continue the discussion would be to say that the "and" has an abyssal structure. What lies between them is not a third term nor even a disciplinary territory but a space of interminable investigation. And the space across which they talk is not simply neutral. Out of this abyss, questions can arise such as: Does deconstruction threaten to deconstruct feminism? Does feminism disarm deconstruction?

ESTRANGEMENT

In response to these questions, it would be almost impossible to ignore those who believe that, in fact, nothing at all happens, that linking deconstruction and feminism produces no significant interaction whatsoever. While it should be obvious that I do not share this belief – this book would be unnecessary if that were so – nonetheless it is important to pause and consider why the relationship between deconstruction and feminism has often been represented as nonexistent, as a case of cross purposes in a different sense of the phrase.

Derrida's own insistence on deconstruction's estrangement from feminism has, for a long time, been a convenient card to play on the theory table. In a particularly strong assertion of his position Derrida writes in *Spurs* (1978):

And in truth the women feminists, against whom Nietzsche multiplied his sarcasms, are men. Feminism: it is the operation through which a woman desires to be like a man, like a dogmatic philosopher, demanding truth, science, objectivity; that is to say, with all masculine illusions, with the effect of castration which is attached to them. Feminism desires castration – also that of woman. Lost the style.[29]

Feminism, according to Derrida, buys into the illusion of castration, which he defines as "the operation of woman contra woman, no less than of each sex against itself and against the other."[30] For Derrida, feminism elides difference, and thus loses its style, by trying to make everyone into a castrated man. Through this operation, feminism produces a leveling effect, and if Derrida is to be believed, one which finds its source of energy in the very ontological and hermeneutical principles that Derrida's version of deconstruction is out to attack.

If this apparent resistance to feminism on Derrida's part does not seem significant enough, there is always his 1985 interview in which he bluntly claims that "deconstruction is *certainly* not feminist ... if there is one thing it must not come to, it's feminism."[31] As the interview continues, he makes the disparity between deconstruction and feminism even clearer, with deconstruction moving into position for a hostile take-over bid. Derrida explains:

> So I would say that deconstruction is a deconstruction of feminism, from the start, in so far as feminism is a form – no doubt a necessary form at a certain moment – but a form of phallogocentrism among many others.[32]

For me, the key phrase here is "in so far as feminism is a form." I would suggest that Derrida's version of feminism resembles what I referred to earlier as theory. This "feminism" consists of knee jerk accusations of "phallocentrism" or "patriarchal sympathies" in response to particular (and predictable) textual features. Pushing this point further, Derrida accuses some feminists of hastily focusing on particular themes and then saying, "Well, there you have it" – it's patriarchal and phallocentric.

Insofar as deconstruction could be against such reductive, formal, theoretical ventures (of whatever sort), I would have to agree with Derrida. Deconstruction is indeed against that kind of feminism. But it is also important – and this may sound defensive – that Derrida takes the time to insist that such a feminism is "no doubt a necessary form [of phallogocentrism] at a certain moment." The question here is where necessity comes from. Is it necessary for feminism to become phallogocentric in order for it to accomplish its work? Or is feminism a form to which phallogocentrism is constrained in order to widen its market, while protecting its economy?

If feminism is merely a form of phallogocentrism, then Derrida, however much he gestures at historical necessity, would be equating all of feminism with a teleological search for the essence of woman. Thus, he would be reducing all feminisms to one and the same feminism. Lost the style, for Derrida as well. However, if phallogocentrism is a contingent deformation (or perhaps formation) of feminism, it would be possible to think of feminism as something other than a desire for a world of only castrated men. In a more recent interview with Jacqueline Rose, Derrida seems to be pursuing this guarded relationship when he replies, "I am not against feminism, but I am not simply for feminism."[33]

Derrida's remark turns back to *Spurs*, where his opposition to anti-feminism can also be found:

> Beyond this double negation, woman is recognized and affirmed as affirmative power, as dissimulatress, as artist, as dionysiac. She is not affirmed by man, rather she affirms herself, in herself and in man. Castration, in the sense in which I spoke of it earlier, does not take place. Anti-feminism is, in its turn, overturned; since it only condemned woman as long as she was, so long as she answered to man, from the two reactive positions.[34]

To put this in context, Derrida's argument is that woman is twice castrated, once as "truth" and then again as "untruth" ("the two reactive positions"). That is to say, woman in the first place embodies the truth as castration, as that which is lacking and must be sought. However, as castrated she is herself lacking, a figure of untruth. In the third (non-dialectical) move which I have quoted above, castration does not take place, and anti-feminism is overthrown. The very point of this whole exercise is that the graphic – of the hymen, of the truth and non-truth of woman – "always subtracts a margin of control from the meaning or code."[35] To try to sum up this series of moves, Derrida's complex deconstruction of hermeneutical or ontological certainty and control does not come out simply for or against feminism.

If an ungenerous reading of Derrida's remarks – which may turn out to be deserved – must judge him as too readily dismissive of the diversity within feminism, nonetheless they do make clear that deconstruction's relationship to feminism is not best understood as simple. If we cannot locate within Derrida's work a moment in which his text speaks simply in the affirmative of the relationship between deconstruction and feminism, a moment can be found when Derrida concedes that "there is a strong link between ... deconstruction*s* and feminine studies, women's studies."[36] This formulation casts the discussion into the plural, seeking to articulate the multiple points of intersection between the two crossdisciplines.

And yet the question of how to read remains. To offer a restatement of my earlier proposition: while Derrida's skepticism may be read either as a dismissal of feminism's connection to deconstruction or alternatively as an insistence on the complexity of that relationship, other writers have moved in a different direction in order to dismiss deconstruction's link to feminism. From their perspective, the problem begins not with feminism but with deconstruction. Feminism has no truck with deconstruction because deconstruction, unlike feminism, has "no political allegiances" (Denise Riley); "subsumes everything in language" (Jane Tompkins); is an "endlessly diffracted light" (Nicole Ward Jouve); "attempt[s] to neutralize feminists" because "the possibility of women's difference has not entered the deconstructive imagination" (Margaret Whitford); "displace[s] female writers ... and readers of texts" (Tania Modleski); is "an arrogant apolitical American adolescent with too much muscle and a big mouth" (Jane Marcus).[37]

While I do not mean to discount the feminist objections to deconstruction out of hand – in fact, I will expand on what is at stake here in Chapters 2 and 3 – for now it is worth noticing that the guiding criticism in the remarks I have cited is that deconstruction both refuses to take gender difference seriously enough and does not provide a proper ground for political action. To make the same point another way, Elaine Showalter offers a more theatrical assessment of this information and goes on to predict the denouement. Showalter explains how "some pioneering feminist critics" see "glittering critical theories," like Derridean deconstruction, as "golden apples thrown in Atalanta's path to keep her from winning the race."[38] While Showalter herself expresses a desire to avoid such a "hostile polarization," nonetheless, she looks at deconstruction with mild and rather dismissive amusement, suggesting that for all its surface glamour, in the final analysis deconstruction may in fact be upstaged by feminism. When the curtain rises on the final retrospective act, we may witness "in the critical histories of the future," a scene in which "these years will not be remembered as the Age of Structuralism or the Age of Deconstruction, but as the Age of Feminism."[39] The suggestion here is that the real politics of feminism wins out over the mere seductive pleasures of structuralism or deconstruction.[40]

While Showalter's theatrical sensibility is tempting, I would still suggest that the curtain should rise on a different scene, which will offer neither the catharsis of tragedy nor the satisfaction of epic triumph. The production I have in mind is more modest in its proportions and probably less fun to sit through. The characters themselves – deconstruction and feminism – are not completely distinct from one another; the script has abandoned the rhetoric of opposition and has turned instead to disciplinary crossing. The relationship between feminism and deconstruction also is not performed as if it were part of a script for a British bedroom farce. Granted, it is difficult to avoid the conjugal rhetoric of "engagement," "relationship," "seduction," and "romance." And I would not want to do so completely, insofar as there is something sexy going on between feminism and deconstruction. Nonetheless, these goings on are not necessarily heterosexually aligned, as is the case in most West End farces.

The tendency to think that feminism is on the side of woman, decon-struction suspiciously male, produces a script in which male deconstruc-tion, if successful, makes a date with female feminism. The passive/active subscriptions should not go unnoticed here. Such is the scenario that Brodzki and Schenck do a good job filling out:

> To the extent that they can (each) be monolithically represented, fem-inism and deconstruction have been set up within American critical discourse as a couple, and a heterosexual couple and privileged couple at that. There is something inherently gendered (or is it sexy?) in the pairing of schools so readily identifiable with women and men, female and male practitioners ... deconstructionists, or theorists, are male, and feminists, who take responsibility for gender, properly female.[41]

They have a point, but I want to argue that this need not be the case, in fact, has often not been the case.[42]

While I will develop the connections to gender and sexuality in the next chapter, for the moment I want to state as clearly as possible that there is a sense in which feminism already "is" deconstruction, and deconstruction "is" already feminism. And yet, with this said, they also do not collapse into one another and eliminate their differences. The works of Judith Butler, Gayatri Spivak, Barbara Johnson, Joan Scott, and Drucilla Cornell would be good examples here: are they better character-ized as deconstruction or feminism? Is there even one way to answer this question in each case? Does the reduction to "deconstruction" or "feminism" prove unsatisfactory? Labels are dangerous things, but none-theless the point of this exercise should be clear enough. In these examples, there is not some mad heterosexual mating ritual taking place between feminism and deconstruction or a battle of the theoretical sexes suing for divorce on the page.[43] To say simply that any of this work is either only deconstruction or feminism, or even first of all one or the other, would be to miss the complex ways in which it is politically deployed and ethically implicated.

TOOL-BOXES AND PEDAGOGICS

But if the rhetoric of conjugal bliss or stormy marriage proves inadequate, how can the "relationship" between deconstruction and feminism best be characterized? What is the most effective way to understand their inter-action, their disciplinary crossing?

Different answers to these questions have already been implicitly sup-plied in a variety of discussions of feminism and deconstruction, and I think it is worthwhile to go over the general ways in which they line up. First, the "tool-box" reply. Mary Poovey makes this position clear when she claims that deconstruction "has provided and continues to offer an essential tool for feminist analysis."[44] More specifically, Poovey believes that the tool of deconstruction can perform three tasks for feminism: 1. "deconstructive strategies could enable feminists to write a history of the various contradictions within institutional definitions of woman that would show how these contradictions have opened the possibility for change"; 2. deconstruction can "challenge hierarchical and [binary] oppositional logic"; 3. deconstruction offers the idea of the "in-between" which constitutes "one tool for dismantling binary thinking."[45] In Poovey's hands, deconstruction could seem like an entire tool-box, but actually it's just one tool that accomplishes several tasks. As far as Poovey is concerned, feminism simply uses deconstruction to dismantle binary opposition and therefore perform a "project of demystification."[46]

Poovey's understanding of deconstruction's handiwork is shared by Joan Scott, who also stresses that:

> If we employ Jacques Derrida's definition of deconstruction, this criticism means analyzing in context the way any binary opposition operates, reversing and displacing its hierarchical construction, rather than accepting it as real or self-evident or in the nature of things.[47]

But unlike Scott, Poovey finds deconstruction a less than perfect instrument for feminism. She is critical of deconstruction's inability to provide "tools for analyzing specificity" and argues that "the recuperative mode of deconstruction provides no model of change."[48] She even predicts, in a turn that echoes Showalter's remarks, that

> feminists practicing deconstructive and other poststructuralist techniques from an explicitly political position will so completely rewrite deconstruction as to leave it behind, for all intents and purposes, as part of the historicization of structuralism already underway in several disciplines.[49]

In short, as far as Poovey sees it, deconstruction is destined to outlive its usefulness for feminism and thus be discarded on the tool-heap of history.

The value of Scott's and Poovey's work would seem to me to be that it imagines ways to understand the relationship between feminism and deconstruction other than as pseudo-scary characters in scripts with titles like "Daughter of Deconstruction" or "Bride of Derrida." Their work reveals the way in which an attention to deconstruction changes the work of feminism but not necessarily in any patrilinear or patriarchal way. Scott's analysis of the historical categorization of gender is, as I will discuss in Chapter 2, an especially important instance of this. However, the supposition that deconstruction must, in turn, be cast off by feminism, points up the limitation of Scott's and Poovey's work: the tendency to understand deconstruction as only a tool for breaking apart binary oppositions.

First, in the simplest terms, I think it would be misguided to believe that once a binary opposition has been deconstructed it remains deconstructed forever. That would presuppose that either there is some kind of natural identity that hides behind the false differentiation imposed by the binary or that the removal of the binary leaves us in undifferentiated, neutral metaphysical bliss. By suggesting that acts of deconstruction will need to be repeated, I also do not mean to imply that the binarisms are themselves in any way natural and thus self-asserting. There is not a metaphysical equivalent to gravitational pull. Nor, however, is there a universal register in which acts of deconstruction are recorded and promulgated.

Second, and more significantly as far as Scott's and Poovey's work is concerned, to construct the relationship between deconstruction and feminism as analogous to that between tool and user is to reduce deconstruction to an identifiable theory or method which comes with a set of instructions for limited use. Indeed, to follow this line of thought, deconstruction must eventually become nothing more than a phallic object reserved for invigorating applications within the theoretical boudoir. Thus, the feminist rallying cry of "sisters put down your tools."

By contrast, I would still like to hold out the hope that a more complex relationship between feminism and deconstruction is possible. And one of the ways to begin to understand this is through the second category of response, which I will call the "pedagogic" answer. In this metaphoric formulation, both feminism and deconstruction would have lessons to learn from one another, without necessarily needing to discard one another in the interests of historical advancement. Barbara Johnson's fine essay, "Gender Theory and the Yale School," follows this line of inquiry, first of all arguing that deconstruction could spend time as feminism's student.[50] Leaving aside for a moment the slide between "gender difference" and "sexual difference" in her argument (I will focus on this movement in Chapter 2), Johnson delivers a compelling account of the ways in which gender haunts the work of such professed deconstructors as Geoffrey Hartman, J. Hillis Miller, and Paul de Man. For Johnson, Hartman makes "a promising start for an investigation of gender relations" but ends up turning the literary woman into literary child;[51] Miller points to gender difference but notably fails to "follow up on the implications of a parricidal daughter"; de Man may paradoxically demonstrate that the philosophical tradition is a men's club, but like his fellow deconstructors, he too fails to articulate the wider implications of the gendered terms he has raised.[52] Johnson even continues to explain how feminism teaches her own deconstructive work a thing or two, detailing how the question of sexual difference haunts her previous book.

But Johnson does not stop even here. Reversing the figural roles of student and teacher, she follows up in "Deconstruction, Feminism, and Pedagogy" with the suggestion that feminism can learn a lesson from deconstruction's valuation of self-resistance, while deconstruction can learn to place less value on self-resistance by listening to feminism. Even though I disagree with Johnson's final assessment of the split between feminism and de Man's writing in particular – I am not convinced that "de Man's writing is haunted by the return of personification," while "feminist writing is haunted by the return of abstraction" – the implication that both deconstruction and feminism change as a result of one another is an attractive way of imagining at least part of the terms for their relationship.[53]

However, before one gets too carried away here, it is of interest to see what happens when Robert Scholes designs the metaphoric classroom instead of Barbara Johnson. According to Scholes, the pedagogic scene is a one-way traffic in knowledge: deconstruction learns from feminism that it's simply "wrong."[54]

On this score, I want to argue that it's actually Scholes who is off course and who perhaps stands to learn something from deconstruction and feminism. One thing he might learn – and I will discuss this at length in Chapter 4 – is that the evaluation to be made is not epistemological (whether a crossdiscipline is right or wrong) but ethical (whether it's just or unjust). In avoiding any engagement with ethical issues, Scholes himself produces an unjust argument, which results from his apparent desire to dismiss any possibility of a relationship developing between feminism and deconstruction:

> But deconstruction did come along and found itself upon the impurity of class concepts. Which means – in the present context – that we should be aware that feminism and deconstruction – and you can see it in the very names – are founded upon antithetical principles: femin- ism upon a class concept and deconstruction upon the deconstructing of all such concepts. This is why attempts to reconcile them should provoke the horrified fascination of an acrobat attempting an imposs- ible feat – even if in academic life there is usually a net under the performer.[55]

The horror. The horror. Yet who exactly is horrified? The acrobat? The spectator? Both? Scholes is right to conclude that deconstruction and feminism can't be reconciled: there is no bottom line of sameness. But this is not to say that some ground of pure difference (onto which the acrobat presumably falls if the net is removed) exists either. If feminism is founded on the class difference of women/men, the horror of it all may be that this difference is not stable. As feminism has learned all too often, what it means to be a "woman" is hardly self-evident, and who is or is not included in the class of "women" is a matter of deeply divided debate. All of which may begin to sound a lot like deconstruction ... if we're not careful how we perform our act.[56] And this is precisely the moment at which Scholes gets frightened. As Scholes himself puts it: "From the heights of deconstruction we are given a glimpse into the bottomless abyss of textuality, a vertiginous perspective in which constructs are erected upon constructs, without foundation and without end."[57] For Scholes, the class of gender difference, the possibility of reading like (not as) a woman or a man, relies on the foundations of visual certainty, which the relationship between deconstruction and feminism denies. Thus, the vertigo inflicted on Scholes by deconstruction is particularly horrifying to him, because his entire argument is predicated on the fact that he knows what a woman looks like and thus knows that he is not one; he knows for certain that, at best, he must always read like a man, never as a woman.

I will return to the significance of the groundless solidarity between feminism and deconstruction in Chapter 4. What's important at the moment is the bottom line for Scholes and his picture theory of gender: with prevailing rhetorical conditions allowing the distinction between male/female to slide into that between men/women, Scholes stands on this slippery surface so that he can go on to argue that "a male critic . . . may work within the feminist paradigm but never be a full-fledged member of the class of feminists."[58] To translate this back into the rest of his argument: feminism teaches deconstruction that men can never really be feminists and must always read like men; therefore men, like deconstruction, are always wrong.

Scholes doubtless has perfectly good intentions in his essay: an interest perhaps in ensuring that men in the academy do not simply appropriate feminism as a way to recapture the power taken away from them by feminism in the first place.[59] Even more importantly, Scholes's argument could be employed to explain why men who feel as if they can oppose abortion and reproductive rights by speaking like, as, and therefore *for* women, have no right to do so. Nonetheless, the disturbing implications of his lesson override some of the benefits. For it seems to me that one can also walk away from his essay with the following conclusion: if a man can never read like or even as a woman, can never really be a feminist and thus can never be "right," all he can do is look up (not down) and try to enjoy the show. This act of passive viewing is, however, even more dangerous than the high wire act could ever be. The spectator's position can be highly irresponsible because it allows the viewer to ignore the obligations that feminism and deconstruction impose. While I am not accusing Scholes personally of advocating the potential consequences of his argument, nonetheless, ignoring responsibility in the guise of conceding authority (to women) can, in worst-case scenarios, become precisely the justifications which silently condone work-place sexual harassment (only "the woman" can speak out about her own oppression, be allowed to "read" the situation, as it were); or even worse, rape (she never said no, and I read it like a man); or to return to my earlier example, to oppose women's reproductive rights precisely by not speaking out in their favor (voicing an opinion would be pretending to speak as/like a woman). The pedagogic scene, as all too many of us have discovered, is not always a liberating one and often cannot account for the injustices committed as a result of reading like/as a man or woman.

THE ABYSS

The space between feminism and deconstruction is not, *pace* Scholes, that of the classroom. Gender difference is as vertiginous an abyss of difference as that which frightens Scholes, as he peers down "from the heights of deconstruction." This is the truth of castration anxiety. If Kant called the faculty of judgment a bridge over an abyss, we can say that this is in some sense one structure of the relationship between deconstruction and feminism. That is to say, their relationship is groundless in the sense that there is no common element between them. What makes it worth talking about, as I shall show, is that each opens onto the abyss (whether as de Manian aporia or *vagina dentata*) in an analogous fashion.

One way to characterize this opening is in terms of "displacement": feminism and deconstruction have a displaced relationship which is also a displacing relationship. Unsettling both the relationship itself and the social structure in which it takes place as event, the displacing effect is one of distortion (*Entstellung*) rather than transcription (*Verschiebung*), deferral rather than arrival.[60] This is not to say, however, that feminism and deconstruction are displacement itself. I do not want to risk reducing feminism and deconstruction to a method or theory of displacement. As I hope I have made clear early on, this book is not modern in the sense that Descartes would have understood. It is not about a search for rules, for methods, which when applied are guaranteed to produce a certain result or repeatable responses. Even displacing ones. The conversation between deconstruction and feminism will not necessarily generate predictable dialogues or gestures. The emphasis here is on change, without the desire for some kind of epistemological technology which can freeze the frame of motion.

And yet motion can have direction, and for some time now I have postponed acknowledging the directions that my argument about feminism and deconstruction might take. In response, let me say first that displacement must not be thought of as a movement from one ground to the next – the ground of deconstruction to the ground of feminism, for instance – but as a displacement which must concede that the grounds don't exist, that the relationship between feminism and deconstruction is foundationless. So one way to view the direction of this book is not only as a move away from a grounded certainty of what feminism and deconstruction are or will be, but also as a denial of any solid ground of post-feminism or beyond deconstruction. There is no morning after. No point of arrival and no mourning after.

The question to which my argument gives rise is one that Mark Krupnick has already asked of deconstruction: "what kind of consensus could it be, founded on the ground(lessness) of difference, on the play of displacement?"[61] My partial answer, and it will only ever be partial, is that in the case of deconstruction and feminism the relationship is not one of consensus (political common *ground*) but rather that of groundless solidarity. This means a deferral of consensus but *not* at the cost of political solidarity or ethical judgment. Hence the *ms. en abyme* – the infinite displacement brought about by feminism and deconstruction: the displacement of the subject, of identity politics, of the subject of feminism and deconstruction.

In putting it this way, of course, I do risk pushing my entire argument off into the abyss of infinite deferral and displacement. And if this were indeed the case, it would seem that the argument against deconstruction because of its nihilistic effects would have merit. However, by looking down into the abyss but not necessarily falling into it, I hope to see that there are no native grounds of either feminism or deconstruction: no subject, no object, no person or thing, that is a natural inhabitant of feminism and deconstruction. I would even go so far as to suggest that a belief in the native or proper will finally merely perpetuate forms of oppression. Rather than search for the establishment of grounds, this book will be about the possibility of locating the abysses and the bridges that are built over them. What kind of bridge can span the absolute rift? Thus, the argument that follows will look at limits, political and ethical limits, and ask: where are these bridges, these lines, being drawn and to what purpose, what effect? Whom do they benefit? Whom do they harm?

And yet this book will also defer offering any unified answers to these questions, having already pushed totalizing theory into the abyss. It will not, however, jump in after it, and instead will set about building some bridges, laying down some lines of connection, of crossing, even in the absence of decidable grounds. Lines to be broken, directed, diverted, tangled, and reworked.

OBLIGATIONS

The groundless spanning of the abyss enfolded within both deconstruction (the aporia of cognition) and feminism (the primary separation of sexual difference) finds its analogy in ethics as the problem of doing justice. If, as Derrida suggests, "there is a duty in deconstruction," and if there also is a duty in feminism, "to whom or to what is the duty owed?"[62] The question is not merely academic to the extent that duty must exceed the walls of the academy. The location of that obligation is not something to be determined. It is this sense of the indeterminate that enforces an ethical judgment. Since that whose call we must answer cannot be identified, there are no original grounds which can serve as a model for future judgments. To use Derrida's words once again, "the origin of the call ... comes from nowhere ... something of this call of the other must remain nonreappropriable, nonsubjective, and in a certain way nonidentifiable."[63] The obligation of feminism, I shall go on to argue, is an obligation to a sexual difference that, in effect, comes from nowhere. I say "comes from nowhere" in the sense that it is an ontological fact onto which meanings may subsequently be grafted, meanings that it has been the business of feminism to contest. However, it exceeds any meaning that might attempt to explain it, to do away with it. As I hope to show in the next chapter, feminism is about keeping sexual difference open as the space of a radical uncertainty. We do not yet know what women can do ...

Chapter 2

Questions of women

UNDETERMINED OR DETERMINED?[1]

We do not yet know what women *are*. It remains uncertain what it would mean to be a woman (to be part of the group "women"), just as it remains uncertain what precisely would constitute knowledge of women. There are neither epistemological nor ontological grounds which would settle the issue once and for all. This is not necessarily a political limitation for feminism. Women are yet to be determined and so are their (political) actions. We do not yet know what women *can do*.[2]

And yet we do know what women *have* been and done. Women have been determined. After all, we operate everyday under the assumption that we readily understand to which group the word "women" refers. We can speak with some confidence about women's achievements, women's rooms, women's poverty, women's studies, women's sports, women's magazines, women's rights, women's bodies, and, of course, just simply women. How could we *not* know what women are? Any belief in the indeterminacy of women and women's actions threatens to be crushed by an avalanche of common sense and popular opinion.

I do not want to dismiss the importance of this landslide of determinations, nor do I wish to close down the possibility that women are yet to be determined. Women both are determined and are yet to be determined. There are established, pre-conceived notions of what women can be and do, at the same time that "women" remains a yet to be determined category.

Another way to describe this condition of "women" would be the *mise en abyme*, a structure of infinite deferral. Originally a heraldic term, a *mise en abyme* is a representation in which the relation of part to whole is inverted: the "whole" image is itself represented in part of the image. Thus the Quaker Oats man appears on the Quaker Oats box holding a small box, which depicts the Quaker Oats man holding a box with a Quaker Oats man. . . . and so on *ad infinitum*. The *mise en abyme* thus opens a spiral of infinite regression in representation. Representation can never come to an end, since greater accuracy and detail only allows us to see even more Quaker Oats boxes. This is rather odd, since we are accustomed to think of accuracy and detail as helping us to grasp an image fully, rather than forcing us to recognize the impossibility of grasping it.[3]

To think of feminism in these terms would be to suggest that each new attempt to determine women does not put an end to feminist questioning but only makes us more aware of the infinite possibilities of women. That is to say, women may be represented, but the attempt to represent them exhaustively only makes us more aware of the failure of such attempts. Hence the infinite regression that I specifically call the "*ms. en abyme.*"

Some may want to stop me here and argue that feminism cannot risk such uncertainty; others might jump to the conclusion that indeterminacy implies that we should stop representing women altogether, since we can never get it right, as it were. However, I would reply that such arguments are tantamount to suggesting that Quaker Oats are likely to cause starvation, because people will gaze endlessly at the box. Caught in the infinitely regressing spiral of representations, they will be unable to open the box and actually eat.

If these responses are not what I'm after here, the question still remains: what does it mean to argue that representations of women are placed within the structure of the *mise en abyme*? To begin with, it would mean that there is no original woman which is then unproblematically reproduced or fully represented – even by feminism. This claim actually is part of a larger argument about the nature of representation. Representation, I would argue, need not be a matter of representing an object for a subject, as Western philosophy has a tendency to assume. Part of the value of the *mise en abyme* is the way in which it upsets the assumed relationship between subject and object in the scene of representation. The subject and object infinitely change places within the *mise en abyme*; there is no set sender or receiver of the representation. The infinitely receding object in the *mise en abyme* closes down the possibility of a stable subject/object relation. On the one hand, the object cannot be grasped by the subject; it slips away into infinity. On the other hand, this produces a parallel regression in the subject or viewer of the *mise en abyme*. As the object recedes into itself, the subject is destabilized; it loses not merely its capacity to grasp the object but also its grasp on itself. The subject thus is faced with its inability to know what it knows, to see what it sees. In this sense, the subject becomes the subject of a representation that exceeds it. Seeing that they have been fooled, viewing subjects see themselves as fools, as *objects* of a visual joke.[4]

The importance of this abyssal indeterminacy for feminism becomes evident when we consider what happens when women function as either calculable objects *or* subjects. Detailing the horrors brought about by the objectification of women has become a standard feature of feminist accounts of the representations of women. Feminism has illustrated time and again that the exploitation of women has come about through their continued commodification as sex objects and domestic slaves. Whether Debbie does Dallas or the dishes, the result is the same: objectification in the eyes of the patriarchy.

If feminism has focused on the problem of women as objects, it has not always paid sufficient attention to the problem of women as subjects. In fact, feminism has tended to see women's attainment of the position of the subject as a cause for celebration. However, we shouldn't put on our party clothes too quickly. The horror of objectification should be matched with the horror of calculable subjectivities which, as Derrida reminds us, has taken the form of "crowds in concentration camps or in the police computers or those of other agencies, the world of the masses and of the mass media."[5] The achievement of a definitive or calculable subjectivity is, as Derrida points out, not solely liberatory. Indeed, the constraint of subjectivity, even when subjectivity seems to offer agency, is clear when we realize that women become subjects only when they conform to specified and calculable representations of themselves as subjects. To return to the analogy of the police computer: only once you have been assigned a licence number and undergone testing and classification, are you "free" to drive a car. And the driver's licence has become, in the United States, the primary instance of subjective identification before the law. There is thus a similarity between being objectified and assuming a subject position already determined: subject positions are occupied by objects. Debbie may not be doing Dallas or the dishes this time, but when Debbie does driving she is still conforming to pre-existing, restrictive criteria in order to take up the subject position "woman." Moving from the back seat to the front is not the same thing as getting out of the car.

By contrast, the *mise en abyme* acknowledges the subject/object positions assumed by representation, but it also makes those positions infinite and ultimately incalculable. Women ultimately will never be determined as either subject or object. And this will be the case no matter how many representations are put into the abyss, for as Derrida argues, "the *operation* of the *mise en abyme* always occupies itself (activity, busy positing, mastery of the subject) with somewhere filling up, full of abyss, filling up the abyss."[6] Derrida's remark calls attention to the paradox of the *mise en abyme*: the more you try to fill it up with representations, the emptier it becomes.

While this may sound rather strange – most paradoxes do – it is nonetheless possible to illustrate what Derrida has in mind and why it would be of concern to feminism. On the one hand, the abyss fills up with representations of women. What it means to be or act as a woman is continually more determined. Women are, for instance, mastered as a subject/object of knowledge by the accumulation of work within women's studies; or to use a different kind of example, their sexuality is continually more defined by the stereotypes of the mass media. While these examples certainly have differing political agendas behind them, nonetheless, both participate in the operation of the *mise en abyme* in that they both determine what we understand women to be as either subjects or object. The accumulation of representations seems to narrow the options and leave *less* room for uncertainty. Or as Derrida would put it, "the authority of representation constrains us, imposing itself on our thought through a whole dense, enigmatic, and heavily stratified history. It programs us and precedes us."[7] Thus, the work of the *abyme* is a sort of filling up the image with more and more definitions and representations of itself. The avalanche of determinations seems to fill up the abyss, which no longer appears to be bottomless (despite Hollywood's attempt to define the ideal woman as blonde, heavy-breasted, and bottomless).

On the other hand, however, the abyssal operation is infinite. The very filling up leaves one "full of abyss." The series of images in the *mise en abyme* is without end; each additional image changes all the others in the series without ever completely filling up the abyss, which gets deeper with each additional determination. It's not, then, the case that the mass media will ever define all possibilities for women's sexuality or that women's studies will ever finally arrive at the truth of women. Women may yet be and do an infinite number of things. What women have been will, in turn, be retroactively altered by that which they have yet to be. The subject/object relationship is perpetually destabilized in the wake of an increasing number of possible (re)presentations.

With this said, I would like to suggest that the *mise en abyme*, turned *ms. en abyme*, is more than a mere analogy for the ways in which I want to emphasize questions of women. While the operation of the *mise en abyme* is not limited to representations of women, it is especially important for women, because it demonstrates that if there is no object or thing-in-itself called "women," neither is there an adequate account by a subject of the phenomenon "women." By questioning the subject/object relationship – by putting it "into *abyme*" – deconstruction challenges the phenomenological claims which have often served as the foundation of feminism. That is to say, deconstruction argues that we will not become conscious of the true essence of woman through an endless recourse to descriptions of experiences of or by women. Such descriptions will only function as yet another representation in the *ms. en abyme*. Feminism can thus neither confirm aesthetic interpretations nor be certain that its political procedures are just.

And yet if there is no truth to be found in experience, where will feminism turn to bear witness to the injustices done to women? While I will return to the problem of experience at the end of this chapter, in general this question calls attention to the fact that it is particularly important for feminism to leave open "questions of women," including the question of what "women's experience" might mean and how it would be possible to do justice to women. That is a long way of saying that feminism must be willing to understand the necessity of indeterminacy. It cannot be exhaustively determined which questions should be asked of and about women and which answers should be accepted. Neither feminism nor deconstruction can ever be certain that they have either asked the right questions or provided the correct answers.

This is not, however, the same thing as being condemned to the land of relativistic nihilism, where political action – or any action for that matter – becomes impossible. Uncertainty, as I have tried to stress, is neither an absolute obstacle to action nor a theoretical bar to political praxis. I would even go so far as to suggest that mainstream culture in the United States is suffering from too much certainty and false beliefs in the possibility of easy answers. Such is the disingenuous feature of self-help manuals that proffer knowledge and promise action on subjects ranging from "Fulfilling your Femininity" to "The Superwoman Syndrome" and "The Cost of Loving."[8] Even supposedly "enlightened" feminists have suffered from too much certainty. I think here of feminism in the United States which felt (and unfortunately sometimes continues to feel) no need to examine its white, middle-class, heterosexual biases, huddling instead under the false banner of the "common oppression" of women. This "version of Sisterhood," as bell hooks points out, "was informed by racist and classist assumptions about white womanhood, that the white 'lady' (that is to say bourgeois woman) should be protected from all that might upset or discomfort her."[9] The "white lady" who participates in this version of feminism has not stopped to question whether all women are oppressed in the same way and to the same degree, whether her liberation is purchased at the cost of the further oppression of other women.

The troubling erasure of difference under the banner of common oppression does not end, however, with the recognition of racial differences. The oppression of women is constructed around a variety of specific historical, national, and class parameters which cannot be accounted for only on the basis of racial difference. In fact, feminism's use of the word "oppression" to describe the various forms of discrimination against women finally ends up undermining the seriousness with which it should treat overt forms of political oppression of women. As June Jordan puts it: "If I, a black woman poet and writer, a professor of English at a State University, if I am oppressed then we need another word to describe a woman in a refugee camp in Palestine or the mother of six in a rural village in Nicaragua or any counterpart inside South Africa."[10]

Feminism must be wary of its appeals to the common oppression of women or even to a common language of women. For if feminism thinks that it has all the answers about women, if it never questions its own composition and exclusionary practices, it is destined to practice some of the worst forms of social injustice in the name of liberation. And feminism cannot avoid this problem by simply being more careful, by listing a number of qualifiers every time it mentions "woman." The alliance between feminism and deconstruction provides a way to explore how women exist in relation to a matrix of differences such that, to use Judith Butler's words, "it would be wrong to assume in advance that there is a category of 'women' that simply needs to be filled in with various components of race, class, age, ethnicity, and sexuality in order to become complete."[11] The problem, then, is not that feminism may accidentally forget black or Palestinian sisters. Rather, a feminism that believes it knows what a woman is and what she can do both forecloses the limitless possibilities of women and misrepresents the various forms that social injustice can take.

While my argument has credited undecidability (especially as it plays a role in the operation of the *mise en abyme*) with undermining received understandings of what women are and can do, it is important to stress that undecidability is still not a point of arrival, as Derrida reminds us.[12] The undecidability of what women can be or do is not meant to be merely the point of arrival (the end of Chapter 1) or even the point of departure (the beginning of Chapter 2). Rather, the abyssal relation that I hope to inscribe within this rhetorical structure is one which joins feminism with deconstruction in order to take up, but not necessarily to answer, questions of women.

Like the images of the *mise en abyme*, undecidability functions as part of a relation; undecidability forms part of a situation of representation, political action, or ethical judgment, for instance. It is not enough to say simply "it's undecidable." We may not yet know what women can do or be, but feminism has an obligation, at the very least, to think about what this might mean. To be faced by an inexhaustible uncertainty is not to be excused from asking what effects it has. I am not arguing that woman incarnates or figures the undecidable.[13] The fact that women will not be determined in advance should not make women any less determined to ask what they may turn out to have been.

It will come as no surprise, then, to say that the point of this chapter is not to put forth a new theory of woman or to answer definitively the question: "What is woman?" I am suspicious of the universal particular which the singular form "woman" forces us to consider, and likewise I would not want to suggest that there is something that all women have in common. That would return my argument to a comfortable seat under the banner of "common oppression." My interest here is to explore the ways in which "women" is a *permanently contested site of meaning*.

The question of what it means to be a "permanently contested site of meaning" is not simple. I do not just mean that people argue about what the word "women" means, but that more profoundly, "women" marks a point of difference within language itself. To use Lyotard's term, "women" is the locus of a differend. "Women" marks a point of dispute where language itself becomes a problem, where one person's injustice cannot be registered in the language of the other. Lyotard refers to the Holocaust and Stalinism to show how systems of representation can victimize, since the oppressed are unable even to register the wrong that is done to them.[14]

These events from the grand stage of history should not, however, mislead us: the possibility of a differend can arise on the slightest occasion. Even in the kitchen. And the sense of the differend allows us to understand the feminist struggle to be recognized as not simply a struggle to assert an identity, but as a struggle to assert a difference, to bear witness to injustices done to women that simply cannot be expressed in the language of the patriarchy. This is the condition of so much feminist struggle: women's complaints make no sense within the terms of patriarchal language.

To take a fairly simple example, "chairman/person" makes no difference in the patriarchal idiom, since the universal is always assumed to be masculine whether or not, in this case, it is specifically marked as "man" or "person." In patriarchal terms, the difference makes no difference, and those who argue that it does should just shut up and stop complaining about such a silly linguistic convention. The injustice done to women cannot, therefore, even be registered in the patriarchal idiom – the case of the differend.

But this is only one end to the story. That these terms *do* make a difference, and that this difference is difficult to calculate once it has been registered, became the source of confusion at the 1992 U.S. Democratic Convention. To put the problem in context, the Democrats had made women's rights a part of their platform, calling the 1992 elections "The Year of the Woman," the year in which women were an unprecedented presence in federal elections. In keeping with this platform, the convention's presidential nomination roll call was presided over by a woman. And here is where the confusion began: what to call her during the state roll call. Was she to be referred to as the chairperson, the chairwoman, the chair, or perhaps the party secretary? Variations on a theme became so contradictory that finally one male delegate referred to her as "Madam chairman." My point here is not to deride the Democratic Party for choosing a woman to chair the convention; this was, by any account, a bold move in a country where sexism still pervades politics, especially at the federal level. What seems to me significant is the linguistic confusion which surrounded this choice. *How* the difference should be registered and *what* difference should be registered was not altogether clear to the delegates responding to the roll call vote. That the voice of (political) authority may be that of a woman, that the "chairman" may not be the universal (male) particular has yet to be registered in the same fashion as the roll call (or *role* call) vote. Gender had clearly marked the Democratic Convention, but the difference that mark makes is yet to be determined.

Lest I give the impression that the only mark of indeterminacy that matters is the linguistic slippage which occurs in political forums, I want to turn to another instance in which women's complaints made no sense within the terms of patriarchal language. Ironically, this was one of the events which led up to the proclaimed "Year of the Woman": Anita Hill's statements in the U.S. Senate confirmation hearings of Clarence Thomas in October 1992. Hill attempted to tell the all male, all white committee that she had been sexually harassed in the work-place by Thomas. The committee, along with Thomas himself, responded with remarkable maneuvers that attempted to discredit her as a witness and discount the relevancy of her testimony for the confirmation. The series of discrediting moves that followed were, in effect, an instance of what Freud called kettle logic: she's lying, you can't prove what she says is true (or false), and even if she were telling the truth, what she says doesn't matter. In the attempts to respond to Hill's charges, it became clear that the white patriarchy could not hear what she had to say. But what became equally clear was that the white patriarchy was not alone in its inability to do justice to her voice. Kimberlé Crenshaw rightly points out that "the particular intersectional identity of Hill, as both a woman and an African American, lent dimensions to her ideological placement in the economy of American culture that could not be translated through the dominant feminist analysis."[15] And what's more, "that black people across a political and class spectrum were willing to condemn Anita Hill for breaking ranks is a telling testament to how deep gender conflicts are tightly contained by the expectation of racial solidarity."[16] Hill's situation was one of the differend: the Senate created a forum in which Hill raised her voice but was not heard, and tragically it was more than the Senate committee who failed to listen.[17] And part of the reason this happened, to use Crenshaw's words again, was that:

> In the absence of narratives linking race and gender, the prevailing narrative structures continued to organize the Hill and Thomas controversy as either a story about the harassment of a white woman or a story of the harassment of a black man. Identification by race or gender seemed to be an either/or proposition. . . .[18]

However, Hill's situation should not forever be confined to the differend, nor should feminism be content with the absence of narrative structures which prevented Hill's story from being heard at the time.[19] As Sarah

Pelmas also points out, we must anticipate a future justice, the symbol for which "might be the recent Doonesbury comic strip featuring the alternative hearings with Angela Wright's testimony, or perhaps the bumper sticker: I believe you, Anita."[20] Or perhaps the primary elections that followed in which women won an unprecedented number of nominations in both Republican and Democratic races. Or perhaps the prominent role women played in the 1992 Democratic Convention, where speakers referred to Hill on a number of occasions. Or perhaps Carol Moseley-Braun, the first African American woman to be elected to the U.S. Senate.

These examples remind us that there is a problem *with* representing women as well as a problem gaining representation *for* women. And the answers do lie in persistent considerations of women in isolation from other differences. This is not just a semantic quibble of interest only to literary deconstructors; there is a sense of urgency with which I raise these points as a feminist. Feminism, I would argue, cannot afford to ignore the problems posed by representation if it is to be successful in pressing its claims for a social justice which goes beyond that which Justice Thomas might understand.

It is for that reason, then, that I want to continue by examining the various ways in which critics have thought the difficult representational status of women. My intention in the rest of this chapter will be to call attention to three moments in recent feminism, each of which marks a point where the categorical function of the term "women" has been subjected to an analysis that imperils the supposed coherence of that very category. First, those attempting to write the history of women have had to grapple with historiographic methods which themselves determine how the question of women may be phrased. Second, the recognition of women as necessarily located within a network of representations leads us to confront the categories of gender and sex as frameworks for identifying women. Third, the very difficulty of this identification positions women as undecidably divided between language and materiality; women risk becoming either inessential representations or essential presences. Given these three focuses, the rest of this chapter will argue that women pose the questions *for* feminism every bit as much as they provide the basis *of* feminism.

HER-STORY OR HIS-STORY?

After centuries of Western history that has been in the strict sense his story (the narratives of "great" men), historians have gradually turned their attention to the problem of historically representing women. What would it mean to write the history of women? What would her story look like? These are by now familiar questions, as are the hoary chestnuts of his-story versus her-story. Nonetheless, I want to begin on this familiar territory in order to trace the ways in which women have become a problem for historical representation as much as they have become its ostensible subject.

First of all, history has become the ground on which feminism can challenge the exclusive universality of the (Anglo-Saxon) male subject. Within the discipline of history, as Joan Scott argues in *Gender and the Politics of History*, new knowledge about women has surfaced, which questions the central role that male subjects have traditionally played in historical narratives.[21] In a sense, this new knowledge may more precisely be understood not as "new" *per se* but rather as old, hidden knowledge which has been discovered as a result of a full-scale re-evaluation of what counts as historical knowledge. That is to say, the type of information considered worth knowing, in order to uphold our obligation to representing the past, has changed along with the re-evaluation of women's place in history. History is not what it used be.

But history is more than a matter of obtaining information, as any historian knows, and historical knowledge is as much a result of methodology as anything else. In the absence of a well-established historiographic tradition, to continue with Scott's analysis, "the subject of women has been either grafted on to other traditions or studied in isolation from them."[22] This absence of a tradition of specifically feminist methodologies has given rise to several different versions of her-story, which Scott does a good job delineating. According to Scott, we can find three distinct her-story methodologies that "developed in tandem with social history": 1. those which claim women's "essential likeness as historical subjects to men"; 2. those which "challenge received interpretations of progress and regress"; and 3. those which offer "a new narrative, different periodization, and different causes," so as to "discover the nature of the feminist or female consciousness that motivated" the behavior of both ordinary and notable women's lives.[23]

Scott does not, however, recite these approaches without reservations. She warns us that if social history assumes that "gender is not an issue requiring study in itself," her-story methodologies, while they study gender, nonetheless do not adequately "theorize about how gender operates historically." Thus in the end, Scott faults social history for being too integrationist, and her-story approaches for being too separatist.[24]

Singling out feminist literary history, Christina Crosby offers an even harsher critique of her-story feminism. Crosby argues that for feminists like Elaine Showalter, Sandra Gilbert, and Susan Gubar:

> To historicize is first to discover women where there had only been men, to see women in history, and recognize a fundamental experience which unites all women, the experience of being "the other." ... Such

a reading obviously is no longer wholly within the discourse which produces history as man's truth, no longer accepts that history has only to do with men. Yet in a fundamental way this feminist reading is still within the "space of formation" of that discourse, for where once history revealed the truth of man's identity as a finite being, revealed man's fate, now history reveals the truth of women's lives, the fate of being a woman, of being "the Other." The closed circle of recognition is still inscribed, for all women are women in the same way, and this discovery of identity is predicated on a whole series of exclusions. . . . A feminism that conceptualizes "women" as a unitary category which can be recognized in history works within the circle of ideological reflection, guaranteeing that women will be found everywhere and will be everywhere similar.[25]

Crosby draws much of her own argument from Audre Lorde's similar criticism of white feminists who likewise fail to address the differences between women. As Lorde points out, by all accounts, her-story threatens to be a colorless narrative, where, as Crosby underlines, "unity is achieved at the expense of the differences of race, and class, not to mention ethnicity, sexual preference, age, and all the other differences which divide women."[26]

Lorde and Crosby offer well-deserved criticism of her-story narratives, and I have no desire to become an apologist for discriminatory and exclusionary histories. However, I am reluctant simply to dismiss her-stories altogether. What if, for instance, bell hooks's *Ain't I a Woman*, Susan Cavin's *Lesbian Origins*, Esther Newton's *Mother Camp: Female Impersonators in America*, and Barbara Christian's *Black Women Novelists: The Development of a Tradition* were to be included in the list?[27] The methodologies which these texts employ and their interest in developing a history of women are still common themes in each of these cases. The danger in this kind of thinking is, of course, the false belief that writing the true history of women is simply a matter of inclusion – of completing the list of texts which I have begun above.

What it is important to recognize, I would argue, is that *her-story is not one story*.[28] An injustice is committed when any *one* history purports to speak for all women everywhere, when it does not underline the incompleteness of its own narrative. I would want to make clear, in a way that Crosby does not, that her-stories are valuable, but feminists must continue to examine how these narratives determine women, carefully looking at both what materials are included *and* excluded.

One way of going about this would be to argue that women's history or the history of women should be written and studied along with both discussions of the political implications of these histories and considerations of the alternatives. This seems to be Scott's solution, since she is careful to stress that it is not clear what the feminist rewriting of history might entail. Given this hesitation, she ventures that feminist history will become:

> not the recounting of great deeds performed by women but the exposure of the often silent and hidden operations of gender that are nonetheless present and defining forces in the organization of most societies. With this approach women's history critically confronts the politics of existing histories and inevitably begins the rewriting of history.[29]

Along these lines, in *"Am I That Name?"* Denise Riley tries to get around the problem by emphasizing that "women" is an unstable category in history. According to Riley, "the history of feminism has also been a struggle against over-zealous identifications" of women.[30] And rather than become the additional force which resolves the controversy, Riley's work encourages feminism to continue with the struggle. As Riley puts it, the indeterminacy of women is "no cause for lament"; "it is what *makes* feminism."[31]

In this sense, Riley provides a useful perspective from which to view some of the ways in which indeterminacy has played (and continues to play) a role in feminism. She recognizes that the purpose of a history of women might be something besides discovering the answer to the question: "What is woman?" But this vantage point is not without its own blind spots. No fan of deconstruction herself, Riley would undoubtedly not wish to align her work with Derrida's, and it seems appropriate that she is willing to take the role of indeterminacy only so far. While her overall line of argument is compelling enough, there is little that is indeterminate about the historical chapters themselves. Riley's book consists of a fairly straightforward traditional history of the category of women at selected moments in Western cultures. It would not be unfair to describe her project as a history of women which purports to tell the truth about the historical progress of the changing determinations of "women."

Here it is possible to see that her-story and history share a tendency to equate women with truth. In each of these instances, "woman" has a history insofar as she is associated with truth: woman is either the truth upon which history (or her-story) focuses, or she is the untruth which it is history's job to expose. One way or another, the narrative tries to relay the truth that woman has been, is, or will be.[32]

The consequences of this historical association of women with truth has been a much debated topic, partially provoked by deconstruction. When Derrida reads Nietzsche and considers the figure of woman in *Spurs*, he rejects the association of woman with truth altogether. As far as he is concerned:

There is no truth of woman, but it is because of that abyssal divergence of the truth, because that non-truth is "truth." Woman is one name for that non-truth of truth.[33]

If Derrida is to be believed, woman is not truth, nor is there a truth of woman. The question of woman, according to Derrida, actually suspends the *decidable* opposition between the true and the non-true.[34] The problem has been, however, that history, philosophy, and certain kinds of feminism (as I tried to make clear in Chapter 1) have figured woman as truth in order to assuage hermeneutic anxieties by appealing to a true meaning of the text of gender. History, philosophy, or feminism could thus each claim to provide the true meaning of the text: the truth of woman. Derrida's analysis, however, has found its critics. Ruth Salvaggio accuses Derrida of sharing with Lacan a suspicious "quest for woman," which presumably is just another macho affectation.[35] Rosi Braidotti is even harsher and claims that Derrida ignores "the reality of women" and that his argument in *Spurs* has caused vast numbers of otherwise critical feminist theorists to be seduced both by him and deconstruction.[36] Turning Derrida's argument back on itself, Gayatri Spivak contends that Derrida actually does precisely what he finds fault with: identifies woman with truth by identifying her instead with the absence of truth.[37] In light of such criticism, does the importance of *Spurs* lie in its function as a cover-up for sloppy philosophy, machismo, and the seduction of innocent (though otherwise tough-minded) feminists?

Without sounding too much like an apologist for Derrida, I would like to say that his critics have missed a crucial point in his argument. The oversight is most evident in Spivak's case, where, as Drucilla Cornell points out, the critique of Derrida rests on a confusion of "Derrida's reading of Nietzsche with an acceptance of [Nietzsche's] position." What Cornell understands too well, and what Derrida's critics too often fail to recognize, is that "woman cannot be contained by any definition, including Nietzsche's name for her as the non-truth of truth."[38] Innocent feminists have nothing to fear and the philosophical standards bureau has no cause for alarm.

In rightfully calling attention to this aspect of Derrida's argument, Cornell nonetheless chooses to ignore the way in which Derrida's text moves between *woman* and *women* in making this argument. Derrida thus insists on the indeterminacy of woman in the singular, while at the same time proposing that women can be adequately determined by this single figure. Woman is indeterminate, according to Derrida, but all women fall under the singular rubric of woman. Derrida is cutting corners here, in a way which marks a limitation to his concern for feminism. My somewhat belabored emphasis here on the plural "women" is meant to underline what is at stake in writing her-stories or histories of women.

Within these discourses a temporal predicament exists that threatens to return *women* to a single historical definition or figure of *woman* as truth. That is to say, history or her-story understood as continuous progress (which takes its strongest form as dialectical history) is oriented "towards a notion of woman's 'truth,' " to use Derrida's phrase, and risks determining what women can be and do.[39]

The historical movement which appeals to the truth in order to determine women takes several temporal forms. This is best understood by looking at three tenses in which history can be written: the past, present, and future. To begin with, history written in the past tense defines what women *were*, attempts to discover what the truth of woman was in the past. The present is understood in terms of the past, and feminists are asked (in the name of the truth of woman) either to respect their elders or to be grateful that they no longer have to be part of the bad old days.

On the other hand, history written in the present tense tends to explain how women have always been what they are. Here the story may either trace the truth of an eternal femininity (the historical proof of the ahistorical truth of woman), or may, like a certain materialist feminism, only celebrate the past insofar as the truth contained in it responds to present concerns. In either case, the present determines the past insofar as we look to the past to show us what we are, and are not, now.

Finally, at the opposite extreme, the future tense might downplay the need to write history at all in favor of a concern for what women will be. This would be a feminism that believes it has nothing to learn from the past, because the past is always a compromised, imperfect version of what the future holds: the truth of woman.

Without implying that any dialectical progression is contained in these three ways of writing history, I want to ask what a history would look like that did *not* ground itself on the truth of woman or set out to determine what women will be and do. As I have already pointed out, women are determined, but not exhaustively. To write of women is thus always to incur an obligation: no feminist has not been a daughter, no woman is not indebted to past sisters. At the same time, there can be no just history of women that does not subject its methodology at every turn to the deconstructive effect of women's radical indeterminacy. This is part of what Derrida is getting at when he postulates:

A history of paradoxical laws and non-dialectical discontinuities, a history of absolutely heterogeneous pockets, irreducible particularities, of unheard of and incalculable sexual differences; a history of women who have – centuries ago – "gone further" by stepping back with their lone dance, or who are today inventing sexual idioms at a distance from the main forum of feminist activity with a kind of reserve that does not necessarily prevent them from subscribing to the movement and even, occasionally, from becoming a militant for it.[40]

While Derrida is right to insist upon the diffusion of feminine identity rather than upon its dialectical recovery, to stress the irreducible and the incalculable, he has not, to my mind, sufficiently considered how these could be understood given the temporal conditions of historical narratives. For that reason, I would propose that any history of women should not be written in the past tense, or even the present or simple future tenses – all of which necessarily ground themselves on the truth of woman – and should instead be written in the future anterior. The writing of history, that is, should expose itself to the *political* question of what women *will have been* and thus destabilize any claim to positive knowledge or restrictions on the non-category of "women."[41]

Distinct from the three historical tenses of past, present, and future, history written in the future anterior doesn't claim to know in advance what it is women can do and be: the radical potentiality of women does not result from a break with the past, nor is it to be found in any form of assurance provided by the past or the present. Instead, the future anterior emphasizes radical uncertainty and looks to its own transformation. It would be a history that is a rewriting, yet is itself always already to be rewritten. Put another way, history written in the future anterior is a message that is handed over to an unknown addressee and accepts that its meaning in part will have to depend upon that addressee. History rewritten for a public that will have to rewrite it ceaselessly.

With this said, it is worth issuing a caution that what I have just outlined is not intended to be understood as itself a history – be it that of the progressive realization that the category of women is a representational construct, or be it the history of critics' increasing disregard for "real" women in favor of their own theorizing. Such would be the two sides in the debate between "constructionists" (who privilege theory) and "essentialists" (who privilege real women). Thus, it would be easy for me to argue that once constructionists and essentialists understand the truth of deconstruction (the magic third term), they will drop what they're doing to write proper histories of women.

However, there is no proper account of women to which deconstruction can appeal, although this is not the same thing as saying that there are no women. Deconstruction neither determines the representational space of women nor does it get rid of the category of women altogether, despite some protests to the contrary.[42] I want to argue that feminist analysis must be a deconstruction of representation that keeps the category of women incessantly in question, as a permanently contested site of meaning. Therefore, no history of progress should be allowed to suggest a final goal, an end or solution, to the questions of women. For instance, sweeping away false constructions of "women" does not then reveal the real women behind them, nor does the perspective of "real women" correct the false constructions of men and their patriarchal discourses. We do not simply add Laura Mulvey to Sigmund Freud, Luce Irigaray to Jacques Lacan, Drucilla Cornell to Jacques Derrida, Julia Kristeva to Roland Barthes, or even Judith Butler to Kristeva.

This is not to dismiss the importance of the historical, only to caution against too much faith in histories of progress. Feminism is not made all at once or at the same time. Thus, feminisms have their histories; no feminism exists in a pure present, standing on foundations entirely of its own making. In different ways and at different moments, debts have been incurred by feminists, debts whose very inescapability marks the limitations of a merely progressive understanding of feminism. The history of feminism is not a history of simple progress, of leaving the past behind. Rather, if feminism has a history, it is one of debts and obligations. There will be no point in the history of feminism at which it will have become obsolete to read Simone de Beauvoir. One is not born a feminist.

GENDER OR SEX? ✓

The history of women, then, should be written in a kind of suspension, written in a present that is not at ease with either its past or its future. The category of women imposes an uncertainty which is also an openness, and feminism should not be afraid to forbid itself epistemological author- ity. Between clear and distinct knowledge and ignorance lies politics. Yet before turning to the ungrounded politics of women's solidarity, it is important to interrogate what kind of category "women" constitutes. A significant debate has taken place within feminism as to whether women is a category of gender or of sex, and as to the precise nature of the distinction between gender and sex.

It will be no surprise that I say right away that this distinction is not necessarily a helpful one. However, it is important to take account of the fundamental issue that feminists have sought to get hold of by means of it: is "women" primarily a natural or a cultural category? The rough distinction between sex and gender can be made as follows: either sex is privileged as a biological attribute upon which a gender ideology is imposed, or sex is denied as merely the ideological mystification that obscures cultural facts about gender. Thus, if women are a sex, they are oppressed by gender; if women are understood as a gender, they are oppressed by sex. I fear that the desire to decide this issue is a significant problem for feminism. Whichever way feminists argue – whether women are understood as naturally sexed or as culturally gendered – the result is a kind of vicious circle.

Briefly, if women are a sex, we end up telling an inverted narrative of the Fall, in which Adam hands Eve the apple of gender stereotypes so that she loses touch with her true essence, her sex. Women's struggle, then, is to rediscover her sex behind the mask of gender. As with all Fall narratives, there is a basic problem: on what grounds does woman know what this sex is that she has lost? And if she knows it, has she really lost it? This produces women who, being somehow closer to their sex than others, have to function as priests to explain to their sisters that they know better than those sisters what those sisters really are. It would be surprising were feminism to have escaped the model of priestly authority employed by the patriarchy throughout Western history; however, that is not a sufficient reason to make women into the mirror images of those who have oppressed them. The notion that there is a truth to the feminine sex introduces a mode of legitimation to feminist politics that implicitly divides and hierarchizes women between those with authoritative access to that sexual nature, and those who require their instruction. In insisting on this kind of division and hierarchy, I am not arguing for a feminism where women are undifferentiated, all alike. Quite the contrary, I am arguing against the homogenizing tendency in the understanding of femininity as a natural sexual category. Hierarchy and homogenization go hand in hand. Hierarchy is always grounded on the assumption that differences are differences of degree, along a homogeneous scale. If femininity is a natural category, then differences between women are merely the effect of degrees of false consciousness, and liberation arrives when all women have come to authoritative consciousness of their own, identical, sexual identity.

   In opposition to this, some feminists have argued that sex is not natural at all, that there is no natural identity behind the masks of gender, there are only the masks. Accordingly, women would be understood to affirm their gender identity as a common experience of oppression and misrepresentation. Gender thus would be constituted as the ensemble of representations of women: housewife, mother, Barbie Doll, whore, madonna, Madonna, etc., etc. Here stereotyped gender roles are seen as based around chromosomal variations that give rise to biological differences; however, the differences have no meaning in themselves any more than do differences in eye color (also the product of chromosomal variation). Following out the consequences of this position, in future societies, parents may conduct pre-natal examinations to discover their fetus's eye color, and may pay no more attention to its sex than they currently do to its likely height. Of course, I exaggerate, but the point remains that for some feminists the meaning of gender arises exclusively within culture. Here, however, a problem arises which parallels that of sex. Gender is culturally determined, yet "culture" is made up of an ensemble of gender determinations. It is hard to know whether to blame culture for gender stereotypes or gender for cultural stereotypes.

In each case, the problem is one of identity, whether natural or cultural. To oversimplify for a moment, we might say that the concern to preserve gender identity as the grounds of a feminist politics at all costs leads both sides of the gender/sex debate into a parallel mistake. On the one hand, a notion of sex identity produces a quasi-religious mystification. On the other hand, the proclaimed demystification of sex turns culture into a mystical and all pervasive force. Where do gender stereotypes come from? Culture. What is culture? A set of stereotypes. Within this rubric, the identity of women is wholly negative: a shared experience of oppression. Yet this is an experience that no one really has, since experience is ideologically falsified by those very stereotypes. Paradoxically, then, the refusal to accept the myth of sex leads ultimately to disempowerment; women preserve their community only by insisting that it is man-made. This is the problem that Susan Faludi alludes to, in her discussion of the conservative backlash against U.S. feminism, when she remarks that "examining gender differences can be an opportunity to explore a whole network of power relations – but so often it becomes just another invitation to justify them."[43]

For the moment, let me say that the strict opposition between sex and gender, nature and culture, is the product of the desire that women have an identity above all – be it natural or cultural. I would like to suggest that the way out of the impasse between these stark extremes is not to resolve the argument between the two straw-women – earth mother and stereotype victim. Rather, a closer examination of the stakes in the gender/sex distinction may lead us to understand women as a category without recourse to a notion of identity as such.

In pursuing this closer examination, I want to understand the philosophical rather than the historical significance of the distinction. While historical work has made valuable contributions to feminism, my focus concerns contemporary issues in the West, without making any universal or ahistorical claims. For my purposes here, it is enough to remember, as Joan Scott helpfully points out, that the "concern with gender as an analytic category has emerged only in the late twentieth century."[44]

In the absence of strictly historical analysis, then, how is it possible to judge the distinction between gender and sex? One way to answer this question would be to consult the distinctions Kant draws between three kinds of judgment: *a priori* judgment which is universal and necessary; analytic judgment which establishes the truth or falsity of identity without recourse to experience; and synthetic judgment which needs to consult experience. An *a priori* judgment on the distinction would argue that the difference between sex and gender is determined in advance of either individual experience or rational analysis. An analytic judgment would argue that the difference between sex and gender is not a matter of experience but primarily a theoretical issue of identification – sex understood in its categorical distinction from gender within an autonomous system of philosophical categories. The synthetic judgment would insist that the experience of sex and gender is the correct basis on which to draw the distinction. Within this model, the *a priori* would privilege "sex" because sex is proposed as a category before thought: sex determines thought. The analytic would tend to privilege "gender" in assuming that the difference between sex/gender is a matter for thought, that mental representation by concepts determines the understanding of gender. Finally, the synthetic would argue that both sex and gender could be understood on the basis of experience alone.

The value of this kind of distinction is that it allows us to sort out with some degree of clarity the assumptions underlying particular accounts of the nature of the category of "women." However, what is primarily important for my purposes is to note that in the case of "women" this kind of classification of judgment breaks down in an interesting way. Kant's schema is useful in that it locates the category of experience within a network of distinctions. Against this backdrop, we can see that what takes place, crucially, in feminist thinking is a displacement of the notion of experience. We could even go so far as to say that the feminist challenge to philosophy is a refusal to accept the rigid distinction between analytic and synthetic judgment: a tendency to critique each in the light of the other.

Feminism's indeterminacy has been at its most powerful in insisting on experience against gender-neutral theorizations of the "nature of woman" and in critiquing the gender-neutral self-evidence of experience in the light of theorizations of gender. On this count, Elizabeth Weed offers an important warning about the dangers of a feminism that unproblematically grounds itself on "women's experience":

> For those outside mainstream feminism, "women's experience" has never ceased to be problematic. The common ground of sisterhood, long held as white feminism's ideal, was always a more utopian than representative slogan. Worse, it was coercive in its unacknowledged universalism, its unrecognized exclusions.[45]

Weed's remarks are timely, and I will discuss the epistemology of "experience" in more detail in the last section of this chapter. For now, I want to focus on how the distinction between gender and sex attempts to deal with the categorical problem of "women." The role of psychoanalysis has been crucial in suggesting that apparently "natural" attributes of sex are in fact the effect of psychic representations of gender. This is somewhat paradoxical, since Freud himself was, of course, primarily concerned to return patients' aberrant psychic representations to what he considered to be the natural sexual roles of male activity and female passivity.[46]

Rather than follow in Freud's patriarchal footsteps, a number of feminists have found Lacan's rereading of Freud a valuable contribution towards an understanding of gender-roles as masks rather than norms. And it is important in the context of my discussion of feminism and deconstruction to look more precisely at what Lacan's work has involved. Lacan makes his position on the relationship between gender and sex clearest in his by now famous parable of the two children on the train:

> A train arrives at a station. A little boy and a little girl, brother and sister, are seated in a compartment face to face next to the window through which the buildings along the station platform can be seen passing as the train pulls to a stop. "Look," says the brother, "we're at Ladies!"; "Idiot!" replies his sister, "Can't you see we're at Gentlemen."[47]

What the two children see, of course, are the signs over the station toilets, and what strikes the reader immediately is that the children have each made a mistake and don't know it. But while the children probably could be convinced that they had misunderstood where they were, it is unlikely that they would also understand the significance of their original error. Such is the stuff of parables, and the psychoanalyst steps in to identify six important points:

First, like the children we are ignorant of the structure that holds the gender/sex relationship in place. As a result, we are likely to be susceptible to the power the structure holds over us without even realizing it. That is to say, we will not be able to recognize the extent to which sex/gender systems control and limit our actions.

Second, each child understands where they are in terms of the other: the sister sees "Gentlemen," the brother "Ladies." This aspect of the parable not only calls attention to the force of binary logic in the gender/sex relationship but also underlines the way in which it is based on difference more than identity: we satisfy our prescribed gender role more through a knowledge of what we are *not* than what we are. And yet this knowledge is not the result of direct experience, since we are forbidden direct access to the place of the Other: the girl is not allowed to go behind the door marked Gentlemen; the boy is forbidden entry to Ladies. Something of the other sex/gender always remains a secret.

Third, sex/gender differentiation occurs as the result of language, not of natural or biological fact. In making this point, Lacan is not attempting to develop yet another instrumentalist account of language to explain sex/gender differentiation. Saussure's insistence on the unmotivated character and differential functioning of the sign is important to Lacan here. Gender is not established on the basis of any intrinsic sexual properties of the subject, but rather in opposition to the sign of the other gender. The signified meaning of woman or man arises from the interplay of the opposed signfiers of gender, from the presence or absence of the phallus. But this is not to argue that there is a one to one correspondence between signifier and signified, which Saussure's work might lead us to believe. As Lacan demonstrates, at the most basic level, the signifier (or sound image) "Ladies" refers both to the signified (concept) of a set of toilets *and* to the group of women in general. A similar multiple correspondence occurs with the signifier "Gentlemen." In each case, this crucial multiplication of signifieds suggests that woman might refer to more than a biological female, man to more than a biological male. Ultimately, as Jane Gallop notices, the "whole normalizing moralism of biologistic psychology" is upset because a natural correspondence between biological sex and proper gender roles does not exist.[48] That is to say, in Lacan's parable the "normal" has no biologistic grounds to which a psychological moralism could appeal.

Fourth, the entire system of assigning signifiers to signifieds is, as Saussure understood, ultimately arbitrary. There is no natural or justifiable reason why one toilet or group of people should be called "Ladies" and the other "Gentlemen." Nor is there any *a priori* justification for enforcing this division. Rather, enforcement is justified through a number of social conventions. Significantly, Lacan's parable makes no mention of the classic psychoanalytic notion of the Oedipal complex and resulting castration anxiety as the primary avenue for gender differentiation. The very absence of this central paradigm – where the girl is supposed to spend her life trying either to represent the phallus or to get the phallus (for instance, penis envy leads to the desire for children, which stand for the phallus) and the boy acquires a life-long preoccupation with the need to have the phallus that, at any moment, could be taken away from him – suggests that gender differentiation is not necessarily tied to parenting or reducible to developmental Oedipal interactions.

Fifth, no matter how much we might point out the arbitrariness of the division of individual subjects on the basis of sex/gender correspondence, this system is nonetheless rigidly enforced. The little girl must still sit in the seat which makes her think she is at "Gentlemen," the little boy must believe himself to be stopped at "Ladies." Lacan's parable would indicate, then, that it is no accident that public restrooms in the West continue to enforce a code of urinary segregation based on sex and gender distinctions. It is perhaps a further irony that the pictures which accompany or replace the written designations on Western toilet facilities do not necessarily bear a strict resemblance to those individuals who are hailed by them. Women will not necessarily wear the familiar skirt which inevitably adorns the women's room, and men in kilts and djellebas will not particularly resemble their trousered counterparts. But the fact remains that there must, underneath it all, be a moment of visual accountability. Women who fail to resemble sufficiently stereotypic women will be likely to find themselves accosted by law enforcement officials and asked to prove why they should be using the women's not the men's room – presence of the wrong set of genitals indicates the presence of a pervert.[49] Obviously, the stakes here go beyond who is simply allowed to use which toilet. The enforcement of sex and gender divisions aid and abet heterosexist societies and also lead to unjust divisions of labor that correspond to economic disparity.[50]

Sixth, Lacan's parable does not so much suggest that anatomy is destiny (in the fashion of much Freudian analysis), as it implies that culture has handed out tickets for gender seats on the basis of anatomy. Females are suppose to stand in the line that makes them into women, males line up to become men. Or as Jacqueline Rose points out, it is "not that anatomical difference *is* sexual difference (the one as strictly deducible from the other), but that anatomical difference comes to *figure* sexual difference, that is, becomes the sole representative of what that difference is allowed to be."[51]

The Lacanian six-point analysis goes a long way in explaining how the two-party system of male and female sex is made to correspond with the appropriate gender. I would even argue that the catchy parable is helpful for understanding that the entire gender/sex system rests upon arbitrary, socially constructed criteria. However, Lacan's train does not carry feminism as far as it needs to go. The ride on the gender/sex railroad may prove informative, but it hardly exhausts the possible terrain that can be covered nor takes into account whether or not the entire train needs to be derailed.

Deconstruction intersects with feminism precisely here: as an extension of the psychoanalytic account of the structure of gender/sex, an extension which involves a switching of tracks. To begin with, for Joan Scott, psychoanalysis is not sufficiently historical and lays too much emphasis on the individual. Nonetheless, her analysis in *Gender and the Politics of History* begins in much the same place as does Lacan's. She sets up the now familiar opposition where gender is a socially constructed category imposed on the pre-determined sexed body. But Scott is not altogether comfortable with the residue of biological determinism that this relationship implies, nor is she pleased with the way in which gender has been isolated from other categories of difference. As a result, she urges that "a genuine historicization and deconstruction of the terms of sexual difference" need to take place. This, she contends, would shift the emphasis away from sex and onto gender so that gender could be "redefined and restructured in conjunction with a vision of political and social equality that includes not only sex but class and race."[52]

In *Technologies of Gender* Teresa de Lauretis, like Scott, places sexual difference on the side of biological determinism and gender on the side of cultural construction. Also like Scott, de Lauretis privileges gender, which she understands as not only a classificatory term in grammar but also a representation of a relation that is an ongoing social construction.[53] For her, sexual difference "constrains feminist critical thought within the conceptual frame of a universal sex opposition," which makes it difficult, if not impossible, to articulate differences among and within women (2).

However, de Lauretis is even less satisfied than Scott or Lacan with the simple distinction between sex and gender. As a result, she proposes that "we need a notion of gender that is not so bound up with sexual difference as to be virtually coterminous" with it (2). According to de Lauretis, we must unravel and deconstruct the sex/gender relationship so that gender is no longer seen either as unproblematically proceeding from biologically determined sex, or as an imaginary construct that is completely beside the point.[54] Alternately, she proposes that "gender is not a property of bodies or something originally existent in human beings"; rather it is a "product and process of a number of social technologies" which create a matrix of differences and cross any number of languages as well as cultures (3). In short, de Lauretis's feminist theory of gender "points to a conception of the subject as multiple, rather than divided or unified" (x).

But de Lauretis's deconstructive engagement with the sex/gender distinction only goes so far. She wants to retain a notion of the subject, arguing that deconstructions of the subject effectively "recontain women in femininity (Woman)" and "reposition female subjectivity *in* the male subject" (24). For de Lauretis, "gender marks the limit of deconstruction, the rocky bed (so to speak) of the 'abyss of meaning'" (48). I am less inclined than de Lauretis, however, to believe that we have indeed hit rock bottom, that at the bottom of the deconstructive abyss lie the jagged edges of gender.

Rather than abandon feminism's alliance with deconstruction where de Lauretis does, Judith Butler goes on to question even our basic presuppositions about the sex/gender relationship. Butler sees no reason to believe that sex, as natural fact, precedes cultural inscriptions of gender: "Gender is not to culture as sex is to nature."[55] As far as Butler is concerned, then, Lacan's two children on the train do not first each receive a (biological) sex and then a gender (a cultural meaning for that sex). Instead, gender as a discursive element actually gives rise to a belief in pre-discursive or inner sex. That is to say, sex is retrospectively a product of gender so that, in a sense, gender comes *before* sex:

> It's not that there is some kind of *sex* that exists in hazy biological form that is somehow *expressed* in the gait, the posture, the gesture; and that some sexuality then expresses both that apparent gender or that more or less magical sex. If gender is drag, and if it is an imitation that regularly produces the ideal it attempts to approximate, then gender is a performance that *produces* the illusion of an inner

sex or essence or psychic gender core.... In effect, one way that genders gets naturalized is through being constructed as an inner psychic or physical *necessity*.[56]

If sex is the retrospective projection of gender, its fictional origin, Butler does not however argue that gender is the "real thing." Rather, she calls it "drag" or "performance," a particular kind of imitation. Not the imitation of a real sex but an imitation of an ideal that is its own projection, that does not exist anywhere else. This gender ideal can never be stabilized, but must ceaselessly be repeated with each performance of gender. To put this another way, we might say that gendered bodies are like actors in an unscripted play desperately trying to imitate a life that no one has ever led. They try so desperately because they believe that if they get it right, they will be allowed to leave the stage and lead that life. The significance of this argument (in the somewhat Beckettian formulation I have given it) lies in a refusal of the simple alternatives of sex and gender, nature and culture. Nature is the retro-projected illusion of a real origin to culture, yet that illusion is *necessary* to culture, the very ground of its capacity to represent itself.

Butler's aim is not, therefore, to deconstruct gender in order to reveal the natural sex which gender had obscured. Nor is she suggesting that gender is a cultural rock on which deconstruction founders. Rather, what the work of deconstruction will reveal is that there is no bedrock (to use de Lauretis' metaphor) of gender or sex at the bottom of the abyss. The relationship between sex and gender is a continuously self-deconstructing one which produces structures that are called natural only because we have forgotten that they are structures.

Paul de Man makes this point clearer when he explains that:

> The deconstruction of a system of relationships always reveals a more fragmented stage that can be called natural with regard to the system that is being undone. Because it also functions as the negative truth of the deconstructive process, the "natural" pattern authoritatively substitutes its relational system for the one it helped to dissolve. In so doing, it conceals the fact that it is itself one system of relations among others, and it presents itself as the sole and true order of things, as nature and not as structure. But since a deconstruction always has for its target to reveal the existence of hidden articulations and fragmentations within assumedly monadic totalities, nature turns out to be a self-deconstructing term. It engenders endless other "natures" in an eternally repeated pattern of regression. Nature deconstructs nature....[57]

What de Man wants us to recognize is that the work of deconstruction may reveal that nature is a structure (the "natural" is a cultural construct).

However, this new found "culture" in its turn implies a new nature, behind it as it were. Once this new nature is posited, it in turn gives rise to another deconstruction, another culture, another implied nature, and so on. The point here is not that culture deconstructs a pre-existing nature but that culture actually produces nature as its fictional origin.

To understand how this works specifically with regard to the sex/gender relationship, it is worth taking a closer look at some commonly held assumptions about sex. It would not take much of an argument to point out that sex has traditionally been understood in the West as a biological feature which requires no cultural assembly. Human beings come in two sexes, male and female, and each individual is supposed to be decidably one or the other.

But what happens when some assembly is required in order to make sure that there are still only two discernible sexes (and genders)? It is the answer to this question that best illustrates how gender actually gives rise to two "natural" sexes. The best presentation of this information to date is Suzanne Kessler's excellent essay, "The Medical Construction of Gender."[58] Kessler looks at what happens when physicians are faced with infants with genitals which are not unambiguously female or male. In these instances, Kessler notes that "case management involves perpetuating the notion that good medical decisions are based on interpretations of the infant's real 'sex' rather than on cultural understandings of gender" (10). Physicians assume, and parents are led to believe, that each infant has a natural sex and that the medical task is simply to reveal it. As Kessler puts it, "the emphasis is not on the doctors creating gender but in their completing the genitals" (16).

In discovering this "natural" sex, Kessler observes that doctors tend to refer to an "underdeveloped phallus" rather than an "overdeveloped clitoris," which suggests that an infant is first of all male until proven otherwise. And more often than not, he is proven otherwise. "What is ambiguous," she notices, "is not whether this is a penis but whether it is 'good enough' to remain one" (13). Thus, as Kessler explains, "as long as the decision rests largely on the criterion of genital appearance, and male is defined as having a 'good-sized' penis, more infants will be assigned to the female gender than to the male" (13). Again and again, the principle criterion for femaleness is the absence of *sufficient* maleness:

> The formulation "good penis equals male; absence of good penis equals female," is treated in the literature and by the physicians interviewed as an objective criterion, operative in all cases. There is a striking lack of attention to the size and shape requirements of the female genitals, other than that the vagina be able to receive a penis (20).[59]

The point of Kessler's article is to illustrate how physicians create a "natural" sex on the basis of shared cultural values about gender roles

(18). Kessler concludes that "the belief that gender [and sex] consists of two exclusive types is maintained and perpetuated by the medical community in the face of incontrovertible physical evidence that this is not mandated by biology" (25). The upshot of this, to return to Lacan's example of the two children on the train, is that as far as medical science is concerned, individuals are not allowed to stand in the aisles when the train pulls into the station; everyone must sit in a single seat, use a single toilet, be hailed by one and only one of two sexes/genders.

✳   ⌊What Kessler so thoroughly demonstrates is that physicians begin with cultural gender stereotypes and work backward to discover a supposedly natural sex which comes in only two types: female and male.⌋ The exclusivity of the two types is then assured in that the male type is given priority, and the female defined as "all those not having a good sized penis." While Kessler deals with extremes, it is nonetheless easy to see that the more common relationship between sex and gender works in precisely the same way. First, sex is established in relation to visual criteria (breasts or beards, clitoris or penis), and gender roles (clothing, mannerisms, voice tone, jobs) are established on the basis of sex-identification. However, it is the awareness of gender-roles that leads us to go looking for supposedly natural sexes.

But it is not only medicine's attention to genitalia or the general public's visual acumen that indicate how gender works to construct sex. In *Gender Blending* Holly Devor takes a revealing look at hormone studies:

> Human behavior patterns commonly used in hormone studies as indicators of biologically based femininity include: interest in weddings and marriage, preference for marriage over career, interest in infants and children, and an enjoyment of childhood play with dolls. Evidence of biologically based masculinity is defined in terms of childhood enjoyment of toys and games requiring high levels of activity, in self-assurance, and in holding career aspirations as more important than parenting.[60]

Devor goes on to explain that by the age of two, children understand that they are members of a gender grouping which consists of stereotypes like those used for hormonal studies.[61] "Popular conceptions of femininity and masculinity," she observes, "revolve around hierarchical appraisals of the 'natural' roles of males and females." What this leads to in mainstream North American society is a patriarchal gender schema that "reserves highly valued attributes for males and actively supports the high evaluation of any characteristics which might inadvertently become associated with maleness."[62]

Taking Devor's and Kessler's work into consideration may lead us to wonder whether the West could ever understand the un-naturalness of its own assumptions about nature and break away from gender stereo-types. On this score, feminists attempting to critique received assumptions about the naturalness of sex and gender roles have found Lacanian psychoanalysis helpful, even though it can be complicitous with the very positions that feminism opposes. Because Lacanian psychoanalysis has displayed a less than loyal relationship to feminist projects, it is worth taking some time to trace how Lacan managed to support both the feminist and patriarchal causes. And in so doing, I hope to perform a deconstructive reading which shows, as Elizabeth Grosz urges, "how psychoanalysis both participates in and departs from phallo(logo)centrism in ways that are not clearly distinguished."[63]

As I tried to make clear earlier, Lacan's work has been useful for feminism insofar as it outlines the traditional understanding of the sex/gender relationship in the West. But beyond this point, in his now well-known *Encore* seminar, Lacan also began a controversial discussion about the psychoanalytic nature of feminine sexuality. Here Lacan is quick to stress that "there is no such thing as *The* woman, where the definite article stands for the universal."[64] On first glance, this statement sets Lacan's work apart from beliefs in static gender-roles or strict correlations between sex and gender. Going even further, Lacan argues that this division of woman upsets the phallic sexual relation which, as Rose and Mitchell point out, "the woman has classically come to support" (137). As an alternative, Lacan proposes a feminine sexuality that would be supplementary and not complementary to phallic sexuality, "a *jouissance* beyond the phallus," as he puts it (145).

But all is not well for feminism in *jouissance* land, where women are not having as much fun as Lacan claims. Feminist critics of Lacan's theory of feminine sexuality have been numerous – too numerous, in fact, to do justice to them all here. But I would like, nonetheless, to chart the trajectory of some frequent and well-founded objections. To begin with, despite all his protestations to the contrary, Lacan actually threatens to return women and women's sexuality to the same rigid, psychoanalytic models from which he claims to be departing. On this score, it seems particularly apt that a statue (Bernini's *Santa Teresa*) serves as his central example of feminine sexuality. Lacan brashly contends that:

> You only have to go and look at Bernini's statue [of Saint Theresa] in Rome to understand immediately that she's coming, there is no doubt about it. And what is her *jouissance*, her *coming* from? It is clear that the essential testimony of the mystics is that they are experiencing it but know nothing about it. (147)

In one look Lacan thinks he knows all about women's pleasure – a *jouissance* that the mystics themselves could not know. And since the statue is not going to talk back to him – such is the benefit of taking your examples from marble slabs – the woman herself is hardly going to contradict him. Lacan, it would seem, returns women's pleasure to a state of passivity which would even make Freud happy.[65]

This is not a particularly feminist conclusion on Lacan's part, to say the least, and Luce Irigaray quickly exposes his phallocentric hands:

> The question whether, in [Lacan's] logic, [women] can articulate any- thing at all, whether they can be heard, is not even raised. For raising it would mean granting that there may be some other logic, and one that upsets his own. That is, a logic that challenges mastery.
>
> And to make sure this does not come up, the right to experience pleasure is awarded to a statue. . . .
>
> In Rome? So far away? To look? At a statue? Of a saint? Sculpted by a man? What pleasure are we talking about? Whose pleasure? For where the pleasure of the Theresa in question is concerned, her own writings are perhaps more telling.[66]

Examples of feminine pleasure, like Lacan's, are nothing more than a solace for men, guaranteeing to them that there is something foreign, fantasmatic, other to what is intolerable in their world.[67] Understanding woman as always and only a fixed model (even a model such as Saint Theresa, fixed in an attitude of mobility and self-abandon) necessarily reduces woman to the condition of the patriarchy: to be for herself a representation, lost in the act of modeling herself.

Statue of a mystic. Woman as statue. Woman as mystic. Such are the leaps of logic in Lacan's argument and the source of another serious problem with his work. It is easy for Lacan's theory of feminine sexuality to amount to little more than another instance of the mystification of woman as fixed model of the truth. This is the problem with Lacan's work that Derrida outlines in great detail in "Le facteur de la vérité." What Derrida demonstrates is that as far as Lacan is concerned woman is always where she is looked for. Woman has no universal, but she does lack universally. She has no truth, but femininity marks the truth of castration. As Derrida puts it:

> The link of Femininity and Truth is the ultimate signified of [Lacan's] deciphering. . . . He gives to Woman or to Femininity a capital letter that elsewhere he often reserves for Truth. . . . Femininity is the Truth (of) castration, is the best figure of castration, because in the logic of the signifier it has always already been castrated.[68]

Although Lacan refuses directly to make woman a universal – there is no such thing as the woman – before he's done with her, "Woman," "women," and "femininity" (Lacan readily collapses the terms) actually become the psychoanalytic pure particular, an ultimate pre-discursive signifier which comes before the discursive phallus. Hers is the true identity of pre-discursive lack.

So Lacanian psychoanalysis proves at times to be just another form of phallogocentrism, while medical science all too often puts its confidence in conventional, heterosexist paradigms of sex and gender. In these circumstances, all is not well for feminism, despite deconstruction's attempts to intervene. Women seem ontologically determined from the start, even if this "start" is retrospectively projected. It is worth asking, then, whether it is possible to break the established links between sex (as biological factor), gender, and sexuality. What can feminism and deconstruction do to move beyond conditions that inevitably prove oppressive for women?

Monique Wittig finds that the only answer is an all-out destruction of gender and sex. To understand why this must be so, Wittig argues that gender is "the linguistic index of the political opposition between the sexes and the domination of women," while sex is a political and philosophical category "that founds society as heterosexual."[69] That is to say, Wittig's point is that within society women are marked by sex, while within language they are marked by gender. Given this distinction, though, any power granted to sex and gender categories is grounded on ontological falsehoods. Gender, she maintains, "is an ontological impossibility because it tries to accomplish the division of Being."[70] According to Wittig, lesbianizing language performs a linguistic overhaul which reveals, by contrast, that Being is not divided, that the categories of gender and sex only get in the way of understanding ourselves as total subjects. With sex and gender out of the way, with distinctions between women and men no longer operative, society will be made up of ontologically total subjects, thanks to the linguistic revolution of lesbianization.

It may be tempting to believe that total subjects lie on the other side of the gender/sex divide, that all the king's persons and all the king's horses could put the subject back together again. But deconstruction has taught us to be suspicious of such totalizing schemes which, as Butler recognizes, unwittingly set up a "normative model of humanism as the framework for feminism." Butler is quick to point out the serious problems with Wittig's argument:

> Where it seems that Wittig has subscribed to a radical project of lesbian emancipation and enforced a distinction between "lesbian" and "woman," she does this through the defense of the pregendered "person," characterized as freedom. This move not only confirms the presocial status of human freedom, but subscribes to that metaphysics of substance that is responsible for the production and naturalization of the category of sex itself.[71]

Feminism's answer to the problem of established links between sex, gender, and sexuality should not be a philosophical embrace of presocial human freedom and neutralized Being. The dialectical neutralization of Being always ensures phallocentric mastery; presocial human freedom appeals to phallocentric universals.[72] Put simply, there is no liberated, total subject which unfortunately became divided – such is the narrative of the Fall to which I referred at the beginning of this chapter. I have just as little interest in pursuing the possibility of a gender and sex free, total subject as I do in trying to establish the true nature of sex or gender. Feminism should not be about establishing the true nature of sexual or gender difference, nor about abolishing it. Rather, the focus should be on keeping sexual difference – understood as the complex interplay of sex and gender roles – open as the space of a radical uncertainty.

But with that said, I have still not suggested *how* feminism and deconstruction would assure this space of radical uncertainty. For as Cornell reminds us, "we can't just drop out of gender or sex-roles and pick them up again when we feel like it."[73] Sex and gender-roles seem all too often unradically certain. Given a general resistance to change and a social interest in maintaining set gender and sex-roles, I would agree with Cornell that "we must take off from within sexual difference and not simply pretend to be beyond it."[74] The question more precisely becomes how to operate within the established terms of sexual difference, examining where those lines of difference have been drawn, while at the same time upsetting the terms and redrawing the lines.

One such avenue for change has been a combination of hormonal therapy and genital reconstruction which have helped individuals change their first biologically identified sex. One might say, then, that women have yet to be determined biologically. While some view medical sex-change procedures to be the reconstruction of the true sex which nature got wrong, such an argument has all of the problems that go along with other considerations of sex as a natural attribute. I would argue instead that sex change procedures generate a second sex which is neither more natural nor more cultural than the first. The very possibility of change itself calls attention to the unnaturalness of sex and gender-roles. This becomes even more evident when apparently radical medical practices designed to change an individual's sex rely on very conventional understandings of what it means to be either sex: the size of primary and secondary sex traits, voice timbre, quantity of body hair, overall body shape. After all is said and done, the result is still the same old two: female and male, woman and man.[75]

There is nothing necessarily feminist or deconstructive about these procedures, which tend to establish the same divisions of sexual difference, even if through unconventional means. Moving away from medical approaches, Devor appeals to what she calls "gender blending," the mixing of sex and gender such that strangers sometimes "mistakenly attribute them with membership in a gender with which the gender blenders themselves do not identify, i.e. females who think of themselves as women are mistaken for men."[76] Devor argues that an increased attention to gender blending "could serve as a transitional step between the present patriarchal sexist gender schema and a future state wherein the concept of gender would become obsolete and meaningless."[77]

On the surface, Devor's argument resembles Wittig's. But Devor's interest in abolishing traditional gender and sex roles is not to pursue a presocial total subject; her goal is the creation of a diverse range of sex/gender combinations such that the terms themselves could no longer create the grounds for discrimination and prescriptive sex/gender combinations. This interest in multiplication and diversity has been a feature of much of Derrida's deconstructive engagement with issues of sexual difference. Derrida stresses the importance of not understanding sexual difference in terms of sexual *opposition*. That is, we must move beyond understanding sexual difference as a binary opposition, which has long been the problem for both philosophical and psychoanalytic interpretations.[78]

In order to do this, Derrida encourages an examination of the "ready-to-wear," "off-the-rack universals" with which we symbolically determine sexual opposition.[79] His rather unlikely example is a Van Gogh painting of two shoes. What interests Derrida so much are the casual assumptions that Heidegger and Meyer Schapiro have made about the painting. In their consideration of the painting, both Heidegger and Schapiro draw conclusions about the class and gender of the owner of the shoes:

> It is true that neither Heidegger nor Schapiro seems to give thematic attention to the sex of reattachment. The one reattaches, prior to any examination of the question, to peasantry, but passes without warning from peasantry to the peasant woman. The other, having examined the question, reattaches to some city-dwelling painter, but never asks himself why they should be man's shoes nor why the other, not content with saying "peasantry," sometimes adds "the peasant woman." Sometimes, and even most often.[80]

Derrida is fascinated by the way in which both Heidegger and Schapiro jump to such conclusions about two shoes which do not explicitly denote the class or gender of their owner. He argues that a whole set of ready-to-wear assumptions about sex and class have been unthinkingly applied in order to reach these conclusions and even to assume, as both Heidegger and Schapiro do, that the two shoes form a pair. What is genuinely remarkable is the stunning obviousness of Derrida's observation that these shoes are *not* a pair, and that no one seems to have been able to see this before. While Van Gogh's shoes, or Heidegger's and Schapiro's interpretations of them, may not seem of much significance for feminism, Derrida's point is that the conclusions the viewers draw about the shoes rest, in each case, on opposition – left/right, male/female, city/country, peasant/painter – and the ability to *see* these oppositions. In order to talk about, perhaps even to see, these objects, the critics have to insist that there is a pair there, even Schapiro who claims to oppose his own scholarly empiricism to Heidegger's mystic ramblings. While it would be valuable to discuss the implications of each of these pairs, for the purposes of my argument here, I want to underline one point that Derrida makes in his essay: sex becomes visible and thinkable in Western philosophy only when it is thought as a complementary pairing, male and female, penis and vagina, inside and outside.[81]

Derrida proposes an alternative to this way of thinking sexual difference which is not unlike Devor's in its implications. Derrida wants to believe in the possibility of a non-binary, non-oppositional, "sexual otherwise." This would consist of "the multiplicity of sexually marked voices," "of non-identified sexual marks whose choreography can carry, divide, multiply the body of each 'individual.' "[82] Thus, sexualities, like sexual differences, would proliferate, confirming Irigaray's statement that for women there is "no possible law for their pleasure, no more than there is any possible discourse."[83] The cognitive abyss of sexual difference is where we are, before we know where it is we are.

Not all feminists have been comfortable with this news from nowhere, and Derrida's remarks have been often criticized for being merely utopian, for phantasmatically moving away from what women really experience.[84] However, I would have to agree with Cornell that Derrida's attempt to move beyond binary or oppositional definitions of sexual difference is one of the more valuable aspects of his work for feminism. Cornell correctly points out that Derrida's "writing is explicitly utopian in that it evokes an elsewhere to our current system, in which sex is lived within the established 'heterosexual' matrix as a rigid gender identity."[85] And it is such utopian thinking that becomes important for feminism, because it "demands the continual exploration and re-exploration of the possible and yet also the unrepresentable."[86]

LINGUISTIC OR MATERIAL GIRL?

But what, one may ask, does it mean to speak of utopian re-exploration and sexual multiplicity: are these just more examples of theoretical wordgames? Where does such linguistic play leave the materiality of women's bodies? Or the reality of women's experiences? A specific question arises immediately: what is the relation between the utopian and the actual? We are familiar with a tradition of social thinking, from Plato through More to Marx, in which the utopian is held out as the stick with which the contemporary situation is beaten. Yet this is not precisely what is going on with Cornell or Derrida. Rather than holding up a fixed ideal, they invoke the utopian as the grounds of an exploration. This is not the same thing as the dialectic proposed by Fredric Jameson, in which the ideal gives us the ground from which to critique the actual, while the actual experience of that critique modifies the ideal.[87] Rather than modification or adjustment, exploration aims at a destabilization of all notions of women, ideal or empirical. This, then, is not the utopianism of ideal models (model cities, model women); it is the literal utopianism of a "no place" (*ou topos*) which undermines existing models of thought.[88] Feminism, that is, must hold open a space of radical indeterminacy within the way it explores the category of women.

In these terms it is perhaps easier to understand what is at stake in the controversy that has raged within feminism over the status of "theory." Replaying the debate over sex and gender in other terms, feminists have either insisted that theoretical attention to the representational status of women in language ignores the real existing conditions of women's oppression, or that in order for feminism to understand those conditions it requires a rigorous theoretical description of woman as a linguistic subject. Bluntly, both of these arguments are straw-women, although their concerns are nonetheless important. The radical epistemological significance of feminism may be briefly stated: feminism upsets the simple opposition between language and materiality that is characteristic of Western philosophy.[89] Saint Augustine and Rousseau placed women on the side of matter and nature, men on the side of language and culture. In these terms, women's philosophy is inherently contradictory: it is not in the nature of women to think abstractly; they are too tied to the material flux and rhythms of nature, to the practical concerns of the household, for them to have access to abstract reason and the public sphere.

Part of the suspicion of deconstruction among feminists no doubt originates in a sense that deconstruction is one more male philosophical plot, little different from those hatched by Augustine and Rousseau. Yet if deconstruction has anything of interest to say to feminism, it is not as a philosophy *of* women nor even a philosophy *for* women. Rather, deconstruction, by subjecting to analysis the binary opposition between language and matter, thought and bodies, interrupts the unquestioned gendering of thought and of existence. Feminism, for its part, places philosophical thought face to face with the practices of gendered bodies. There is no synthesis here, no fusion of language and matter, of bloody bodies and rational minds. Instead, both feminism and deconstruction persistently inhabit the unthinkable paradox that a thinking body represents for the Western tradition.

Thus, feminism will not argue that women are either pure abstraction (ideological construction) or raw bodies (real historical objects). It will argue, however, that women are both at the same time, and that to be both at the same time is an impossible position, a challenge to an entire epistemology. There is no escape from anatomy for feminism, even as feminism refuses to accept that anatomy is destiny. In refusing philosophical arguments which key the subjection of women to anatomically grounded stereotypes, feminism does not attempt to theorize away gender. To do so, given the Western philosophical tradition's assumption that man is the gender-neutral instance of humanity as such and woman a gendered deviation, would be one more version of arguing that feminism is the struggle for women's rights to be men. If we take it seriously, this insistence that gender, while it is not natural, is not entirely cultural either, poses a radical challenge to an entire philosophical tradition. Feminism, that is, is not about answering questions posed to women by men within a philosophical tradition, nor is it simply a matter of trans-valuing women's exclusion from that tradition so as to become glad to be unphilosophical. Rather, feminism should not be afraid to demand that it should have its cake and eat it too.

Feminism cannot afford to lose sight of the body, even for a moment. At the same time, the insistence on the body, though it may be unacceptable within the terms of patriarchal philosophy, is not an abdication of critical thought, or a refusal of intellectual risk taking (risk taking is perhaps the feminist synonym for what traditional philosophy calls abstraction). Despite arguments to the contrary, despite all the calls for sexual multiplicity, decisions about sex and gender are frequently made on the simplest of anatomical criteria. The consequences vary in their political effects: from discrimination against women to discrimination on behalf of women. Hence, the lack of sufficient attention to women's health care, discriminatory treatment of women in the work-place, and violence against women, but also women's communities, women's assistance programs, and women's colleges.

The crucial point to realize is that there is no simple rule that can come to terms with sexual difference. Feminism does not simply want equal status or separate treatment for women. Women and men, that is, are not linguistic concepts between which we simply need to establish an equitable ratio that will resolve all questions arising from sexual difference. Nor are women autonomous material bodies, sexually self-sufficient. This is not meant to imply that women need men, rather that no sex is self-sufficient, as the very possibility of homosexuality shows. Since it is possible to desire a member of the "same" sex, that sex must carry within it the possibility of internal difference. Hence sexuality is not simply a variable which is added on to gender: the fact of homosexual sexual orientation inherently undermines the understanding of gender as a simple opposition between two identities, whether those identities are called sexes or genders. It is because the question of lesbianism opens up an internal difference (the space of a desire) within the proclaimed unity of the female that lesbianism has been so important in feminist theory.

Contrary to popular opinion, the "woman centered woman" is not more female than heterosexual or bisexual women (nor is she simply manly). Rather, the lesbian can only approach her femininity as an uncertain and contradictory site: *one which needs to be theorized* precisely because, *pace* Freud, homosexuality is not a narcissistic perversion (the wide array of gender blending in the lesbian community bears witness to this). Lesbianism is an encounter with woman as a question under the sign of Eros rather than an answer or a truth belonging to Logos. Critical lesbianism thus reminds feminism that it needs to examine the way in which women have been determined as *both* a linguistic and material category, but have not been exhaustively determined as (or by) either.

And in doing so, feminism must do more than unproblematically appeal to the reality of women's experience or the materiality of women's conditions for its answers. As Lacan recognized, "there is nothing more philosophical than materialism."[90] And I would add: except experience. The challenge of feminism to philosophy is that feminism simultaneously relies on and critiques the possibility of experience. Feminism that is interested in deconstruction follows through on this by understanding experience in terms of the body rather than the disembodied Cartesian subject. The body should not be taken as the *ground* of thought, but nonetheless the body's inescapability must be affirmed. As Trinh Minh-ha warns us, "the Body, the most visible difference between men and women, the only one to offer a *secure ground* for those who seek the permanent, the feminine 'nature' and 'essence,' remains thereby the safest basis for racist and sexist ideologies."[91]

The body is not real or essential; we will not find all the answers that we seek within it. However, feminism cannot dispose of the body any more than it can simply inhabit it. The difference of bodies remains a fact – a fact that menaces instead of legitimates our understanding of sexual difference. I would argue, then, that feminism and deconstruction should not ignore that these differences exist, but rather should follow Trinh's suggestions and create "*different* distribution[s] *of* sexual *difference.*"[92]

But the question is how to do this. Derrida's strategy is to denaturalize the rhetoric of the body, which leads him to concentrate on the hymen's graphic and the processes of invagination, without assigning any natural or essential femininity to them.[93] This may seem counter-intuitive to a cultural tradition in which the hymen has been situated as the space of difference within and between women, a marker of feminine difference and differentiation. But Derrida argues that the hymen has no proper, literal meaning, belongs to no woman in particular.[94] The supplemental work of the non-dialectical hymen exists outside the discourse of biological mimesis, at the margins of functional physiology. That is to say, the hymen may be thought to mark a space of material difference; however, there is no real space of difference to mark. Hence, no phenomenology of the hymen, because the hymen is a material/figural abyss about which there is nothing to know, a blank upon blank.[95] For Derrida, then, bodies are always discursive, inscribed and inscribing: rhetorical hymens and invaginations are intended to denaturalize the body, create different distributions of sexual markings.[96]

Irigaray's redeployment of descriptions of the feminine body works in a similar way. Taking the position that phallogocentric discourse has limited our understanding of sexual differentiation and pleasure, Irigaray tries to find linguistic avenues which can begin to speak about women's unspeakable pleasure – pleasure which exists but cannot be articulated by language. As a result, Irigaray writes of the multiple ways in which woman, as a sex which is not one, which is not singular or divisible into one, " 'touches herself' all the time," since "her genitals are formed of two lips in continuous contact."[97] The multiplicity of sexual differentiation and pleasure is also neither limited to individual bodies nor are the boundaries between individual bodies clearly drawn:

> Two lips kissing two lips: openness is ours again. Our "world." And the passage from the inside out, from the outside in, the passage between us, is limitless. Without end. No knot or loop, no mouth ever stops our exchanges.[98]

But this body, these lips, serve to displace the body as a site, rather than to fix it as the legitimating ground of a discourse on the nature of women. I would argue, as have others, that Irigaray's work is best understood *not* as another instance of crude essentialism or as a politically mistaken interest in biology, but rather as a strategy, like Derrida's, for denaturalizing the body by redeploying morphological language.[99] Biological language and anatomical designations do not function definitively: this is a body which will not be contained or fixed. Rather than celebrating a hypostatized female body, Irigaray's use of the rhetoric of biological discourse refigures anatomy, writing *through* and *with* the body rather than writing *of* the body: this is the sense in which Cixous has also spoken of "writing the body."[100]

However much Derrida, Irigaray, and Cixous insist upon refiguring the body as a way to create different distributions of sexual markings, there is another end to such control of the body which takes a decidedly less positive form. Western cultures have stressed the need to refigure the body to such an extent that women have begun to have an impossible relationship with their bodies. A woman's body is never the right shape, and supposedly always needs to be refigured through dieting and surgical interventions. Nine-year-old girls regularly go on diets; cases of anorexia and bulimia amongst women are almost as frequent as the common cold; breast implants, liposuction, and face-lifts are not just exotic operations for those women who can afford them. All of this is as much as to say that a battle with the body is almost the defining feature of what it means to "be" a woman in the West.

Given this situation, the question that needs to be raised in the context of my argument is: how are these refigurations of the body to be distinguished from those called for by Irigaray, Cixous, and Derrida? Put another way, is anorexia a form of writing the body? The quick answers are "there is no difference" and "yes." However, there are significant and important distinctions which need to be explored. First, the problem to address is not one of the violation of an essentially stable instance (the body) which is then deformed. Rather, anorexia is the attempt to erase the instability of the female body (periods stop, for instance), precisely in order to no longer have to live the contradiction between the patriarchal discourse of a stable healthy body and the actual experience of the female body, which by virtue of its own instability, seems to invite the interventions of patriarchal authority. And, of course, that authority establishes impossible aesthetic standards. The anorexic seeks to establish an authority over her own body at the price of that body itself, reducing the body to the fixed term, zero. Which is why anorexics rarely stop at being thin; their "excessive" thinness is an attempt to escape the inescapable. Irigaray, Cixous, and Derrida are not arguing for anorexia; they are arguing against the very lure of ideal bodily stability that constructs the anorexic's double bind.

Yet we might ask how far this refiguration can go, and how much it is dependent on the binaries of sexual difference. Interestingly, one of the major attacks on Derrida has been for assuming the possibility of a certain kind of transsexuality when he insists upon philosophizing from and about the position of woman. Do binary understandings of sexual difference, which all of these writings try to undermine, come back into play to determine refiguration as merely gender-switching? The answer for some feminists would be an unhesitating "yes." When a male philosopher takes up the position of woman, Rosi Braidotti sees just another example of the old misogynist habit of appropriating women's bodies.[101] Margaret Whitford is even more critical and accuses Derrida of "gender tourism" and "metaphysical cannibalism."[102] Boys must be boys, and never play at being girls or they will be held politically suspect.

There does, however, seem to be more at stake here than either Braidotti or Whitford are willing to concede. Spivak better articulates the consequences of Derrida's moves:

> However stubbornly Derrida might insist that female personhood must be reduced out of the female element or the female silhouette, that the vagina has only a figural connection with invagination, the strength of his own methodology will not allow such a totalizing exclusion and

binary opposition to stand.... Even the strongest personal goodwill on Derrida's part cannot turn him quite free of the massive enclosure of the male appropriation of woman's voice.[103]

Barbara Johnson continues Spivak's argument when she explains that:

Jacques Derrida may sometimes see himself as *philosophically* positioned as a woman, but he is not *politically* positioned as a woman. Being positioned as a woman is not something that is entirely voluntary. Or, to put it another way, if you tell a member of the Ku Klux Klan that racism is a repression of self-difference, you are likely to learn a thing or two about repression.[104]

Both Spivak and Johnson acknowledge the debt that Derrida is reluctant to admit: a debt proceeding from the fact that the physical body plays an important role in the meaning of sexual difference. The position of the body matters, as the distinction between the periodicals *On Our Backs* and *Off Our Backs* attests. And just because deconstruction and feminism attempt to undermine essentialist understandings of sexual difference, it does not mean that they completely succeed in doing so. Despite their efforts, essentialist understandings of sexual difference are still very much a part of institutional practices.

Likewise, the institutional non-recognition of Derrida as female figure entails political effects, which get articulated as a suspicion of a biological man's use of words like "hymen" and "invagination" to explain the work of deconstruction. If Derrida is positioned "as a woman" in philosophy, he is still *not* a woman. No refiguration can simply ignore the force of prior figurations, as Derrida would no doubt readily acknowledge. The question is not what it means to be or not to be a woman, rather it is that of what pragmatic force feminism should attribute to the assignation of a gender through institutional readings of sexual markings.

In phrasing the question in this way, I rule out the assumption that those markings are either the signs or the origins of anything like a universal or real "women's experience." The notion of experience implies the reduction of the matter of everyday life to the perception of *a* subject. That is to say, experience presupposes a subject who can be presumed to know. Such an understanding of experience has often been a staple of feminism; utilizing foundational logic, feminism has appealed to the truth of women's experience. And in so doing, it owes a large debt to phenomenology. But this is not necessarily a debt that feminism should keep incurring. I want to argue that feminism can exist without a consensual affirmation of female experience and that it is possible to rewrite the category of experience in terms that elude the knowledge of a subject.[105]

Such an assertion seems to fly in the face of a long tradition of feminist struggle. An entire generation of feminists was dedicated to nothing less than women's liberation, the empowerment of a female subject through acquired self-consciousness. The genre of autobiography is one of the best places to turn to understand what it would mean to speak of a feminism that was not primarily concerned with affirming the female subject's rise to autonomy through self-knowledge. The genre of female autobiography is crucially marked by this ambivalence, once it is recognized that the problem is not that women have simply been prevented from writing their autobiographies (and that feminism means that they should get on with doing so – sisters pick up your pens). Although it is undeniable that women have suffered from discrimination and exclusion in matters of self-representation, this is not merely a question of historical circumstance. As the texts of writers such as Hélène Cixous, Kathy Acker, and Audre Lorde attest, the category of women's experience is a problem for representation as such. I will discuss the question of identity politics in more detail in the next chapter, but for the moment suffice it to say that feminism shares with deconstruction a challenge to the notion of subjective experience as adequate to account for human existence.

In this sense, the genre of women's autobiography should be understood as a strategic necessity at a particular time, rather than as an end in itself. This is because the traditional structure of autobiography as the self-realization of a subject – the liberation of a subject into pure consciousness – is inadequate to the complexity of the question of woman. De Man's "Autobiography as De-Facement" is a crucial essay for understanding the dead end of consciousness-raising as a self-legitimating political project.[106] De Man argues that autobiography is the impossible genre, which does not deny the fact that countless books claiming to be autobiographies get written each year. What interests de Man is that although a book may claim to be an autobiographical account, this is actually an impossible task to fulfill. No text can present an accurate representation of the author's experience.

To show how this is indeed the case, de Man looks closely at autobiography's defining rhetorical trope: prosopopeia – "the fiction of an apostrophe to an absent, deceased, or voiceless entity, which posits the possibility of the latter's reply and confers upon it the power of speech."[107] In the case of autobiography, de Man is quick to notice that the apostrophe is addressed to the author's own absent or former self. Of course, the author can't actually talk to her/his past self and, likewise, that past self can't really reply. It's all a fiction. But fiction has a purpose, even when it disguises itself as factual autobiography. And here the purpose is to disguise the fictional aspect of a subject's experience. De Man contends that what autobiography shows is that there can never be a subject speaking directly of experiences. Whenever we try to explain what is happening to us, these present happenings become past events before we can explain them (even if the past is as immediate as reading this sentence on this page). Thus, autobiography cannot present us with an accurate portrayal of the author's experiences because it cannot present experiences: there is no reliable self-knowledge as such. Therefore, it is *not* that we don't have a "life" (we do) but that we don't have a direct *knowledge* of a private way of understanding. That is to say, we don't have experiences, if experiences are understood as direct knowledge of objects or events.

That the fiction of autobiography reveals the illusion of experience should not be judged as a picky point for only rhetoricians and literary critics to dwell on. There is a serious point to de Man's deconstructive argument which has consequences for feminism. As Scott recognizes, "the unifying aspect of experience excludes whole realms of human activity by simply not counting them as experience at least with any consequences for social organization or politics."[108] If some activity is never noticed, others are likewise forgotten; for it is only at the price of erasing the pastness of the past (amnesia) that the subject can believe itself simply present in autobiography or in politics. The effects of this amnesia are terrifyingly evident in the defense of technological rape (of the earth, of bodies, of women) in the name of "progress."[109] This is the reason juridical problems arise around women's bodies. There are no words for the experiences of women: "abortion" (she is pregnant or she isn't), "rape survivor" (rape is not murder). Feminism has even had to argue for the apparently tautological and self-evident "no means no."

I would like to suggest, then, if feminism and deconstruction are to refer to "experience" at all, it must be with this reserve: that the experience in question is one for which there can be no account.[110] Hence the woman – the voice for which there has been no language. Her experience isn't experience, in any conventional sense. However, to dissolve the category of "experience" is not to dismiss the political. There is a politics to the invocation of "experience," as teenagers are well aware. All knowledge is political, whatever its pragmatic status as a corrective. If anything, the political is re-emphasized. The production and circulation of knowledge takes on a *more* overtly political (social and ideological) aspect, because self-knowledge is no longer the origin, model, or reference point of or for the act of knowing and the knowledge of action.

And this move towards a politics which is not grounded by a notion of subjective experience also fails to propose a politics that would be decidable in any other straightforward way. The political remains the realm of the undecidable, which will not yield a theory of what women should be. Despite their false experience in the world . . .

Chapter 3

Towards a groundless solidarity

POLITICAL DIFFERENCES

Feminism is resoundingly political. One of the slogans that is perhaps most familiar is the claim that "the personal is the political." By this light, it seems, feminism refuses the gendered distinction of a male sphere of public life from a female realm of domestic economy. Feminism insists that politics is not something that happens between men alone: the supposedly natural order of relations between men and women is itself political, a matter for discussion and struggle. Even traditional notions of the nature of the political, which exclude or severely restrict female participation, have a gender politics.

   Deconstruction, however, is widely considered not to be political, to be an ivory-tower evasion of real politics. This general suspicion of deconstruction's politics often takes the shape of questions about deconstruction's constant emphasis on the importance of undecidability: how can an insistence on undecidability lead to political action? Isn't politics about acquiring certainty (or at least consensus) and acting on it? While I will discuss the politics of deconstruction in detail in this chapter, for now let me just say that deconstruction is better understood as a questioning of the terms in which we understand the political, rather than as a simple negation of the political. In this sense, it has much in common with the feminist refusal to accept the terms within and by which politics is conventionally practiced. To anticipate the argument of this chapter, then, I could risk saying that feminism is a deconstruction of the political, were it not that to use the term "deconstruction" in this context is to beg a series of important questions. One thing that most writers on the topic acknowledge is that the invocation of the verb "to deconstruct," as if it were a magic wand or universal key, is a highly un-deconstructive move. As I tried to make clear in the introduction, deconstruction is neither a magical method nor a mystical practice, and we're kidding ourselves if we think that the work of deconstruction necessarily solves all our problems or provides all our answers.

So for now, let me just hold on to the idea that what is at stake for feminism and for deconstruction is not the working out of a particular politics but rather the insistence that the nature of the political must remain open to question, to modification. Issues like abortion, for instance, do not have a simple politics. On the one hand, feminism insists that abortion is a political question. On the other hand, it insists that abortion is a matter of personal choice. For personal choice to be a political question, the conventional distinction between public and private needs to be rethought in a way that might be called deconstructive. Thus, while there is a difference between the public and the private, there is nothing that is intrinsically political or intrinsically personal (experiential). To put this another way, what is considered private is itself a political decision, and the result we are beginning to witness in the United States is that the private increasingly becomes a matter for public scrutiny – to a variety of political ends.[1]

This example is meant to illustrate that to discuss the political nature of feminism and deconstruction is not simply a matter of explaining their political implications, if by implications we mean how fundamentally or inherently non-political points of view or philosophies impinge upon a presumed stable order of discourse called "politics." For feminism as for deconstruction, politics is not "over there." Politics is not simply a discursive or practical mechanism, a stable field of practices that we can point out when it proves convenient. What counts as "politics" is a fundamental political question and one that feminism and deconstruction do not cease to ask.

Discussing "issues" in this chapter is therefore *not* a matter of working out where deconstruction and feminism stand on certain basic questions presumed to be of general interest. It is not a matter for pollsters – although politics, as it is commonly understood, is becoming more and more a question of market research. I want to argue that questions of subjectivity, identity, and solidarity are not matters in which opinion can be calculated. They are matters of opinion in a more radical sense, insofar as a belief in the calculability and decidability of opinion actually suppresses differences of opinion.

The purpose of this chapter is to examine how deconstruction and feminism attempt to rethink the political so as to allow a new range of differences of opinion to appear.[2] And this examination is closely tied up with an investigation of the limits of identity politics. The feminist political movement has often been understood to be at its most powerful when it grounds itself in an essentialist notion of woman and appeals to identity politics. But is this necessarily the case? Do identity politics actually limit the way in which feminism can understand difference and make possible political action? Can there be feminist politics which do not rest on a notion of women's identity, or on a female essence which would seek its political realization? Or does feminism cease to be feminism and start to be deconstruction when it begins to embrace nonessentialist notions of woman? In other words, does feminism lose its own identity thanks to deconstruction?

In attempting to address these questions, I want to explore the political practices made possible by *solidarity* which is not based on identity. The solidarity to which I am referring would, in fact, be a coalition built around a suspicion of identity as the essential grounding for meaningful political action. And while more is at stake here than simply replacing identity with difference, my hope is that political solidarity can be affirmed without losing sight of the difference within it.

In what follows, then, I will begin by focusing on the question of the *ground* of political action, to ask whether political grouping can occur without the assumption of some fundamental identity. To practice a politics without recourse to an identity – as either the hidden identity at the origin, or as the liberated identity which forms the goal – requires us to rephrase the notion of solidarity and community along the lines I have suggested. Finally, I want to argue for the necessity of rephrasing feminist and deconstructive action in terms closer to the traditional discourse of ethics than to conventional understandings of the political. What we stand to learn from feminism and deconstruction is that there are problematic positions about which we cannot speak a single political truth. That is to say, feminism and deconstruction do not give rise to a single politics that is articulated everywhere at every time in the same way.

To call this a move from politics to ethics is not to suggest that we need to start focusing either on moral criteria or on individual choice. I am not, that is, echoing either John Rawls or G. E. Moore.[3] In my argument, the "ethical" names a shift away from the regime of truth. The shift to the language of ethics is an attempt to redefine the political, to get away from the assumption that the political is the discourse of social truth, the practice that aims to establish the true society or to tell the truth about society. Thus an appeal to the ethical as a way of problematizing social responsibility, as a way of thinking the question of community without appeal to the truth of a presocial identity, will allow me to develop an account of feminist community as *groundless solidarity*. But first of all, we have to look at how feminism and deconstruction handle subjectivity and subjection.

SUBJECT TO CHANGE: IDENTITY POLITICS

If anything could be called a common political interest for deconstruction and feminism, it would be subjectivity. Both have examined this issue in some detail, although not necessarily with the same results. In fact, some of the fiercest political battles between deconstruction and feminism have been fought over just what role subjectivity should play in the drama of politics.

To understand why subjectivity is such a central issue as far as deconstruction and feminism are concerned, it is important to recognize the way in which the politics of the modern era are anchored upon the notion of a subject. At first glance, this may seem a little paradoxical, since the determining characteristic of modern political organization is that individuals cease to be subjects, subject to the arbitrary rule of a monarch. Instead, modern individuals supposedly become citizens in a State, bound by laws which supposedly they themselves have decided upon either by staging a revolution or through engaging in democratic discussion. Yet the subject does not go away. No longer subject to a monarch, the modern citizen is now the subject of a State. Yet this subjection is held to be freedom, since the State is nothing other than the collective will of its citizens.

The State as political entity names the incarnation of a national people into a subject. Accordingly, political meta-narratives offer to work out the destiny of the subject. Thus, for instance, "we the people" become Americans, call ourselves Americans, dedicate ourselves to finding out who we are, and struggle to organize ourselves politically so that we can be American. In this sense, political forms are the means to an end, and that end is the realization of a fully autonomous political subject. The instance of individual citizens subject to the State determines the nature of what it is to be an American. So rather than doing away with the subject in favor of the citizen, "the subject" plays such a dominant role that modern politics could accurately be renamed "the politics of the subject."

Given this state of affairs, the ways in which feminism and deconstruction problematize the category of the subject stand to have direct political implications. First, both deconstruction and feminism insist that the supposed freedom of political subjects to make their own laws in the modern state should not be taken at face value. Deconstruction persistently refuses to accept the category of the subject as self-evident or natural. As far as Derrida is concerned, "the subject is a logocentric concept," neither a neutral category of existence, nor a natural category of Being.[4] That is to say, the subject is necessarily always a political subject, produced by and within the *polis*. The subject does not enter into the realm of the political; rather, the subject is produced by the political itself as a way to regulate and control individuals. Judith Butler perhaps puts it best when she writes that:

> [T]he subject is an accomplishment regulated and produced in advance. And is as such fully political; indeed, perhaps *most* political at the point in which it is claimed to be prior to politics itself.[5]

For deconstruction, the subject is a certain logocentric concept which persists in order to enact specific political effects, and no amount of denying that the subject is political will negate this fact.

Deconstruction, however, finds no need to embrace the subject as the foundation of all forms of political activity. A deconstruction of the subject would involve recognizing the abyssal nature of the subject/object relationship, which I traced in Chapter 2. And if the subject infinitely changes places with the object, as the *mise en abyme* suggests, then it is necessary to imagine a deconstructive politics that does not ground itself on the possibility of a stable or coherent subject free to make its own political decisions.

Lest we think, however, that we have left behind the notion of the subject forever, feminism's response to the deconstruction of the subject has often been less than enthusiastic. On its side, feminism is more conflicted than deconstruction over the necessity of the subject. Wendy Brown sums up the situation well when she says that the "postmodern deconstruction of the subject incites palpable feminist panic."[6] While Brown might be accused of unnecessary hyperbole by those unfamiliar with the nature of the debate, a couple of examples reveal the extent to which her assessments are accurate. In *White Woman Speaks with Forked Tongue*, Nicole Ward Jouve expresses the popular sentiment that "you must have a self before you can afford to deconstruct it."[7] Margaret Whitford puts it even more strongly when she suggests that the deconstruction of the subject "continues to leave women in a state of fragmentation and dissemination which reproduces and perpetuates the patriarchal violence that separates women."[8]

As far as Jouve and Whitford are concerned, the deconstruction of the subject undermines the very possibility of feminism. They hold that it is not only desirable for women to become subjects, it is also necessary if feminism is to achieve its political goals. How else, they ask, will women be able to join hands and fight the patriarchy? The battle will only be won by feminism if women first become unified subjects in their own right. The argument then goes that feminism should consequently spend its time trying to bring women together, appealing to a common language, common consciousness, and common experience with which all women can identify.[9] I use the word "identify" intentionally here, because I think that it is important to stress that such feminism understands the subject in terms of identity: the political subject is that which remains identical to itself in the face of contradictions. To be a political subject, then, is to have a political identity, a self, a consciousness to call one's own. What more could a girl want?

But this appeal to the subject counts for more than a rebirth of individualism in the house of feminism. For a feminist appeal to identity also means that not only would each individual woman be a subject, but all women would participate in a common political identity called "Woman." The politics that proceed from this emphasis on women as subjects, united in a common struggle, usually goes by the name "identity politics." And this version of feminist politics would argue, in a very modernist way, that political action is impossible without subjects acting collectively. Hence the argument that the deconstruction of the subject is a luxury that feminism cannot politically afford: no subject means no identity, which means no identity politics, which means no feminism.[10]

Certainly, there is a pragmatic aspect to feminism's appeal to identity politics, and its suspicion of deconstruction in this particular political arena appears to have some merit. If one were to spend all of one's time worrying about deconstructing the subject while also attempting to run election campaigns, argue sexual harassment cases, or explain to students why sexist language is inappropriate, then not much would get accomplished from a feminist perspective. It's not usually very effective, for instance, to attempt to convince women voters that voting for a woman candidate is in their best interest because they also should be in favor of deconstructing the subject. Chances are that the person who did use that argument would quickly learn a few things about the practicalities of political campaigning as it now stands.

Feminism, indeed, cannot afford to ignore identity politics and hope that they will go away magically. Deconstruction or no deconstruction, identity politics continue to have a great deal of political currency, operating effectively across the political spectrum. For instance, representative democracies in which over 90% of elected officials are white men illustrate that identity politics have long worked in conservative ways to assure who gets elected and even who gets to run for office. The question really is how to negotiate the identity politics which are now in place and how to move on to other forms of politics. The value of deconstruction is that it can help us to understand the limitations of playing the identity politics game, as well as open up possibilities for ways of doing politics differently. In that sense, the work of deconstruction can loosen the strong hold that identity politics, that the politics of the subject, have over political life.

In light of these considerations, I want to continue, as promised, by discussing the major drawbacks of relying too heavily on identity politics to solve all of feminism's problems and win all its battles. To begin with, identity politics all too often encourage uniformity and conformity. In the name of "identity" and "identification," such politics demand of women that they all join together solely on the basis of what they have in common, so that difference among women is not just ignored but erased. The question that arises is: must feminism always seek to erase difference by giving birth to a family of identical daughters who all fight for the same causes, who all pretend to share the same feminist goals? In this respect, the danger is that women stop being a *question* for feminism and that identity functions as a normative ideal.[11] Identity politics can thus work to exclude or simply ignore all of those individuals who fail to conform to the correct model of womanhood.

Such is the danger of the "common oppression" argument to which I referred in the previous chapter, even when it tries to become more nuanced by allowing for a set of identities that attempts to be all inclusive. For instance, a heterosexist paradigm which tries to find an identity for all women with regard to their marital status (single, divorced, or married) would have trouble taking account of lesbians. If a woman has a live-in female partner is she "married"? If she's separated from her live-in female partner is she "divorced"? Within this paradigm, there are no names to apply to these cases which do not treat the lesbian woman in terms of her heterosexual counterpart. In the eyes of the law, frequently when it comes to such things as spousal benefits granted by employers, all lesbian women are single. Legally, the lesbian couple often simply does not exist.

In addressing this case of discrimination against lesbians, which results from trying to apply categories designed to describe heterosexual relationships, identity politics can become part of the problem rather than the solution. Identity politics based on common oppression would have to argue that categorizing women in terms of their domestic arrangements oppresses all women equally. While many feminists would agree that all human beings lose when they are positioned in terms of such narrowly defined categories, it nonetheless is a gross oversimplification to say that all women are oppressed equally and in the same way by this convention. The lesbian worker whose partner needs medical benefits does not occupy the same position as the heterosexual female homemaker who is covered by her husband's insurance benefits. Identity politics begin to fall apart when they try to account adequately for the fact that all women are not the same, are not facing the same set of political problems. If feminism tried to argue that all women are supposed to join hands together, identify with a common set of political problems, it would fail to consider the difference, for instance, between the heterosexual homemaker's unpaid labor and the lesbian worker's lack of spousal benefits.

To take this example a step further, it's also not enough merely to establish a hierarchy of oppressions as a response: the lesbian worker is more oppressed than the heterosexual homemaker, the black lesbian worker more oppressed than her white counterpart, and on and on. This is the political pitfall that Pratibha Parmar recognizes when she considers the ways in which identity politics employ a language of "authentic subjective experience." As Parmar explains, identity politics have

> given rise to a self-righteous assertion that if one inhabits a certain identity this gives one the legitimate and moral right to guilt-trip others

into particular ways of behaving. The women's movement in general has become dominated by such tendencies. There has been an emphasis on accumulating a collection of oppressed identities which in turn have given rise to a hierarchy of oppression. Such scaling has not only been destructive, but divisive and immobilizing.[12]

Alongside the "we're all oppressed together" trap lies the "hierarchy of oppression" whirlpool – together they form the Scylla and Charybdis of identity politics. As Parmar points out, the other danger of identity politics is that difference and identity become a matter of hierarchies, where identity is reduced to a place within a hierarchy of oppressions. Individuals battle for the right to speak by collecting oppression markers: the more oppressed and victimized the individual identity, the more moral and political currency it has.

How can feminism speak its differences without drowning in a whirlpool of oppression? Identity politics try to answer this question by examining who is speaking for whom, by paying special attention to which individuals represent which categories of difference. Such a solution frequently assumes that each individual should speak for the categories of difference that they are seen to represent within the feminist community. To return to my earlier example, this would mean that the white homemaker should speak politically only in the name of other white homemakers; the black woman must represent the black woman's perspective; the lesbian is always held accountable for the lesbian perspective.[13]

One advantage of this concern with visible representation and accountability is that it can call attention to the ways in which identity politics have actually served to exclude certain positions. For instance, a feminist movement biased toward white, middle-class, heterosexual women could dramatically change its political focus by listening to the voices of women of color, working women, and lesbians. However, this simplistic approach to difference as a series of identity categories has some worrying consequences. First, individuals become recognizable only as their category of difference. The black woman, for example, always represents the black woman's position so that she cannot be understood as representing a political position that does not necessarily have anything to do with the fact that she is a black woman. Second, the individual is assumed to be able to represent an entire identity category. To continue with the same example, the black woman is supposed to represent all black women under the assumption that all black women must share the same political opinions on any given matter. The result of this form of identity politics is that, in the name of representation, it stands to be complicitous with some of the worst forms of tokenism and stereotyping.

Such an answer to the question of speaking difference can only be arrived at by begging part of the original question: what happens when an individual is marked with multiple categories of difference? Is the black lesbian first a black, then a lesbian, and then a woman? Or is she understood as a lesbian black who is first a lesbian, then a black, and then a woman? Is the white homemaker first a white, then a homemaker, then a heterosexual, and then a woman? Is she politically more aligned with other white women, with other homemakers, with other heterosexual women? Who speaks for those whose differences cannot be named? These are precisely the kinds of questions that identity politics try to answer with a return to a hierarchy of oppression; they merely try to identify which position is the most oppressed and therefore granted priority over the others. That this move proves so unsatisfactory reveals the extent to which identity politics consistently tend to ignore the complexity of the relationship between identity and difference.

In *Woman, Native, Other*, Trinh Minh-ha offers an important corrective to this dead end of identity politics. She argues that:

> Difference understood not as an irreducible quality but as a drifting apart within "woman" articulates upon the infinity of "woman" as entities of inseparable "I's" and "Not-I's" .... Difference does not annul identity. It is beyond and alongside identity. ... The idea of two illusory separated identities, one ethnic, the other woman (or more precisely female), again, partakes in the Euro-American system of dualistic reasoning and its age-old divide-and-conquer tactics.[14]

Trinh's feminist gesture is also deconstructive in its attempt to articulate the interconnectedness of differences and identities. Breaking away from the imperialism of dualistic reasoning, Trinh challenges the unity of the modernist subject and thus calls the very foundations of identity politics into question.

In a way, this is also a subtle return to Hegel's position that difference should not be understood in terms of pure antinomies, of binary oppositions. The Hegelian dialectic functions in contrast to Kantian antinomies in that within the thesis stands the difference of the antithesis, and vice versa. That is to say, neither thesis nor antithesis is purely identical to itself: within "I" there is always "Not-I." However, Trinh also should not be understood as yet another Hegelian, marching toward Absolute Knowledge thanks to final dialectical synthesis. Rather, the move she is making is deconstructive in that for her, as for Stuart Hall, difference is always undermining identity such that it would be more accurate to understand identity as a production "which is never complete, always in process, and always constituted within, not outside, representation."[15]

Identity, then, is neither natural nor stable, and the mistake of identity politics is to assume that it is. But nonetheless, can such a recognition of the proliferation of differences ever make a political difference? Must feminism speak of difference in a way that would satisfy deconstruction? Some feminists might still say that it's only by putting differences aside, by recognizing common political goals in the name of coalition building, that any political action happens. This has some validity, as Parmar persuasively explains, in that the battle to claim positions of oppression and difference can splinter the feminist movement to the point that the only political action it can perform is its own self-destruction. However, a critique of identity politics should bear in mind these crucial questions: *how* will we decide to put aside our differences, *how* will a position of political solidarity be arrived at? These questions should serve as a reminder that feminism can no longer afford to ignore the kinds of concerns about identity that Trinh and Hall raise.

With this in mind, it is therefore important to consider alternatives to identity politics as well as feminist and deconstructive critiques of identity. A modern politics of the subject is not the liberating spirit it may once have been considered to be, and feminism is beginning to recognize the injustices its own political practices have brought about. But where feminism would turn next is certainly not self-evident either, especially since a return to classical political theory would stall on its failure to welcome women into the rank of full citizens. From Plato to Aristotle and Rousseau, women have been written out of the social contract. At the very least, women have been said to have sex-specific flaws which they must correct before becoming citizens (Plato); at the very worst, women are *de facto* excluded from the public sphere, from any engagement with political life (Aristotle and Rousseau). In this respect, identity politics along with, at least theoretically, a representative democracy look like a great improvement. However, as I have tried to illustrate, the problem feminism inherits from the legacy of the universal subject of contract law – from Hobbes to Locke and now Rawls – is that it assumes that there can be no politics without a subject.

This self-validating proposition has served to shut down entire avenues of discussion about what might constitute politics. In her essay "Contingent Foundations," Butler provides an excellent analysis of what is at stake here:

> To claim that politics requires a stable subject is to claim that there can be no *political* opposition to that claim. Indeed, that claim implies that a critique of the subject cannot be a politically informed critique but, rather, an act which puts into jeopardy politics as such. . . . The act which unilaterally establishes the domain of the political functions, then, as an authoritarian ruse by which political contest over the status of the subject is summarily silenced.[16]

The same could be said to hold true for that even bigger political subject: "we the people." For as Butler rightly observes, this time in *Gender*

Trouble, "the feminist 'we' is always and only a phantasmatic construction," which does not need to form the foundation for all feminist politics.[17]

Butler gestures toward the possibility of doing politics without a stable subject (a subject in possession of a verifiable identity). And in this context the question that needs to be asked is: what happens when feminism stops assuming that identities have to be in place before political action is possible?[18] First of all, it would mean redefining what might constitute politics. Certainly, politics would be more than negotiating power between individual subjects.[19] But politics would also involve more than securing the relation of the citizen subject to society, a point which Bill Readings demonstrates in "The Deconstruction of Politics."[20] For feminism to take account of the deconstructive critique of the subject, it must displace the centrality of the subject in our understanding of political action. This will have enormous political implications for our understanding of the nature of political struggle: feminism would seek neither to liberate a female subject nor to secure certain fundamental rights for her. And to say this is, of course, to consider how a feminist politics could also be deconstructive, how a deconstruction of politics could also be feminist.

I have already discussed the problems attendant upon an understanding of feminist struggle as the attempt to realize or liberate a supposedly universal subject, "woman." However, the feminist rethinking of politics does not merely consist of relinquishing this particular utopian ideal and finding other reasons to engage in action. On a more basic level, the deconstructive displacement of the subject means that we need to rethink the way political discourse claims "rights." This entails reassessing the way in which oppositional politics, at least since Thomas Paine, have sought legitimation in an appeal to the "rights" of a subject. For feminism this would mean questioning just how desirable it might be to make political appeals to a "woman's *right* to choose" or "equal rights."[21]

Traditionally, rights-based politics assume the prior existence of a political subject to whom specific rights are then granted. Political subjects come first, rights follow afterward. For instance, "women" are definable political subjects to whom abortion rights or equal rights are then granted. The question becomes that of deciding which rights are the natural and inalienable property of a given subject. Accordingly, the problem of rights becomes a matter of description: what rights belong to which subjects? In the context of this argument, it is important to note that there is nothing intrinsically anti-sexist in the argument about rights, so stated, since it may be argued that men and women, as different kinds of subjects, possess different sets of rights. Of course, once we start talking about *human* rights, then gender ceases to be a factor, and the description of humanity is what counts: the question of what rights animals or fetuses have is in fact the question of whether or not they are human. Here I want to note one important factor, as this issue relates to abortion. Within this understanding of rights as the property of subjects, the only criterion for determining rights is the description of the human subject who is to be their holder. Thus there can be no right to an abortion, only the right to life, for fetus or for mother (when endangered). Sidestepping this debate by claiming that the right to abortion is covered under a more "fundamental" right to privacy – as the U.S. Supreme Court did in its landmark abortion decision Roe v. Wade – is less an end to the discussion than it is a postponement of what is really at stake, however necessary that deferral might have been at the time. Feminism is destined to lose this entire argument, since the equal rights to which women aspire turn out to mean the right to be a hu-MAN.[22]

Feminism, however, need not accept the terms of the debate – whether they are articulated as the right to life, the right to privacy, or the right to equality – because these terms are based on a fundamental misconception about the subject. Subjects do not define rights for themselves; rather, rights produce subjects who can hold them. That is to say, the attribution of a right as "human" is implicitly a definition of the nature of the human: it is supposedly a human attribute to be free, to conduct political discussion without recourse to torture, and so on. The appeal to rights suggests that these are not inherently political questions: such a description of politics contains the mark of the Fall which allegedly has separated mankind from its own nature, stripped it of its rights. If those who advocate political rights are to be believed, the politics in which the newly enfranchised will engage is the struggle to escape from politics and return to nature.

This seems a generally dangerous way of thinking, since it tends to view all forms of equality and injustice as merely temporary, in order to blind us to their deep-rootedness. The abortion argument will not be solved by pious wishes, or any balance between the rights of the fetus-subject and the mother-subject (and even the father-subject). There is no such balance, because these subjects are the products of the rights attributed to them. Rights are like gateways: the fact that they seem to open onto vistas of liberty can lead one to ignore the fact that one has to stoop, bend and contort oneself in order to fit through them.

Deconstruction would urge us to consider – whether within the context of the abortion debate in particular or more generally in discussions of rights politics – that political subjects are provisional.[23] Rather than taking the political subject as a given, or assuming that natural rights are legitimate, a deconstructive politics would turn its attention to the way in which rights actually construct the political subjects who are entitled to those rights. Thus, the appeal to rights is always an appeal to a certain *description* of the human as more human than other descriptions.[24] In

Lyotard's terms, the formulation of a prescription about rights on the basis of a description of the nature of the human is the fundamental operation of Terror, of the *a priori* suppression of difference. You can have rights, but only if you are human in my way.[25] This is a lesson feminism has taught more than any other area of political struggle, since it lives most acutely the differend that constitutes the abortion debate. In the language of the fetus, the mother is a murderess; in the language of the mother, the fetus is a virus. No balance can be struck, since there is no common language that can express the rights of both sides without prejudice. And to appeal to rights in such a case risks hiding the fact, claiming that the prejudices of one side precede argument because they are natural.

To say this, however, is not to argue against feminism or, for that matter, against abortion. It is to argue that the abortion debate cannot be "won" or "resolved" in present terms, in terms of a struggle over rights. Indeed, to continue arguing in terms of rights may well be anti-feminist. An abortion is each woman's choice. To seek to enshrine it as a "right" risks neglecting the sentiments of the woman who chooses not to have an abortion, or who has an abortion and regrets it, or who has or doesn't have an abortion and can't decide whether she did the right thing. An abortion, that is, is not like a vote. You don't use it to express yourself, to feel one with yourself. Abortion is no more or less natural than sex – and feminists know how the notion of "conjugal rights" has served to enshrine marital rape for centuries in the West.

This is a point worth dwelling on for a moment. Conjugal rights imply the right of property which the man as subject has over the woman as object. Accordingly, conjugal rights are precipitated by the understanding of sex as the question that can be regulated by a common language which describes this activity as heterosexual. To put this in the terms I've used from Lyotard, there is no differend in sexual activity according to this assumption: a woman has a certain right to her body; a man has a right to have sex; society regulates the preponderance of these two rights. Two kinds of subjects are produced between whom sex circulates as a commodity. When the woman exercises her rights, no sex takes place; when the man exercises his rights, sex occurs. To take an example using these terms, five minutes of sexual activity once a week doesn't seem very much to ask, compared to the rest of the week when the woman "has" the commodity. That this description of sex seems patently inaccurate has to do with the range of discourses it excludes. That it has received the imprimatur of the church, despite this, might seem strange were it not that we can now understand it as the logical consequence of the attempt to legislate a natural sexual activity. And all such attempts to legislate by appeal to nature will produce similar kinds of injustice. Plenty of women have found "sexual liberation," the affirmation that sex is natural and thus good, to be nothing other than imposition of unlimited sexual service of men. Along the same lines, when it comes to sexual activity, the right to privacy, as Mary Poovey notes, "can actually exacerbate sexual oppression because it protects domestic and marital relations from scrutiny and from intervention by government or social agencies." Poovey concludes, and I would agree, that "in postulating an individual capable of 'free choice,' in other words, the privacy defense ignores the extent to which women have been subjected to violence, *especially* in relation to their sexuality."[26] Of course, the danger we face with Poovey's corrective is the equally unattractive possibility of the State policing all sexual activities. "Protection" can also take the form of "oppression," and certainly sodomy laws, in all their various configurations, have operated as frightening examples.[27]

This case can help us to understand that politics is not simply a matter of according or balancing rights, that a distributive notion of justice is unjust in that it assumes the prior existence of those to whom justice is distributed as self-evident entities. Drucilla Cornell has attempted to redress this injustice by calling for "equivalent rights" rather than "equal rights." Her idea is that "rights should not be based on what men, as conventionally defined under the gender hierarchy, need for their well-being, as if there was only one genre of the human species."[28] This is a first step in getting away from rights politics which are based on presumably universal notions of what it means to be a human subject, which has, as I've tried to show, always really meant what it means to be a male subject. Cornell's argument is especially useful in the cases where feminism must strategically appeal to rights politics. That is to say, however much I want to expose the problems with rights politics, however much feminism and deconstruction stand to gain from developing other ways of doing politics, rights politics retain a great deal of political force, just as identity politics do – in fact, sometimes they are just two ways of describing the same political activity, as many anti-abortion rallies will attest.

By deconstructing the "conventional understanding of gender identity," Cornell's "equivalent rights" provide a way to recognize two important categories of rights:

> The first type of equivalent rights recognizes the legitimacy of nontraditional, intimate relationships, particularly the arrangements of those who engage in homosexual rather than heterosexual love and sexual encounters. The second type of equivalent rights addresses the value of feminine sexual difference. These rights demand the acceptance of one fundamental premise, perhaps the most basic premise of feminism, which is that what is called human is only too often in patriarchal

culture the genre of the male, which implicitly erases the other genre of the human species: the female.[29]

But however much Cornell's position is an improvement over conventional rights politics, it still carries with it the attendant problems of rights politics outlined in this chapter. Cornell's "equivalent rights" are useful as a strategic position, but I do not think they provide a way to move beyond a politics of the subject; instead, we are left with a discourse of rights which provides a wider array of subject positions, but the subject remains nonetheless.

TO BE NEGOTIATED: THE POLITICS OF THE UNDECIDABLE

Given the problems with both rights politics and identity politics, what would a politics without the subject look like? How could deconstruction and feminism negotiate between competing political claims within such a framework? Would this just turn into the politics of anything goes?

Let me say right away that I do not think that a politics without a subject leads to nihilism or a political free-for-all. But I will maintain that a politics which does not have a notion of the subject as its founding principle is a politics best understood as a politics of the undecidable. This is a point worth explaining, because in claiming that the political is the realm of the undecidable, I am not trying to suggest that no political actions or decisions are possible. Rather, the political is better understood as the realm of continual negotiation, as a matter of negotiation in the absence of any accounting procedure. Homi Bhabha stresses the central role negotiation plays in politics when he refers to the words of Nelson Mandela:

> As Nelson Mandela said only the other day, even if there is a war on you must negotiate – negotiation is what politics is all about. And we do negotiate even when we don't know we are negotiating: we are always negotiating in any situation of political opposition or antagonism.[30]

I would stress, as does Bhabha, the importance of recognizing that these negotiations often take place without recourse to pre-established models or methods of calculation which direct the negotiations. This would be very different from identity or rights politics in that a politics of the undecidable would refuse to close down the question of difference or account for it by merely balancing competing claims to rights.

The emphasis here would be on deconstruction's and feminism's insistent questioning of the political, which would be, as Readings acknowledges in "The Deconstruction of Politics," at odds with any conservative attempt to naturalize the status quo.[31] For as I hope I have illustrated thus far, deconstruction and feminism warn us about the dangers of becoming comfortable with a politics grounded in stable subjects or normalizing identities – instances where negotiations are limited by the political models (identity or rights) which precede them. It would also be at odds with establishing a set political order in which negotiations are no longer necessary.[32] To take one extreme example, fascism and other forms of totalitarian politics would have little chance to dominate. But to take another, politically less comforting example, there would also exist the danger that hard-won battles carried out in the name of social justice – political struggles to overcome racism or sexism, for instance – may have to be refought, renegotiated. Within the politics of the undecidable there is still, unfortunately, the possibility of injustice, but it is important to emphasize here that the political would be the space of the contested with regard to the social.

As a way to illustrate more precisely what I mean by the politics of the undecidable, I want to return to the abortion debate and look at Barbara Johnson's analysis of the way in which undecidability plays a crucial role in the political struggle which surrounds that debate. Johnson argues that:

> It is often said, in literary-theoretical circles, that to focus on undecidability is to be apolitical. Everything I have read about the abortion controversy in its present form in the United States leads me to suspect that, on the contrary, the undecidable *is* the political. There is politics precisely because there is undecidability.[33]

While Johnson's argument is limited by her singular focus on the abortion debate as primarily a debate over when "a being assumes a human form" (189), as well as by her failure to discuss the problems with rights-based arguments, there is much to learn from what she does say. First of all, Johnson's argument illustrates the way in which an insistence on undecidability does not also mean the end to political action. For her, political action on the abortion question is possible precisely because of the recognition of the place of the undecidable. On this count, Johnson provides an important counter to much feminist thinking. Just as many feminists have been concerned about the political consequences of the deconstruction of the subject, so too have they taken issue with deconstruction's emphasis on undecidability. Inevitably the problem these feminists underline is that deconstruction's emphasis on undecidability (or indeterminacy) makes politics impossible. The refrain is a familiar one, and echoes some of the feminist arguments made against the deconstruction of the subject.

To take a few examples: Biddy Martin and Chandra Talpade Mohanty cite the "political limitations of an insistence on 'indeterminacy,'" which in their view "implicitly, when not explicitly, denies the critic's own situatedness in the social, and in effect refuses to acknowledge the critic's own institutional home."[34] Similarly, Leslie Wahl Rabine contends that the indeterminacy which guides deconstruction is incommensurate with the women's movement "which has no choice but to take yes-or-no positions on specific issues and to communicate them as unambiguously as possible."[35] As one final example, Poovey, in what seems a striking departure from her own argument about abortion, concludes that deconstruction's politics of indeterminacy must be equivalent to thermodynamic heat death – the ultimate position of inactivity, the entropy of agency.[36]

Each of these feminist writers accuses deconstruction of a politics of indeterminacy, whereas Derrida has been concerned to distinguish the politics of undecidability from the notion of indeterminacy. Much confusion has arisen over these terms in the context of deconstruction, and the distinction is an important one, which we are now perhaps in a position to address, although I did not myself draw the distinction between the indeterminate and the undecidable in Chapter 2. Indeed, I would propose that the specificity of a feminist politics is perhaps to undermine the Kantian grounds on which the distinction is drawn. Derrida has gone so far as to claim that he does not believe he has "ever spoken of 'indeterminacy.' "[37] For him, undecidability is something else altogether:

> Undecidability is always a *determinate* oscillation between possibilities (for example, of meaning, but also of acts). These possibilities are themselves highly *determined* in strictly *defined* situations (for example, discursive – syntactical or rhetorical – but also political, ethical, etc.). They are *pragmatically* determined. The analyses that I have devoted to undecidability concern just these determinations and these definitions, not at all some vague "indeterminacy." I say "undecidability" rather than "indeterminacy" because I am interested more in relations of force, in differences of force, in everything that allows, precisely, determinations in given situations to be stabilized through a decision of writing (in the broad sense I give to this word, which also includes political action and experience in general).[38]

A strange binary opposition seems to be lurking round the corner here: between a good, "political" undecidability and a bad, vague indeterminacy. So why do I refer to indeterminacy, particularly with a view to what women can be or do? In drawing his distinction, Derrida is concerned to avoid the insinuation of a Kantian liberty that he hears behind "indeterminate," the assertion of a freedom from determination (a subjective autonomy).[39] Thus, Derrida contends that actions are not free but multiply determined, the problem being that we cannot decide *among* determinations. Hence uncertainty is not autonomy. In this sense, Derrida's remains a laudably *political* thinking, and in speaking of the "indeterminacy of women," I am not attempting to return to a notion of subjective autonomy, nor to argue that there is any essence of woman that would be free from determination. Rather, I have argued in Chapter 2 that women are multiply determined, in a way that agrees with Derrida's stress on the undecidability of determinations. However, I also want to suggest that these multiple determinations are *open-ended*, a suggestion that underlies my appeal to a non-Kantian indeterminacy for women. The affirmative potential of feminist politics is that such a politics takes the undecidability of the multiple determinations of women, the clash of virgin, whore, mother, etc., as the aporetic space within which a freedom arises. Not a Kantian freedom, not a subjective autonomy, but the freedom of a collective uncertainty, a groundless solidarity. As feminists, we are all concerned for women, yet we don't know what they are. And what binds us together is the fact *that we don't know*. The specificity of feminism is thus its insistence that the politics of undecidability (among multiple determinations) must be understood from a standpoint of indeterminacy, of political *possibilities*.

Leaving aside the confusion between indeterminacy and undecidability, I would argue, therefore, that feminist resistance to the politics of the undecidable is misguided. To return to Johnson's argument, what the focus on the undecidable stands to make clear is that it is precisely feminists who wish to preserve abortion as a difficult decision, a decision that is a woman's choice, that is not decided in advance. Nazis, on the one hand, and fundamentalists, on the other, believe that the question of abortion is always determined: have one if you are "unfit" and don't have one at all. I have been asked how a focus on the undecidable "will help us win the debate on abortion." To win the debate on abortion would be to allow the *undecidable* in so far as abortion would be neither a decision which could be made in advance or made once and for all for all women.

Another way of putting this would be to say that the interpretation of the future (of politics) is always in process without it ever becoming determinable. Prescriptions for political order are not produced from descriptions of past or present politics. To use Gayatri Spivak's words, the politics of undecidability hold out for the possibility of "revolutions that as yet have no model."[40] In this regard, undecidability need not be another name for relativism or nihilism, as I have tried to stress. By acknowledging the undecidable, deconstruction and feminism allow us to imagine other political spaces – spaces of political otherness. This is an acknowledgement that politics is not an order of meaning, that politics will not come to an end and explain what other people are, what their otherness means. Rather, politics is an encounter with difference, the attempt to handle differences. An ethical or just politics must recognize that this handling cannot itself become the object of a contract, cannot be given a determinate meaning. There are differences, they arise, always more of them.

A just politics must seek to handle those differences, to respect them, without implying that what is other can be made identical by means of that handling. This is the lesson of Lyotard's *Differend*. There are differences among women, there are differences between women and men. These differences are not symmetrical, nor do they fit into a simple hierarchical order. All these differences must be respected, but we will never come to the end of them. This is a depressing thought for people who don't like politics, who don't like difference, who just want to get it over with and make everyone happy. For those of us who find that our lives are confusing, that other people are strange, it can be a benefit to realize that 1. it is not other people's fault that they are different from us (this is the psychotic fascist assumption); 2. it is not our fault that we are not like other people (this is the neurotic liberal assumption). The endlessness of politics in this sense has a parallel with the endlessness of teaching, the endlessness that enters teaching once teaching ceases to be the simple transfer of information between a knowing master and an ignorant student.

Spivak sees a specifically pedagogic benefit in Derrida's "deconstructive" lesson in *Limited Inc*. She holds that:

> [It] can teach student and teacher alike a method of analysis that would fix its glance upon the itinerary of the ethico-political in authoritarian fictions; call into question the complacent apathy of self-centralization; undermine the bigoted elitism (theoretical or practical) conversely possible in collective practice; while disclosing in such gestures the condition of possibility of the positive.[41]

Once the understanding of knowledge as information has been relinquished, the process of teaching becomes that of exploring ethical responsibilities, or the "politics of pedagogy": the responsibilities among students and teachers and their responsibilities to a tradition and to a world in which that tradition sits uncomfortably. In this sense, the pedagogic scene is a strong metaphor for the way in which deconstruction enacts an ethical transformation of the political.

Derrida tries to work out what this transformation would mean in the context of a European idea of democracy and the *duty* to respond to the call of European memory. Derrida's point is a complex one, and it is worth quoting him at length:

> The *same duty* [to respond to the call of European memory] dictates assuming the European, and *uniquely* European, heritage of an idea of democracy, while also recognizing that this idea, like that of international law, is never simply given, that its status is not even that of a regulative idea in the Kantian sense, but rather something that remains to be thought and *to come* [à venir]: not something that is certain to

happen tomorrow, not the democracy (national or international, state or trans-state) of the *future*, but a democracy that must have the structure of a promise *and thus the memory of that which carries the future, the to-come, here and now.*

The *same duty* dictates respecting differences, idioms, minorities, singularities, but also the universality of formal law, the desire for translation, agreement and univocity, the law of the majority, opposition to racism, nationalism, xenophobia.[42]

In this passage from "The Other Heading," Derrida makes a number of important moves. First, the political is phrased in ethical terms: as a *duty*. This duty is not the same thing as public virtue, which for Rousseau would be found in nature or for Hegel in reason. Rather, Derrida's use of "duty" is better understood as an obligation to the other, the other that comes from nowhere and everywhere, the other that cannot be located as either subject or object. Our duty to the memory of Europe, the duty "to recall what has been promised under the name *Europe*" (76), is a duty to both the past (a tradition) and the future (a promise). This is not the same thing as uncritically upholding a tradition or forgetting the injustices that have been committed in the name of an adherence to tradition. Derrida is not proclaiming a version of cultural imperialism reminiscent of the arguments put forth by Allan Bloom and E. D. Hirsch in the United States, nor is he trying to argue that there is even a single cultural tradition that must be called European. Rather, the duty of which Derrida speaks is primarily to recognize that the present is *not* culturally self-sufficient, the present does not *ground* a politics any more than do the past (conservatism) or the future (technocracy). The past can only be recalled as a promise (it still awaits fulfillment), and the future fulfillment is dependent upon a past promise.

Thus, for Derrida, to think about European democracy is to negotiate the temporality of the political. Democracy has a context; it has a relationship to the past. But it must also be thought in relationship to the future. In this sense, democracy remains to be thought; it remains to be seen what will happen to it. This is not the same thing, Derrida notes, as a democracy of the future. European democracy extends into the future because it provides a context for what might yet happen.[43] This is very much a politics of the undecidable in that Derrida is trying to stress that the political – especially when it takes the shape of European democracy – should not be allowed to predict the future: the terror of political models occurs when they leave no room for the undecidable, when they precisely try to fix the future. European democracy, in Derrida's view, does not offer a model or a set of rules which create the political future. Rather, for Derrida, and this is the third point I would like to stress, European democracy enacts a promise: a promise to remember a duty (more precisely, a responsibility) to both the past and the future. And this very act of remembering may lead to a critical reappraisal of European democracy itself; that is to say, what has been done in the name of European democracy may prove neither to have done justice to the past nor have been responsible to the future.

Finally, Derrida phrases the duty enacted by European democracy as also a duty to respect difference. This would mean accepting and acknowledging that individuals within the democracy are not all alike, that the very nature of European democracy will change, will become different from itself, and that not all peoples are like those who are governed by European democracy. All of which is to say, that the duty lies in thinking difference in non-hierarchal terms. But this duty to respect difference does not stand by itself; it is juxtaposed alongside a desire for translation, universality, international law, and a concern for global forms of oppression which pit whole groups of people within European democracy against one another: racism, xenophobia, and nationalism.

Given Spivak's and Derrida's rather polemical arguments, how is it possible to take what they're saying and apply it to different political contexts? To which political contexts around the world might they apply? Do Spivak's remarks only have relevance for U.S. universities? Derrida's for the European community? What changes would need to be made if they were to apply to other contexts and political forms? These are questions which cannot be answered once and for all; they must be addressed again and again. None of these specific contexts is a universal model, as both Spivak and Derrida are quick to point out.

Thus the understanding of politics as undecidable is not about refusing to make decisions: it is about refusing to ground decisions in universal laws. We might even go so far as to say that the politics of the undecidable is an insistence that we have to *make* a decision, each time, in each case – that we cannot avoid making a decision by just applying a pre-existing universal law.[44] The question, then, is not how to move beyond or out of deconstruction so that judgments and actions can take place but rather how deconstruction and feminism oblige us both to judge and to act. To avoid a paralyzing relativism – I can't decide therefore I can't act – the politics of undecidability must, in some way, engage with ethics and consider *obligations* and *responsibilities*.

This engagement with ethics, however, is not one which takes the shape of traditional moral philosophy with its emphasis on the subject. Rather, the deconstructive motivation (we could call it agency) to make judgments and take actions begins with the *displacement* of the assurance of a self-present subject. In this respect, Derrida's use of the word "duty" is misleading. The trouble with "duty" is that Kant tries it make it immanent to the subject. Subjects are conscious of their duty and conciously do the right thing if they are to be moral. However, obligation and responsibility insist upon the subject as a *singularity* in a relation to otherness. We are obliged, we are responsible, but we cannot make that into a matter of consciousness. Thus, in what follows, I will argue that the ethics of deconstruction and feminism is an ethical activism which requires that judgments be made, yet which does not supply the means of legitimating those judgments. No recourse to self-present subjects, natural rights, or transcendental truths . . .

Institutional Interruptions

1: INSTITUTIONS?

Before I pursue the issue of ethics any further, I think it is important to underline that the politics of feminism and deconstruction are situated in relation to institutional structures. The phrase "institutional structures" is meant to refer to those codified organizations that in some way serve as regulatory bodies governing social actions. And the range of possibilities that could fall under this umbrella phrase are large: social welfare programs, organized religions, the academy, the military, government agencies, ideas of motherhood, to name only a few obvious examples and suggest the ways in which these structures might overlap. In this context, neither deconstruction nor feminism is a free floating body of ideas, independent of socio-political institutions.[1]

To many these may seem like unduly academic reflections upon feminism, an attempt to drive feminism along with deconstruction into the ivory tower. After all, what is so significant about the institutional situation of feminism and deconstruction? Why would it be necessary to interrupt a discussion of politics and ethics with a reflection on the institutional structures in which deconstruction and feminism exist? The short answer is that it is impossible to understand the work feminism and deconstruction perform without thinking about their relation to institutional structures. A longer answer must consider that deconstruction is singular in its attempt to think the institutional politics of knowledge; likewise, there exists a wide body of feminist writing on the *exclusion* of women from institutions. And although the struggle against exclusion is by no means over, feminism's gains have also brought with them the necessity of some reflection on what it means for women to be *included*, on what the institutional politics of feminism might be.[2]

It is not clear what it means to speak of an "institutional politics," of knowledge or of anything else. In the first place, I want to insist that there is a specific weight to social and political institutions, that institutions are not simply the tools or instruments by which policy is enacted. As we all know, bureaucracy has a life of its own. We don't just have some ideas about education and then set up a university to carry them out, nor do government ministries seek to *solve* the problems they are supposed to address (government ministries seek rather to *manage* problems, and thus keep themselves in existence). The critique of bureaucracy as such (as opposed to denunciations of specific bureaucratic organizations for failing to do their jobs) is the most obvious example of an "institutional politics," of an attempt to think the politics inherent in the institutions by which politics is carried out. More generally, feminism has clearly addressed the gendered nature of social and political institutions that claim to manage society "as a whole." And deconstruction has been exemplary in its insistence that the institutions of knowledge are not neutral, that they have a politics. As Derrida points out:

> Thus, if it is to have any effect, what we sloppily called deconstruction is never a set of technical discursive procedures, still less a new her-meneutic method working on archives or statements in the shelter of a given and stable institution. Deconstruction is also, at least, the act of taking a position, in the very work it does with regard to the political-institutional structures that constitute and govern our prac-tices, our competences, and our performances. Precisely because it has never been concerned only with signified content, deconstruction should be inseparable from this politico-institutional problematic and should require a new questioning of responsibility, a questioning which should not necessarily trust the codes inherited from/of ethics and politics. This means that deconstruction, which is too political for some people, can seem paralyzing to those who only recognize politics with the help of pre-war slogans [*des panneaux de signalisation d'avant la guerre*]. Deconstruction is neither limited to methodological reform that would reassure the established institution nor a flourish of irres-ponsible or thoughtless destruction, whose most certain effect would be to leave everything as it is and to consolidate the most ingrained forces within the university.[3]

Derrida emphasizes that deconstruction is not a set of discursive proce-dures nor a method which takes shape in a given institutional location. Simply put, deconstruction does not rely on signified content alone; rather it takes into account the significance of context. Perhaps an innocuous enough statement on its own and yet increasingly relevant when one considers that context includes "the codes inherited from ethics and politics." If deconstruction is "the act of taking a position," it is also a way of rethinking how we might understand politics in the absence of grand political metanarratives. Hence, a politics of undecidability which questions institutions but not through mere destruction, insofar as the interrogation of codes of behavior sanctioned by particular institutional structures involves at the same time a political *investment* in those institutions.

Once the specificity of institutional politics is recognized, then both feminism and deconstruction have to address the question of their own institutionalization: what happens when feminism and deconstruction become, for instance, a standard feature in the academy? What happens once feminism and deconstruction do not only participate in institutions but become themselves cultural institutions, referred to in the press as presumed to have a certain stability and weight in cultural life? Have feminism and deconstruction unwittingly become examples of, or participants in, those seemingly immobile institutional structures which they set out to disrupt?

These are questions that feminism and deconstruction must continue to ask, for the danger lies in becoming satisfied with a set of answers which makes it seem unnecessary to repeat the questions. Were this to occur, deconstruction and feminism would indeed succumb to unreflective institutionalization. What follows, then, is intended to be some provisional answers, formulated mainly within the insitutional contexts of North America. These answers eventually will prove to be unsatisfactory and incomplete, giving rise to more answers and more questions.

2: ACADEMIC?

The existence of the derogatory catch phrase "academic feminist" marks a further point of feminism's community with deconstruction. The epithet "academic" is not designed to lend intellectual respectability. Quite the reverse. What is being marked is the institutional detachment of feminism and deconstruction from everyday reality. However, there is a kind of double bind here. On the one hand, feminism and deconstruction, by virtue of their mutual dissociation from "reality," are considered insane, too academic. The objection raised against them follows a beautifully simplistic line of argumentation: "life just isn't like that." A slightly more nuanced version would claim that academic feminism, like deconstruction, may indeed respond to the pressures of a certain reality, but that reality is the hopelessly elitist, very select, reality of the academy (principally the university) which actually affects very few individuals. Here, academic feminism and deconstruction are ghettoized as esoteric, not sufficiently mainstream, concerns. Academic feminism is seen to sell out feminism's commitment to everyday praxis, deconstruction presumed to be hopelessly removed in the first place. This position would not stand in the way of an alliance between academic feminism and deconstruction; however, one would be hard pressed to imagine why the alliance would matter, why the result would be anything more than a ridiculously esoteric discourse.

On the other hand, academic feminism and deconstruction also fall prey to the charge of being insufficiently academic. Such critics claim that academic feminism is a contradiction in terms, an oxymoron. The line of reasoning would be that by definition feminism is *not* an academic concern but rather a political agenda, attempting to pollute the academy with everyday concerns. For anti-feminists, feminism corrupts the academy; for some feminists, the academy corrupts feminism. By extension, deconstruction gets dismissed as insufficiently academic, although not necessarily because it is too wedded to presumably nonacademic, political concerns. Instead, deconstruction is more often not taken seriously because allegedly it fails to conform to proper scholarly standards for research. Thus, it's not really philosophy; it's not really literary criticism; it's not really political science; it's not even properly interdisciplinary. The list could grow, while the point remains the same: deconstruction fails to conform sufficiently to the standards of any pre-existing disciplinary practices and hence is not considered academic. Again, such an objection does not so much stand in the way of any alliance forming between deconstruction and feminism as refuse to acknowledge that the result would have any legitimate effect on academia.

What is perhaps oddest about these arguments is that they often exist in the same place. For instance, Allan Bloom will accuse feminism and deconstruction of having both too much *and* insufficient reality in the same book.[4] Of course, the question must be: how could this be possible? Why would critics like Bloom mount an argument around two mutually exclusive claims? I'm sure it's possible to answer this question in a number of ways, the simplest having recourse to something about sloppy argumentation. While that may indeed be true at some level, it also rather misses the point of what is at stake. It would seem to me that a better answer would have to take up *why* it is so important for some to make a case against the serious role feminism and deconstruction stand to have in the academy. Bloom's confused response makes more sense when we think of it as coming from someone who is desperate to make sure that feminism and deconstruction are dismissed from becoming serious academic concerns.

I would argue that all of these objections are intended to eliminate the ways in which both feminism and deconstruction disturb the carefully drawn institutional boundaries of academia. What is especially disturbing, for critics like Bloom, is the way in which feminism and deconstruction challenge the line between the ivory tower and the world. Feminism and deconstruction are thus dangerous because they are neither solely in the ivory tower nor in the world but on the line between them. In this context, the two different ways of dismissing their academic importance are really two sides of the same coin: the current coin of the established institutional realm.

Therefore, my focus on the university has to be understood in terms of a larger view of the borderline between political praxis and theoretical reflection, the borderline I talked about in Chapter 1. The place where this borderline between theory and practice takes on an institutional meaning is in the university, a *political* institution for the *disinterested* pursuit of knowledge. Of course, the paradox here is that the supposed unworldliness of scholarly investigation requires a massive and worldly institution in order to be possible. But the worldly shell around the unworldly kernel doesn't really exist. Administrators, for instance, are not really protecting scholars from undue "outside" political influences; rather more often than not, the concern is to control the precise nature and ideological direction of those influences.

Here I am not only talking about state-funded research for direct political ends: the military's technological campaign, known as "star wars research" conducted in science departments in the United States, for instance. While it's possible to acknowledge, as Derrida does, that "never before has so-called basic scientific research been so deeply committed to aims that are at the same time military aims," it's also increasingly difficult to "distinguish between technology on the one hand and theory, science and rationality on the other."[5] The separation between basic, supposedly politically disinterested, research and applied, politically committed research has broken down to the point that we can begin to wonder whether such a separation ever really existed in the first place.

Significantly, it is not enough to point out this problem in the sciences alone. As Derrida rightly notices in "The University in the Eyes of its Pupils":

> At the service of war, of national and international security, research programs have to encompass the entire field of information, the stockpiling of knowledge, the workings and thus also the essence of language and of all semiotic systems, translation, coding and decoding, the play of presence and absence, hermeneutics, semantics, structural and generative linguistics, pragmatics, rhetoric. I am accumulating all these disciplines in a haphazard way, on purpose, but I shall end with literature, poetry, the arts and fiction in general: the theory that has these disciplines as its object may be just as useful in ideological warfare as it is in experimentation with variables in all-too-familiar perversions of the referential function. . . . From now on, so long as it has the means, a military budget can invest in anything at all, in view of deferred profits: "basic" scientific theory, the humanities, literary theory and philosophy.[6]

Direct political influence is hardly limited to the sciences alone, and it is all too easy to forget that the military is comprised of more than technological hardware. Likewise, corporate influences on universities should not be understood as stopping with their appropriation of technological advances in the sciences – witness the increasing frequency with which corporations endow named chairs in the humanities.[7] On top of this, government granting agencies have increasingly sought to carry out partisan political agendas, by attempting to control what gets thought by determining what projects receive funding. Especially in the cold war years, politically partisan control of the humanities and the arts once was the charge the "democratic" West leveled at its Communist opposition. However, in light of the turn of events at, for instance, the National Endowment of the Arts (NEA) and the National Endowment of the Humanities (NEH) in the United States, it would seem that an interest in political control of the humanities and the arts is itself interestingly bipartisan.[8]

What these examples all have in common, though, is their tendency to call attention to the political function of the academy. I would even go so far as to suggest that how Western societies understand thinking is largely shaped by educational systems. Thought is an institutional event and more likely than not the key institution for thought is the academy, whether it's the advanced research carried out by universities or more basic skills taught in primary schools.[9] This is not to say that educators should fool themselves about the extent of their own political power – certainly not all politics is a result of the academy, just as not all political influence is aimed at academic institutions. However, the point I am trying to make in this particular context is that it would be similarly foolish to claim that feminism and deconstruction are not political on the grounds that they are neutral, philosophical enterprises. Such an argument not only neglects the inextricable connection between philosophy and politics, but also assumes there is something of value to be gained from preserving the fiction that academic thought is apolitical and completely independent from its institutional setting.[10]

Indeed, the institutional setting is precisely the point at which it becomes possible to *read* the connection between thought as defined by and practiced in departments of philosophy and the political world. That is to say, the particular interest of the academy *qua* institution of education is that it is a hinge between the reflective thought of philosophy and the world of political action, and its paradox is the paradox of their relation. To spell out the paradox: the university is supposed to be both the political institution in which nonpolitical thought can occur and the nonpolitical institution in which political thought can occur.

Thus, if I propose to examine how feminism and deconstruction are situated within the university, how they stand to change the university, this is a political question every bit as much as a matter internal to the academy. In what follows, I intend to look briefly at the disciplinary structure of the university, how it operates and to what effect, and then turn to two specific disciplines within and upon which deconstruction and feminism work: philosophy and women's studies. Obviously, this is not an exhaustive account. Rather, my intention here is to take some specific instances in which deconstruction and feminism challenge disciplinary boundaries, interrupt disciplinary procedures, and then go on to explore the possibility that deconstruction and feminism work on and within disciplines while not becoming disciplines themselves. Such an interrogation of disciplinarity by feminism and deconstruction cannot, however, simply remain in the field of political knowledge. For to think the politics of knowledge as such, as feminism and deconstruction seek to do, cannot be to *know* those politics but only to *imagine* them. Any claim to know the politics of knowledge would, as knowledge, itself remain subject to those politics. Therefore, in order to question what is "known-as-political," deconstruction and feminism must speak from the place of ethical responsibility. Taking the necessarily institutional character of knowledge seriously means exercising an *ethical* imagination: we must always imagine the institution within which any act of thinking and judgment might take place. It would be accurate to say, then, that what began as an interruption of a discussion of politics and ethics will end up as a necessary institutional detour, a way of overcoming the simple opposition of politics to ethics.

3: DISCIPLINES?

To understand the basic ways in which deconstruction and feminism engage the disciplinary structure of the university, it is first worth saying a few words about what disciplines are presumed to be and what function they are thought to serve in the modern university. On the simplest level, disciplines focus on specific objects of investigation. To take a couple of obvious examples, biology focuses on living organisms, while art history looks at art objects over time. At least traditionally, disciplines are also concerned with defining the rules and methodology for the proper study of the objects in question.[11] So to return to my examples, not every study of a living organism, technically speaking, contributes to the discipline of biology, just as not every reflection on an art work constitutes art history. The point here is that disciplines are defined as much by what they exclude as what they include. That is to say, disciplines are a way of carving up areas of study and regulating what constitutes proper investigation in each area. Crayfish metabolisms are the business of biology, while art history is left to pursue the development of surrealism – as long as these studies are conducted according to proper disciplinary standards.

Of course, disciplines can overlap. For instance, chemistry comes into play when art historians try to carbon date paintings, just as it does when biologists attempt to work out the chemical reactions of metabolic processes. Yet while disciplines do have areas of overlap, they are still presumed to have specific objects of studies – chemistry should have nothing to say about the aesthetic merits of surrealism over cubism, for instance. Thus, although disciplines may certainly change over time (chemistry in 1990 looks rather different from its 1890 counterpart) and new disciplines emerge (English departments are inventions of the last 100 years), nonetheless each discipline is thought to retain characteristics that separate it from all others.

Within the university, such disciplinary specialization has been marked and maintained by academic departments which take the names of the various disciplines.[12] This serves important administrative functions and also usually locates the studies carried out in the name of each discipline. As a result, the departments can serve as a sort of immigration border patrol, controlling what gets accepted into a particular discipline and making sure that the various immigrants are properly naturalized, so to speak. This also means that the disciplinary structure sanctioned by the university is based on identity and sameness. The other is always elsewhere, outside the borders of the disciplines. Significantly, interdisciplinary studies are not the exception to these rules that they may seem. Situated within the university and regulated in much the same way as any other discipline, interdisciplinary studies also operate on principles of identity, admitting only that which is recognized as proper to the particular interdisciplinary area. An example might be iconology, which melds literary-historical and art-historical interpretative techniques around a strictly delimited series of objects.

All of this may seem rather obvious, especially to those of us who have spent significant portions of our lives in universities. However, there are also more subtle implications of this disciplinary system which I have tried to outline in basic terms.[13] First, I think that it is important to consider whether disciplines are at all self-conscious about their founding principles, about their criteria for inclusion and exclusion. Samuel Weber convincingly argues that as disciplines become more established they become less self-reflective. According to Weber, attention shifts to "the problems and questions emerging *within* the field, the coherence and even history of which was taken increasingly for granted."[14] And Gerald Graff contends that disciplinary boundaries exist precisely to prevent such reflection, since objects of study, once given a department, seem to become self-evident.[15]

This could be a condition that some in the academy would celebrate, arguing that it's better not to get mired in the past and just get on with things. But this pragmatic position tends to forget that disciplines do not always have positive effects: the dangers of disciplinarity reside in the way in which the compartmentalization of a discipline leads one to ignore the necessary play of exclusion that structures what the discipline includes. In their ability to draw clear boundaries between different areas of study, disciplines organize academic institutions in ways that tend to discourage any questioning of the legitimacy of the structure itself. Disciplines amount to a containment strategy designed to prevent conflict and promote the uncritical acceptance of the institution. That is to say, disciplinarity is the regulatory mechanism which assures the continued success of the academic institution itself: by carefully controlling what gets included and excluded at any given point, the academy is able to guarantee its own reproduction. This is the point Wlad Godzich makes in a larger context when he observes that "institutions are fundamentally instruments of reproduction, not in the simple mechanical sense, but rather in that they ensure that regulative processes take place so as to contain what otherwise could threaten to turn into anarchic proliferation."[16]

Since my intention here is not to carry out an exhaustive analysis of the organization of modern universities, I have to ask what all of these observations about disciplines have to do with feminism and deconstruction. To understand the connection, it is worth recalling some of my earlier remarks. As I have tried to show, the work of deconstruction and feminism upsets the structural heart of the university by refiguring what constitutes the "academic." By challenging the border between what is included and excluded from the university, feminism and deconstruction open up the entire debate about what a university should be. Significantly, this is not the only front on which feminism and deconstruction challenge the constitution of the university. Their critical relationship to the academy is also enacted by questioning the legitimacy of the disciplinary structure itself (which may lead back to a consideration of what is included and excluded in the first place). The result, however, is *not* an attempt to get rid of disciplinary boundaries in order to unify all knowledge (and all disciplines) via a common denominator or interpretative methodology. I would even argue that no knowledge is free from the disciplinary construction of objects, and organic theories of knowledge are just an example of a particular form of disciplinarity. Rather, the aim is that by questioning the authority of disciplinary borders, feminism and deconstruction will transform the terms by which the university defines itself and lays claim to authority.

It would be possible at this point to make a number of generalizations about the ways in which feminism and deconstruction question disciplinary borders. But instead of taking that direction, I would like to turn to the specific disciplinary examples that I earlier promised to look at: philosophy and women's studies. My reasons for examining particulars rather than forcing too many generalizations has to do with a desire to situate deconstruction and feminism within the specific disciplinary structures on which they work, and insist that there are ways in which they work *inside* as well as *on* disciplines.[17] My primary aim here is to underline how deconstruction and feminism expose the limits and preconceptions of particular disciplines in order to open up spaces for different forms of knowledge. From here I hope to make a few more general remarks about the future of disciplinarity in the age of feminism and deconstruction.

4: PHILOSOPHY?

I suggested in the Introduction that neither feminism nor deconstruction has found a comfortable home in the discipline of philosophy, at least in British and North American universities. The welcome mat has not been thrown out for their arrival, nor has philosophy necessarily been willing to assume that deconstruction and feminism have always been lodgers. Neither welcomed outsiders nor tolerated insiders, feminism and deconstruction have nonetheless situated themselves in relationship to the discipline of philosophy. This relationship has taken any number of forms: feminist perspectives in philosophy; arguments that philosophy is a patriarchal plot and thus antithetical to feminism; deconstructions of philosophy; and deconstructive philosophy. All of these forms do, however, have one thing in common: they call into question what constitutes the discipline of philosophy, and I would argue (although it is not necessarily evident here) that they also challenge the grounds from which philosophy draws its authority, which is to say they question the grounds of the very discipline that is supposed to ground knowledge itself.

It would not be possible in this context to review all of the supposed challenges that feminism and deconstruction pose to the discipline of philosophy. The most familiar are that feminism seeks to turn philosophy into politics while deconstruction seeks to turn philosophy into literature, just a kind of writing. Yet these claims are too limited: they name disciplinary readjustments rather than a disruption of disciplinarity as such. That is to say, "politics" and "literature" turn out to be the master disciplines, instead of philosophy – this is a matter of struggling for the position of prom queen among the disciplines.

I want to say, on the contrary, that feminism and deconstruction do not seek to reveal philosophy as really something else, but as *other to itself*: paradoxically determined by the very things that philosophy excludes in order to define its own disciplinary coherence. In order to ensure that which is included is "philosophy," certain things have to be "excluded" from philosophy. In the interests of my own argument, I would like to turn to Derrida's essay, "Plato's Pharmacy," in which two of the things that philosophy's discipline excludes, and which nonetheless haunt philosophy, turn out to be women and writing.[18] This essay is important both for what it has to say about deconstruction's and feminism's potential challenge to philosophy, as well as for the ways in which it might turn out to be part of the problem. Put another way, the essay could prove to be the medicine that cures philosophy of its disciplinary problems, or it might just be what poisons it.

This very juxtaposition of remedy and poison to which I have just alluded is, as many will already know, a crucial part of the essay. As Derrida notices, the Greek word *pharmakon* has a double, antithetical meaning: it can be either a remedy or a poison.[19] And the implications of this observation so interest Derrida that he devotes much of the essay to tracing the connection between the *pharmakon* and writing in Plato's work, especially the *Phaedrus*. While I will not attempt to summarize this complex essay, I will offer two possible readings which have particular importance in this context.

On the one hand, "Plato's Pharmacy" can be situated as part of the tradition of filial inheritance which constitutes the discipline of philosophy. It would even be possible to take Derrida's conclusions about Plato's indictment of pictorial mimetics in the *Republic* and apply them to philosophy in general: "it is all about fathers and sons, about bastards unaided by any public assistance, about glorious, legitimate sons, about inheritance, sperm, and sterility."[20] From father to son, from Plato to Derrida. It only remains to be decided just what kind of Platonic son Derrida is. Of course, this view of the family scene does not seem to include mothers or daughters. Mothers are either hiding at the periphery of the picture – "drawn upside-down in the foliage, at the back of the garden," in the case of the *Republic* – or they disappear quickly and dramatically. Significantly, one of the few women allowed to make an appearance in the Platonic family scene is Orithyia, when Derrida cites the passage from the *Phaedrus* in which Socrates skeptically retells the myth of her disappearance: while playing with Pharmacia, she was allegedly cast into an abyss by Boreal.[21] Thus, although Derrida challenges Plato's work and reveals this picture of the family scene, the essay could nonetheless be read as just another instance of the son (Derrida) killing off the father (Plato) so that the father's ghost can live on in the son's writing.

But this is not the only reading we can give to this essay. On the other hand, Derrida as Platonic son is not an altogether welcomed guest in the halls of philosophy, nor has he given his father's ghost a comfortable house to haunt. Derrida's essay could also be read as a feminist gesture, insofar as it reveals the extent to which philosophy has thus far limited itself to patriarchal and patricidal writing. In this sense, Derrida makes visible the family scene that Platonism has tried to hide. For as he observes, "'Platonism' is both the general *rehearsal* of this family scene and the most powerful effort to master it, to prevent anyone's ever hearing of it, to conceal it by drawing the curtains over the dawning of the West."[22] Thus, by making (deconstructive) observations that "slip away from the recognized models of commentary," Derrida could be opening the way for the feminist (re)writing of philosophy.[23]

This is not to suggest, however, that Derrida alone will create a space for feminism within philosophy, nor is it to discount the importance of a large body of feminist work that engages with the discipline of philo-sophy.[24] The point that I am trying to make – a point that I think Derrida's essay underlines – is that renegotiating the limits of philosophy and the limits of writing is one way for feminism to upset philosophy's foundation of filial inheritance. What count as proper philosophical commentaries, methodology, and topics will be challenged by feminism and deconstruc-tion. Significantly, Derrida as possible Platonic son, rather than adding even more ground to secure the foundation underneath the house of philosophy, removes a crucial cornerstone: philosophy's filial line of inheritance. The lever that removes the cornerstone does not even need to provide any physical pressure; the work is merely to point out that the cornerstone was never there in the first place.[25] In this sense, Derrida's own writing evokes the *pharmakon* about which he speaks, calls up the specter that has always haunted philosophy. This is not something new; the *pharmakon* is not a miracle cure, a new wonder-drug – it is something inherent in the condition of philosophy. Thus, Derrida paradoxically repeats the double-edged gesture of all philosophical critique, not so as to simply renew philosophy but also so as to set philosophy against itself. Derrida's *pharmakon* may cure Platonic philosophy by giving it a new vitality and interest, but it does so by poisoning traditional philosophical discourse with deconstruction and feminism, poisons which turn out not to have been introduced from *outside* philosophy but to have been the necessary obverse of all of philosophy's miracle drugs.[26]

5: WOMEN'S STUDIES?

If feminism's and deconstruction's relationship to philosophy is that of uneasy insider/outsider, the situation with women's studies is very differ-ent. While deconstruction's place in the academy is less than clear, women's studies is thought by many to be a discipline created by feminism as a response to a society and a university structure that did not meet its needs. Almost by definition, then, women's studies is an attempt to rethink the disciplinary organization of the university. First, by refusing to limit itself strictly to the academy, by appealing to a wider community of women, it has challenged the division between academic and popular feminism. Second, by potentially appealing to scholars belonging to almost every traditional discipline, it has provoked a re-evaluation of the disciplinary borders which have divided feminism from itself.

In these respects, women's studies has promoted a radical rethinking of the disciplinary structure of the university. For as Jane Gallop (following Elaine Marks's lead) suggests, women's studies is not "a mere region of knowledge supplementing traditional disciplines."[27] Rather, according to Gallop and Marks, women's studies alters the very subject of knowledge by calling "into question what is considered knowledge in any discipline."[28] Women's studies, then, is not simply one more interdisciplinary program; the radical epistemological move on the part of women's studies deconstructs the whole notion of the university. In this respect, the general concerns of women's studies closely match what Derrida envisions as some of the results of a deconstructive interrogation of the university. It would not be an exaggeration to claim that, in the name of feminism, women's studies sets out "to transform the modes of writing, approaches to pedagogy, the procedures of academic exchange, the relation to languages, to other disciplines, to the institution in general, to its inside and its outside."[29]

In making my deconstructive case for the close affiliation between feminism and women's studies, however, I do not wish to leave the impression that feminism is restricted in the academy to women's studies. Women's studies is an important, but certainly not the only, institutional location for feminism; moreover, feminism is directed at concerns other than women. Likewise, not all of women's studies is feminist; it is possible to make women the subject or object of investigation without bringing feminism into the picture.[30] That is to say, women's studies is more than feminism, just as feminism is more than women's studies. And in this sense, there is a way in which feminism, at the heart of women's studies from the beginning, is also an outsider to women's studies.

I would argue, however, that part of what makes feminism such a potentially disruptive force within the academy is precisely this lack of complete congruence with women's studies. While feminism may most readily be recognized by the academy as located within women's studies programs or departments, it also has invaded any number of disciplines. Feminists have at times even been suspicious of the risk of ghettoization that women's studies as a discipline may encourage. In short, the work of feminism is not to construct its own cell in the academic beehive but rather to challenge the notion of institutional construction, of academic disciplinary isolation, *tout court*.[31]

Thus far I have painted a very positive picture of women's studies, arguing for its subversive, feminist effect on the academy. But does women's studies always work in the best interests of feminism? Could Gayatri Spivak be correct when she suggests that, in fact, women's studies is just another branch office of humanist philosophy?[32]

Women's studies has been known to conform to very traditional understandings of what women are supposed to be and do. For instance, charges of racism and homophobia have been levied against women's studies programs for finding their disciplinary coherence in an idea of woman that is predominantly white and straight. The problems with identity politics, which I discussed in Chapter 3, have also long haunted women's studies. Even the disciplinary innovation, which has been the hallmark of women's studies, can fall by the wayside when women's studies installs itself into the academic framework like any other discipline. Women's studies students answering multiple choice questions by filling in circles on computer scan sheets with number two pencils is hardly a radical departure from the daily grind of the academy.[33]

At the same time that women's studies tries to challenge disciplinary boundaries and constitute a new field of knowledge, it risks instituting its own rules, regulations, and laws that can prove just as oppressive as those of any other discipline. For example, women's studies may want to reflect on its traditions and methodologies, but is a course on the classic texts of women's studies necessarily the answer? By relying on a notion of "classics," would women's studies just be creating an exclusionary canon where it should be critiquing the very notion of a classic?

There are, however, practical considerations behind the need for women's studies to act like its neighboring disciplines. However much it might seem undesirable for women's studies to consider itself a discipline at all, it cannot altogether ignore the constrictions of university budgeting. If women's studies is to be a part of the academy, there comes a point when it must think about the practicalities of funding: how will the staff be paid? Do the instructors give their time to women's studies for free? Are students forced to take overly large classes? In what ways will the program have contact with the larger community?[34]

These are only a few of the practical questions which begin to take over the economic life of women's studies. But budgetary questions should not be an excuse for women's studies to engage in exclusionary practices which reflect a desire for disciplinary uniformity. Christina Crosby is right to suggest that "dealing with the fact of differences is *the* project of women's studies today."[35] And these differences will not be done justice if women's studies does not reflect on its own practices. For as Crosby recognizes, "the challenge is not to purify women's studies or the academy, but to question constantly our most powerful concepts."[36] If an important feature of women's studies is its interrogation of what constitutes the university, then women's studies also should not forget to interrogate what legitimates the division between its own inside and outside.

And this is perhaps where deconstruction comes in again, at the point where disciplinary institution blinds women's studies to its own exclusions and inclusions, at the point where women's studies might take itself, its functioning, and its purpose for granted. This is not to suggest, however, that deconstruction comes in from the outside as a methodology that will rescue women's studies. The impossibility of that particular relationship should be the lesson of the *pharmakon*. Rather, deconstruction is what allows us to think the strange articulation of feminism and women's studies, by reminding us that the theoretical analysis and practical politics of feminism cannot simply take on institutional forms. By making institutional critiques, feminism and deconstruction can remind women's studies that it is an institution, while women's studies can remind feminism and deconstruction that they have to take the institution seriously.

6: THE FUTURE OF DISCIPLINARITY?

Having thus far considered some of the specific ways in which feminism and deconstruction engage philosophy and women's studies, I now want to fulfill my earlier promise of risking some generalizations about the future of disciplinarity. I think that I have made it clear that feminism and deconstruction do not completely stand outside the disciplinary structure of the university. However, I hope that I have made it equally clear that neither are they entirely within that structure. Thus, I have insisted that feminism and deconstruction do not become disciplines themselves, although they continually cross disciplinary borders.

This is the sense, as I mentioned in the introduction, in which feminism and deconstruction are "crossdisciplines" (or ̶d̶i̶s̶c̶i̶p̶l̶i̶n̶e̶s̶). Deconstruction and feminism do not make disciplinary structures entirely disappear from the university; rather, they radically rethink them in terms of *difference* rather than identity. That is to say, the crossdisciplinary work of feminism and deconstruction seeks difference where before there was only a margin demarcating interiority from exteriority. That means if disciplinarity is to be thought under a logic of *difference* instead of identity, it is no longer possible to place a thought comfortably within a single discipline or ignore it as extraneous to that discipline.

It would be possible, then, to understand deconstruction and feminism not as systems of rules but as an endless *search* for rules. Judgment lies in the process of this search, which demands responsibility without allowing the comfort of finality. Every action must be judged *as if* it implied the foundation of a discipline, but no judgment or set of judgments can be that foundation. Thus, feminism and deconstruction do not seek to become new disciplines, to achieve full institutional identity. The disciplinary recognition they seek is rather a conflictual one – they claim the right to cross disciplinary borders in the name of thinking the very politics of institutions (and, in the case of the U.S., specific disciplinary subdivisions). This involves a simultaneous recognition of the institution as both a necessary and a limiting condition for thought and action – institutions cannot be entirely done away with, but they must not be simply accepted as such either.

Therefore, feminism's and deconstruction's critique of institutions is political but does not remain entirely so. They do not believe that the problem of institutions can be solved politically by making better institutions. Few people will want to argue that we do not need better institutions, yet we still have to reflect on what we mean by "good institutions." Is a good police force identified by Orwellian efficiency? Or by a certain tolerance and readiness to let things slide? Is a good university one that cares for students, for knowledge, or for professors? Or is it one that serves the State? And what happens when these interests conflict? The answer to these questions are political, but they also involve a reflection on the nature of the good, which moves us back into the realm of ethics . . .

Chapter 4

Groundless solidarity

ETHICAL ACTIVISM

Throughout this book, I have had recourse to the name of ethics in order to indicate the difference that feminism and deconstruction make. In neither case is the word "ethics" an obvious term: for deconstruction it might seem to imply a little too much by way of subjective agency; for feminism it might seem too individualistic and lacking in political articulation. With these objections in mind, the difference that ethics names can be roughly characterized in two ways. On the one hand, ethics insists on responsibility. That is to say, the presumed autonomy of the rational subject is reminded that it is not isolated. On the other hand, ethics insists on judgment. That is to say, it reminds those who wish to rely on meta-languages that nothing goes without saying – that any attempt to describe society exhaustively runs the risk of totalitarianism.

What is at stake here, however, is not a return to ethics as a traditional branch of philosophy. While the focus will still be on the two differences I have just described, I appeal to ethics in order to destabilize both the notion of the subject and the social. I understand the subject as neither sovereign nor autonomous but as always caught up in a network of responsibilities to others. Accordingly, I have sought to make a link between the problems of solidarity that are so central to feminist politics and the deconstructive attack on Cartesian subjective self-presence. With regard to the social, I have invoked the ethical as marking a necessary margin of undecidability in the question of political organization. Feminism, then, is more aptly called an ethics than a politics, if by politics we imply the instrumental articulation of social forces towards a determinate end: the attempt to build a just society, for example. Thus, feminism is concerned with social justice, certainly, but that is not the same thing as the notion that a society could achieve stasis as just, once and for all. Indeed, feminism has good reason to be suspicious of such a totalizing notion, given that images of the just society have tended to be constructed at women's expense, based on the equitable exchange of women between men, for example. Ethics reminds politics that no social form can be instituted that will put an end to the problem of justice.

So what kind of ethics is it, then, that deconstruction and feminism desire? How does it differ from the Kantian notion of the subject as free agent, or from pragmatism, or from moral philosophy? In this chapter, I want to focus on three aspects of the ethics which would arise from an engagement of feminism with deconstruction. First, a turn away from subjective autonomy produces an ethics which is not a question of individual choice or individual care for the other. Second, by taking a distance from pragmatism, this ethics gives rise to an account of *groundless solidarity*. And third, by distinguishing itself from moral philosophy, it seeks to preserve justice as an unanswerable yet urgently necessary question. In short, then, the ethics of feminism and deconstruction is not a moralism but an *ethical activism*. And in what follows, I hope to show that the engagement of feminism with deconstruction will give rise to a solidarity that rethinks the political as a foundationless activity of judgment.

TURNING AWAY FROM SUBJECTIVE AGENCY

I have already discussed in Chapter 3 how feminism and deconstruction problematize the category of the subject. My concern there was to show what kind of politics can take place without a subject as the privileged instance. Significantly, a politics that is not centered on a subject (the politics of the undecidable) is a realm of continual negotiation in which action is phrased in ethical terms as a duty. It is this connection to ethics, the necessary linkage of politics and ethics in the absence of the subject, that I want to explore now.

In the still influential wake of Kant, it may at first seem strange, if not absolutely impossible, to speak of an ethics that does not appeal to autonomous, rational subjects who act impartially. Kant's belief that "the principle of autonomy . . . is the sole principle of morals" has held considerable sway.[1] Perhaps Kant's most ardent contemporary support appears in the form of John Rawls's contractual theory of justice. Rawls's decidedly ahistorical theory is aimed at finding general principles which govern social life, but significantly, those principles of justice are chosen by rational agents, "situated behind a veil of ignorance."[2] Rawls's whole point is that rational, autonomous subjects can act out of ignorance of the actual pragmatic context of a judgment (and thus with no sense of self-interest) in order to create a moral society on universal principles. The particular case is considered only insofar as it illustrates the general principle. For Rawls, ethics and activism (indeed any kind of pragmatic implication in the actual) are fundamentally at odds.

By putting such emphasis on Kant and Rawls, I do not mean to suggest, however, that they are alone in espousing the centrality of the subject to ethics. Philosophical positions as distinct as subjectivism, ethical egoism, and much analytic philosophy have all made this appeal. I also do not want to dismiss all of these philosophies out of hand, simply because they have a theory of the subject with which I think deconstruction and feminism stand at odds. It is obvious, for example, that my appeal to duty and obligation – rather than an ethics of care, of the good, or of the useful – has a Kantian echo. But importantly, what deconstruction and feminism together have to say about ethics is in no sense strictly Kantian, nor does it follow the possible Kantian lead of Rawls. I will say more about the deconstructive rejection of the categorical imperative later in this chapter; for now it is enough to stress that the ethics to which the relationship between feminism and deconstruction give rise neither appeals to an ethical subject, nor pleads the case for a moral *a priori*, a meta-obligation to be moral. It is possible to see deconstruction as giving rise to an ethics without a subject (more precisely, an ethics in which the subject is at stake, is not the absent center of judgment) that can help us to be more suspicious of appeals to identity politics in the name of feminism.

One of the clearest indications of this deconstructive shift away from an ethics of the subject occurs within the pages of Paul de Man's *Allegories of Reading*:

> Allegories are always ethical, the term ethical designating the structural interference of two distinct value systems. In this sense, ethics has nothing to do with the will (thwarted or free) of a subject, nor *a fortiori*, with a relationship between subjects. The ethical category is imperative (i.e., a category rather than a value) to the extent that it is linguistic and not subjective.... The passage to an ethical tonality does not result from a transcendental imperative but is the referential (and therefore unreliable) version of a linguistic confusion.[3]

De Man's notion of ethics, as J. Hillis Miller points out, is a far cry from conventional Kantian versions which revolve around subjectivity in the more traditional sense.[4] For de Man, the ethical condition emanates from language rather than experience and is thus the result of a linguistic confusion rather than a transcendental imperative.[5] This does not make ethics any less necessary (the necessity that compels an ethical judgment is linguistic, not subjective or transcendental), but language provides no assurance that the right can be reconciled with the true. To use Miller's words, "surely one should want to dwell within the truth, and surely one should want to do what is right, but according to de Man it is impossible to respond simultaneously to those two demands."[6] The ethically right cannot be derived from the epistemologically true. As Lyotard reminds us in *The Differend*, these are heterogeneous language games.

The engagement of feminism with deconstruction does not, then, pro-

vide a rationale for deciding what is true or false (whether upon epistemological or political grounds), and ethical decisions are not made on the
basis of pre-established norms (were this so, then we would be back in a
politics of determinacy). Rather than judging on the basis of a system of
rules, political activism becomes the search for the rule that may do
justice to the case. This search is necessarily endless, since we do not
know what a woman may be, what the limits of our solidarity will turn
out to have been. Any feminism that sets out to achieve a defined goal
on the basis of predetermined principles, any feminism that thinks it
knows just what woman is and what she should be, will turn out to have
been lacking in solidarity, will simply be doing the patriarchy's work for
it: answering the question "what do women want?" and setting men's
minds at ease.

It is in this way that deconstruction and feminism reveal that ethical
judgments are actually groundless. Which is not to say that these judgments are without cause or without purpose. Their groundlessness might
better be explained by saying that we have to try do the right thing, here,
now, where we are. We must judge where we are, in our pragmatic
context, and no transcendental alibi will save us. For example, the watch-
word "all men are *potential* rapists" reminds us of the permanent necessity
of judgment (in "all" cases) while not providing an absolute or universal
rule: they are "potential rapists," which means that in this case, at this
time, they may not be rapists. This is an ethical slogan precisely in that
it does not allow a predetermined essence (e.g. men are essentially rapists)
to obviate the need to judge each man on a case by case basis. To have
the potentiality to be a rapist does not mean that all men are on the
point of actually committing rape, just that they may be, and women must
take that into consideration in dealing with them. Every day, in every
contact, the possibility of rape cannot be eliminated. However, it would
also be possible, though unfortunately not very likely, for all men to
potentially be rapists and at the same time, at a particular moment, for
no man to actually be a rapist. Or, in deconstructive terms, we always
have to judge, in each case, because the grounds themselves have no
grounds, rape as a permanent possibility is never a certainty.[7]

This produces a terrain of judgment which would resemble the landscape at Cornell University, which Derrida describes in "The University
in the Eyes of its Pupils." As Derrida puts it, "the abyss, the hole, the
Abgrund, the empty 'gorge' would be the impossibility for a principle of
grounding to ground itself."[8] One can perfectly well stand on the bridges
which span these abysses and link the various portions of the campus,
but the bridges themselves are not grounded. In this sense, the bridges
allow us to stand poised over the abyss of ethical judgments in search of
their rules.

While the landscape of metaphors helps to explain groundless ethical judgments, it is nonetheless somewhat difficult to grasp what it might mean to proceed without foundations, since the words that the patriarchy have left us for this are anarchy and chaos. It is for that reason that I would like to say a bit more about groundless solidarity. Groundless solidarity is the possibility of a community which is not grounded in the truth of a presocial identity. Solidarity forms the basis, although not the foundation, for political action and ethical responsibility. That is to say, groundless solidarity is a stability but not an absolute one; it can be the object of conflict and need not mean consensus. This would be very much in line with Derrida's discussion of stability:

> To account for a certain stability (by essence always provisional and finite) is precisely not to speak of eternity or of absolute solidity; it is to take into account a historicity, a nonnaturalness, of ethics, of politics, of institutionality, etc. . . . A stability is not an immutability; it is by definition always destabilizable.[9]

There is a sense in which groundless solidarity could be said to constitute a moral community, but only in a very limited and restricted sense. This notion of community could not be equated with organic totality, or have a natural foundation any more than it would lay claim to absolute solidity. The community of groundless solidarity could cross national borders, just as it might be the meeting place for any number of different ethnicities, religious affiliations, and sexualities, for instance. Groundless solidarity, then, could be understood as a political coalition brought together on the basis of shared ethical commitments, but it would make no claim to inclusiveness (all communities are formed on the basis of some type of exclusion). What continually destabilizes this community of groundless solidarity is the difference contained both within and without it, a difference which works to destabilize any clear separation between individual and community, between self and other.

Jean-Luc Nancy has best explained the sense of community which could be evoked here. Nancy is not willing to set individuals and the community in opposition to one another, nor does he conveniently pose self and other in opposition:

> Community is what takes place always through others and for others. It is not the space of the *egos* – subjects and substances that are at bottom immortal – but of the *I's*, who are always *others* (or else are nothing).[10]

Nancy makes clear that his assessment of community does not constitute a return to groups of autonomous subjects. For Nancy, community is "a whole of articulated singularities," which are not grounded:[11]

> It is a groundless "ground," less in the sense that it opens up the

gaping chasm of an abyss than that it is made up only of the network, the interweaving, and the sharing of singularities: *Ungrund* rather than *Abgrund*, but no less vertiginous. There is nothing *behind* singularity – but there is, outside it and in it, the immaterial *and* material space that distributes it and shares it out as singularity, distributes and shares the confines of other singularities, or even more exactly distributes and shares the confines of singularity – which is to say of alterity – between it and itself.[12]

It is possible to conclude from Nancy's remarks that the Other, to whom there is an ethical responsibility, is neither a material particular nor a universal abstraction. The subject, if it would be possible to speak of one at this point, is not autonomous but instead caught up in a network of responsibilities to others, as I remarked earlier. In effect, the Other, to whom responsibility is owed, is not precisely locatable as either subject or object. The Other does not affect a subject, a Cartesian ego, but a singularity – which is what is at stake in Nancy's distinction between the ego and the I. Hence the problem of the Other is not a problem of intersubjectivity: no amount of agreement between subjects can make the Other go away. Whereas the notion of intersubjective dialogue presumes that two subjects can come to terms, agree and become one so as to put an end to otherness, the invocation of singularity insists on the radical difference that constitutes any speaking position. This is not merely a difference from other people, it is a difference from history. This is why whites in America have a *historical* responsibility for the sins of their forebears, although they may not have committed any individual acts of racism. They have a responsibility to the Other which no amount of goodwill or equal rights legislation can wash away. This is an ethical responsibility that the singularity assumes precisely because it recognizes that the individual is not an autonomous subject responsible only for its own action. The singularity is responsible to an Other that exceeds and precedes it; it owes a debt that can never be *fully* repaid, but must be honored, be recognized, with consistent attentiveness.

This returns my argument to a point that I have mentioned on more than one occasion in this book: that the call to responsibility to the Other comes from nowhere, is neither absolutely human or inhuman. To make the argument clearer, I want to quote in full a passage from Derrida's interview, "Eating Well," to which I have referred in previous chapters:

The origin of the call that comes from nowhere, an origin in any case that is not yet a divine or human "subject," institutes a responsibility that is to be found at the root of all ulterior responsibilities (moral, juridical, political), and of every categorical imperative. To say of this responsibility, and even of this friendship, that it is not "human," no more than it is "divine," does not simply come down to saying that it is inhuman. This said, in this regard it is perhaps more "worthy" of humanity to maintain a certain inhumanity, which is to say the rigor of a certain inhumanity. In any case, such a law does not leave us any choice. Something of this call of the other must remain nonreappropri-able, nonsubjective, and in a certain way nonidentifiable, a sheer supposition, so as to remain *other*, a *singular* call to response or to responsibility. This is why the determination of the singular "Who?" – or at least its determination as subject – still remains problematic. And it *should* remain so. This obligation to protect the other's otherness is not merely a theoretical imperative.[13]

The obligation to otherness is a debt that cannot be calculated: what single lump-sum payment could compensate non-whites for the history of racism, for example? Justice does not involve paying one's debts. Believing that one's debts can be paid is a fundamentally irresponsible belief: the desire to wash one's hands of responsibility to others. Rather, justice involves recognition of the debts that cannot be paid, the debts that set a limit to one's autonomy. To recognize such debts as unpayable is not to write them off, either – it is rather to commit oneself to an endless work of reparation without the final solace of redemption. This, for instance, is the debt America owes its native peoples.

TAKING A DISTANCE FROM PRAGMATISM

Ethics here names an approach to the problem of doing justice, which acknowledges the radical contingency of discursive pragmatics. On the surface, this argument has something in common with anti-foundational pragmatism. The initial resemblance is, however, misleading, and for that reason, it is worth slowing down to trace some of the differences and similarities.

First of all, there may appear to be a strong resemblance to the work of pragmatists like Joseph Margolis, which rejects the tradition of foun-dational or transcendental questions, the "second-order questions about what makes human knowledge conceptually possible."[14] In this regard, feminism and deconstruction share Margolis's suspicions (if I can be allowed that word) of foundationalist theories which claim "a fixed, cer-tain, or strongly privileged cognitive access to the real world, on which all other cognitively relevant claims depend, however weakly."[15]

But in the long run, the work which feminism and deconstruction produce together is very different. Feminism and deconstruction do not suggest, as does Margolis, that "what we need to explore are the alterna-tive possibilities that transcendental reflection can generate about plausi-bly stipulated (but hardly necessary) conditions for a viable realism and communicative practice."[16] Reconciling realism and relativism, which is

Margolis's main concern, is of little interest here. Margolis's pragmatism seeks to be a philosophical practice which joins epistemological and onto-logical questions, since pragmatism names for Margolis a realism based in relativism rather than in a positive assurance about the nature of the world. Pragmatism is thus, for Margolis, a matter of being *realistic*, with all the mixture of assurance and reservation that the word conveys.

Thus, rather than a radical assault on foundationalism, Margolis's ver-sion of pragmatism ends up being a kind of caveat about the status of knowledge, appropriate to the pursuit of knowledge in the secular age. God is not so much dead as *absconditus*. American philosophical pragma-tism thus continues to derive from William James's overriding desire for *reconciliation*, despite the absence of an Absolute Truth that might serve as an *a priori* ground for that reconciliation. A feminist pragmatics, it seems to me, should have no interest in reconciliation, and should instead be concerned with insisting upon (gender) difference as irreconcilable.

Despite this objection, the attraction of pragmatism to feminism is based on the way in which anti-foundational pragmatism provides a way for feminism to begin asking ethical questions about scientific technology once the distinction between values and facts has collapsed. One good example of this is Christie McDonald's consideration of surrogate mother-hood.[17] In the wake of technological advancement (especially with regards to reproduction), McDonald wonders whether there has been "a change in the norms by which situations are judged, case by case."[18] Practically speaking, the answer would appear to be "no." McDonald's careful analy-sis of the surrogacy case of Baby M leads us to understand just how much we have neglected to consider the new ethical dilemmas with which science presents us:

> One of the things that was clear in the case of Baby M was that neither recourse to historical tradition (the Bible, for example) nor recourse to legal precedent would yield all the answers needed.... There is perhaps only one thing about which there is no doubt in this case: surrogacy contracts put the traditional structure of the family and the role of maternity in question.[19]

All of this is not to say that technology *per se* is bad or good; rather, technology presents us with ethical choices which cannot be made simply on the basis of familiar criteria, either *a priori* or *a posteriori*. To use McDonald's words:

> It is not a question, then, of whether technology represses or liberates.... It is a question of taking responsibility for the transform-ation of social relations through science and technology.[20]

Here McDonald's formulation of feminist ethics moves in a direction which is closer to Richard Rorty's rather than Joseph Margolis's notion of pragmatism, given Rorty's interest in solidarity. Rorty has usefully emphasized the role solidarity plays in ethical obligations, and he has situated that solidarity as an effect of culture.

More precisely, for Rorty, solidarity entails a "process of coming to see other human beings as 'one of us' rather than as 'them.' "[21] That is to say, "our sense of solidarity is strongest when those with whom solidarity is expressed are thought of as 'one of us,' where 'us' means something smaller and more local than the human race."[22] Rorty acknowledges that we may indeed belong to different groups, form solidarities based on different similarities, but each group is held together on the basis of the fact that "we can have we-intentions, intentions which we express in sentences of the form '*We* all want. . . .' "[23] In every instance, just as Wilfrid Sellers would argue, our ethical obligations come from the "we" communities with which we identify.[24]

In order to understand what Rorty is getting at with these statements, it's worth turning to a more extended passage in which he marks the importance of solidarity with its moral context:

> The view I am offering says that there is such a thing as moral progress, and that this progress is indeed in the direction of greater human solidarity. But that solidarity is not thought of as recognition of a core self, the human essence, in all human beings. Rather, it is thought of as the ability to see more and more traditional differences (of tribe, religion, race, custom, and the like) as unimportant when compared with similarities with respect to pain and humiliation – the ability to think of people as widely different from ourselves as included in the range of "us."[25]

I have quoted this passage at length because I think there are significant problems with Rorty's claims, which mark the difference between his use of "solidarity" and my own references to "groundless solidarity." While Rorty repeatedly emphasizes that his version of human solidarity is not meant to suggest that there is anything essentially human which binds "us" together in a community, it is rather difficult to see what else "we" are supposed to recognize in each other except a common humanity, if not a narrow ethnocentrism.

Rorty may think that he overcomes this objection when he says things like: "it is the ethnocentrism of a 'we' ('we liberals') which is dedicated to enlarging itself, to creating an even larger and more variegated *ethnos*."[26] Rorty certainly seems to believe that such qualifying statements provide an escape from ethnocentrism, but, in fact, they reveal Rorty's anti-foundational pragmatism to be little more than old-fashioned liberal humanism writ large, capable of appealing to those who want to reaffirm the value of the "melting pot" for political philosophy. While McDonald offers a timely reminder that in the "absence of certainty about absolute values," we do not yet know what kind of negotiations can take place,[27] Rorty seems altogether too happy to come to terms with such uncertainty or undecidability by believing in communities which take their ethical cues from the recognition of "usness." In the long run, as even the cover of his book would suggest, Rorty's pragmatism seems to owe more to individualism than to solidarity. Put strongly, Rorty unwittingly returns us to another version of the ethics of the subject.

However, what is most disturbing about Rorty's schema of obligation and solidarity is that there is no space left for the possibility of an obligation to the unrepresentable, the incommensurable, the radically Other. Assimilation is the only basis on which solidarity is formed. There is, I would argue, a real danger in understanding solidarity as based on similarity rather than difference, on the recognition of sameness ("usness") rather than on a recognition of the Other. Acknowledging new beliefs is more than a matter of accommodation. As Drucilla Cornell does a good job of demonstrating, feminism may be beyond accommodation anyway.[28]

This is also the important point that McDonald recognizes, for although she stresses, like Rorty, a "shared responsibility for the future of the human race," she does so only in a context which recognizes that the human self is *contingent*, that we may not yet know of what a self consists and who the other is (45). Witness the case of Baby M. In this respect, McDonald has offered the best analysis to date of the problems facing a feminist ethics in the age of technological reproduction. However, I think that her argument is at its best when it leaves behind the acknowledged debt to Rorty and becomes something that might more accurately be called deconstructive. With regard to abortion, to return to my discussion in Chapter 3, we can see how a deconstructive reading practice allows feminism to develop the question of justice in a more significant way than does pragmatism. The pro-choice movement within feminism relies on a solidarity based on difference, on the possibility of a respect for differences when it comes to a woman's right to choose whether or not she wants an abortion. If Rorty were to apply his understanding of solidarity to the pro-choice movement, he would conclude that it would be based on the ability of all members to be able to say: "We all want the right to choose." While this is correct to some extent, I would argue that to say simply that this similarity forms pro-choice solidarity hides more than it reveals. The pro-choice movement works because of the recognition of *difference* within the movement itself.

Again, this move to the recognition of difference may seem to place my own argument back in the pragmatist camp. After all, for William James and the philosophical pragmatists who follow him, the key question is "what difference would it practically make to any one if this notion rather than that notion were true?"[29] James goes on to make clear that "if no practical difference whatever can be traced, then the alternatives mean practically the same thing, and all dispute is idle."[30] While James's emphasis on the practical consequences of difference may seem parallel to the ethics suggested by feminism and deconstruction, what James does not mention, and what feminism and deconstruction allow to be considered, is that it is not always possible to know in advance, to predict, the difference that a difference would make. The pro-choice movement advocates the possibility for others to have the right to choose to have or not have an abortion. In its broadest interpretation, it sets up no terms or conditions to which all women must adhere; rather, it holds open the possibility for differences around the issue of abortion. It is precisely an obligation to differences, to others who do not choose the same thing for the same reasons that forms the groundless solidarity of pro-choice feminists.

APPROACHING AN IMPOSSIBLE JUSTICE

It would be possible to summarize this argument by saying that ethical judgments are always necessary, yet they are always threatened by the displacing action of other judgments. And one of the things deconstruction and feminism do is make us aware of the necessity as well as the precarious status of ethical judgments. In the name of the ethical, the judgments that deconstruction and feminism make always contain a simultaneous questioning of their ethical status. At the same time they pass judgment they also ask the question: "What's next?"[31] In this abyssal scene, any answer to the question will also necessarily lead to a reposing of the question. That is to say, just as there are no grounds for ethical judgments, there also is no end to judgment.

It is this aspect of the ethics to which the engagement of deconstruction and feminism gives rise that most clearly marks the distinctions from moral philosophy, including the popular albeit controversial feminist ethics of care. By this point, some of these distinctions are obvious. An alliance between feminism and deconstruction would hardly serve as a spokesperson for the moral *status quo* à la Hume, who turns to a combination of utility and sympathy as the basis for understanding given moral rules, which he assumes are so obvious that they need not be interrogated.[32] Feminism's and deconstruction's continued interrogation of the status of ethics, their persistent posing of the question "What's next?" does not sit comfortably with appeals to *a priori* moral rules.

Other work in contemporary moral philosophy seems positively anti-feminist in its approach. Although she is not stressing the connection between deconstruction and feminism, Marilyn Friedman does a wonderful job delineating the gender bias in contemporary moral theory which stakes its claim on the necessity of impartiality. According to Friedman, even the nonfeminist critics of impartiality, such as Alasdair MacIntyre and Michael Sandel, have overlooked the gender bias that lurks in such philosophy.[33] As Friedman points out:

> Hypothetical disasters abound as thought experiments in these discussions. The moral world of mainstream ethics is a nightmare of plane crashes, train wrecks, and sinking ships! Wives and children drown in this literature at an alarming rate. The nonfeminist impartiality critics never acknowledge how infrequent these emergencies are in daily moral life, nor, therefore, how rare is the need to sacrifice someone else's wife in order to save one's own. And for these infrequent occasions, the nonfeminist impartiality critics never discuss the possibility of investing our moral energies in efforts to *reduce beforehand* those breathtaking contests for survival and love – for example by better FAA regulation of airline safety.[34]

For Friedman one of the worst offenders in this "moral world of mainstream ethics" – and I would have to agree with her – is Bernard Williams, who has developed the notion of moral luck.[35] Friedman calls particular attention to the conclusion Williams draws from one of his central examples: "the painter who *abandons* wife and children altogether and heads off to Tahiti to develop his art will be retroactively justified if he thereby acquires the good fortune to create great paintings."[36] Friedman gets it right when she suggests that Williams's big moral take-away point comes down to a value hierarchy in which "wife trumps stranger, but great paintings trump wife."[37] Hardly the stuff of an ethics which has acknowledged any obligation to feminism.

Of course, one strong alternative to the impartiality philosophers is the feminist emphasis on an ethics of care which takes into account the particularity of women's experience. This has taken a number of forms, most notably Carol Gilligan's *In a Different Voice*.[38] An ethics of care proposes that somehow women, and hence feminism, can offer culture a kinder, gentler world on the basis of some inherent feminine goodness. Another way of looking at this would be to say that an ethics of care is a feminist rewriting of the Aristotelian "good life," where this time true friendship is between women, who contemplate *ethos* and find the highest *eudaimonia*. As Alison Jaggar notices, Gilligan's work has not only "encouraged the current revival of neo-Aristotelian approaches to ethics," it has also given rise within (and outside) academia to an entire industry of writing on so-called ethics of care.[39]

But Gilligan in particular has also come under fire from all sorts of philosophical camps. An empiricist could claim that while Gilligan is on the right track by searching for the particularity of women's moral experience, the data she presents on this count are faulty. That is to say, women care but not necessarily in the way Gilligan claims.[40] Others, like Nel

Noddings, want to reaffirm the experience-based, phenomenological approach of an ethics of care, while meeting the objections of pity and self-sacrifice as the necessary result of any ethics of care.[41] In a more deconstructive account, Drucilla Cornell outlines the ways in which an ethics of care, and Gilligan's work in particular, necessarily demands a normative context.[42]

Cornell's objection gets close to what I think is an unresolvable problem for all moral theory, including ethics of care. As John Rajchman so directly puts it: "the piety of moral theory is to try to say what is good for each and all of us, and where and how to find it."[43] Rajchman's criticism, like Cornell's, refuses the appeal to the universal that structures the possibility of moral theory. In fact, ethical *activism* is distinct from moral *theory* precisely in that it refuses the passage to the universal that theoretical critique seeks to effect. Such a distinction is what would separate ethical activism, as I am defining it here, from activities like the feminist anti-porn movement. Anti-porn feminists, as Laura Kipnis points out, are trying to construct a politically correct notion of femininity against other " 'unreconstructed' versions." The danger here is that feminism, to borrow Kipnis's words again, threatens to be reduced to "another variety of bourgeois reformism" in which "the policing of popular representation seems like only a path to more domination."[44] By contrast, the ethics resulting from the engagement of feminism and deconstruction do not set a moral standard or ideal, nor do they propose shared moral perspectives for women. In this respect, ethics would not have its foundation in sexual difference. It would be more accurate to think of the work of deconstruction and feminism as *creating* an ethics that has responsibility to issues of sexual difference.

This distinction between foundations and creation could easily be gendered with an eye on the tradition of epic. The patriarchal gesture *par excellence* is the founding of a city. Romulus, born without a mother, maps out an abstract structure on a blank terrain and names it, by the legal fiction of paternity, as his, as Rome. Women, meanwhile, create in the sense of giving birth, a messy process which is only given its meaning by the application of the patriarchal power of naming when the play of umbilical continuity and separation can be given its rule – that of the father.

While the distinction between foundations and creation is important, at the same time it is also a bit misleading. I do not mean to suggest that feminism and deconstruction serve as an ontological ground. My remarks about creating should not be taken to imply an essentialist argument by which woman embodies a creative principle and man the abstract rationality of form. I will leave such binary oppositions to St. Augustine, having no wish simply to reverse their hierarchy. I do want to argue, however, that the force (or creativity) of a feminist and deconstructive ethics pro-

ceeds from a certain *difference* from the patriarchal tradition of foundations, whether in philosophy or in urban planning – which are becoming
more and more the same thing. Creating, then, is an unstable and experi-
mental process which takes place in the absence of ontological grounding.
And the absence of ontological grounding is what distinguishes this from
moralism.

It is significant to note here that my argument for ethics in the name
of deconstruction and feminism does not situate sexual difference as the
absolute ethical difference. This distinguishes it from Irigaray's insistence
that the Other is that which "differs sexually from me."[45] While Irigaray's
ethical centering of sexual difference may seem preferable to Levinas's
patriarchal ethics which is founded on sexual indifference,[46] there is a real
danger in according sexual difference such a privileged role. Indeed, the
question of the place of sexual difference seems to me to be badly posed
and to lead to one of two impasses. Either, as for Irigaray and Spivak,
sexual difference is accorded an ontological privilege (ethics is solely a
question of intimacy), or critics spend their time trying to calculate the
exact ratio of importance to be accorded to sexual as against ethnic, class,
or other differences. In the latter case, it is easy to see that what is at
stake is an attempt to put an end to the ethical pull of the problem of
difference and to turn it into a purely epistemological question, a matter
of calculation. I would argue that sexual difference is neither primordial
nor calculable (in the manner of the utilitarian philosophers). By contrast,
I would underline that feminism needs to remain open to the fact that
sexual difference is one difference among many – not the only or always
the most important difference, not the absolute mark of otherness. In
general, justice is not a matter of calculation, nor is it derived from first
principles.

That is to say, ethics is not something that the moral person simply
recognizes so as to understand that immorality doesn't pay. I would
strongly suggest that ethical consequences are precisely *not* decidable –
calculated once and for all; statistical inference should not be understood
as a final judgment. As Derrida recognizes:

> A decision can only come into being in a space that exceeds the
> calculable program that would destroy all responsibility by transform-
> ing it into a programmable effect of determinate causes. There can be
> no moral or political responsibility without this trial and this passage
> by way of the undecidable.[47]

One way to read this passage in the context of my own argument would
be to say that the politics of undecidablity intervene as the mark of
ethical impossibility.[48] We cannot be sure that we have judged justly or
committed the right political act. This is not to suggest, as Cornell well
knows, that a recourse to undecidability alleviates responsibility. As she

points out, "we cannot be excused from our own role in history because we could not know so as to be reassured that we were 'right' in advance."[49] There are no assurances, and for that reason we are more not less responsible.

It is this element of calculation that distinguishes law from justice. To use Derrida's words again:

> Law (*droit*) is not justice. Law is the element of calculation, and it is just that there be law, but justice is incalculable, it requires us to calculate with the incalculable; and aporetic experiences are the experiences, as improbable as they are necessary, of justice, that is to say of moments in which the decision between just and unjust is never insured by a rule.[50]

If, however, justice is incalculable and ethical responsibility is not mere obedience to laws, where does this leave the Law and the legal–juridical system? First of all, feminism and deconstruction should together remind us of the dangers of leaving it to the legal–juridical system to decide ethical issues. It would be unjust to place too much faith in the "saving force of legislation." Laws like the Neighborhood Playgroup Act and the Parental Responsibility Act, which are designed to insure parental responsibility and enhance the rights of children, also evoke "Orwellian visions of an intrusive government that oversees and regulates our most private decisions."[51] We would not have very far to go to see just how frequently "women were victimized by policies designed to protect them – policies that, for this very reason, denied them the chance to make basic decisions for themselves."[52]

Law is not, however, necessarily negative, the police always repressive. This is Derrida's deconstructive lesson. "A red light is not repressive," nor would be a law enforcement officer attempting to stop an act of domestic violence.[53] Significantly, there is a sense in which giving things a name gives them a legal reality, as Cornell notes is the case with "date rape," and we could add other terms here like "sexual harassment" and "domestic violence."[54] But laws are not just in themselves, and as Derrida recognizes, "one obeys them not because they are just but because they have authority."[55] Part of the problem, of course, becomes deciding when the law is unjust and what authority has legitimated or allowed the unjust action. The danger is believing that the legal system, or any other third party, would always be capable of making that decision itself.

Thus, to assign to some third party the task of arbitrating ethical issues, to make it the business of a particular discipline (philosophy) or sector of society (the legal system), would be to shirk responsibility. There is no meta-language that can deal on our behalf with difference. Ethical responsibility is not mere obedience to laws; it neither begins nor ends with the law. Rather, as Derrida would have it, "responsibility is excessive or it is not a responsibility."[56] To repeat myself a bit, this means that justice remains unrepresentable, that it is impossible to do justice to justice, to carry out one's responsibility entirely.[57] But even though justice is unrepresentable and impossible, one should not stop trying to be just.

This requires that we envisage feminist and deconstructive politics differently, a difference that I have tried to mark in appeal to the terms *ethical activism* and *groundless solidarity*. These are not political programs; they are rather ways of rephrasing modes of political organization and understandings of political action.[58] They assume political action to be both endless and contingent. And in each case, they attempt to distinguish between a political *movement*, which attempts to think its own uncertain relation to tradition, and a political *project*, which ignores tradition and looks toward the new Jerusalem. Recently, we have begun to hear talk of post-feminism and of the death of deconstruction. I want to suggest that both of these reports are mistaken. Certainly, the appeal to deconstruction as an interpretative method within literary studies has reached its limit. And at the same time, the gains of feminism have produced a situation in which the meta-narrative of the affirmation of female identity has foundered precisely because its realization can only be imperialist. To put this another way, we don't need more lessons in how to be a woman; feminism is no longer only the search for an authoritative, subjective, speaking position. In a sense, then, we have to learn to negotiate outside the horizon of authority. No more authoritative deconstructions of literary texts, no more authoritative statements on the essence of woman. To speak without recourse to the meta-language of authority is to speak as singularities, to attempt to do justice in singular cases, rather than to be just once and for all. It is this dispersal of the modernist horizon of social justice that feminism and deconstruction work for. That work is not without its moments of achievement, but it is an endless work, an abyssal politics . . .

Notes

1 UNNECESSARY INTRODUCTIONS

1 Their names appear throughout this book. As a further note, I persist with
  the use of the rather nondescript term "relationship" as a way to hold open
  the question of how to understand what happens with deconstruction and
  feminism. The alternatives likewise present problems: "alliance" suggests too
  much agreement; "conjunction" is too grammatical; "intersection" seems to
  present two unified fronts which require a traffic light; "negotiation" makes
  it appear like they are trying to close a business deal; "reconcilliation" happens
  more frequently to bank accounts and suggests that they have to be friends
  and reach political consensus; "compromise" misleadingly implies a need to
  meet halfway on something. And yet for all these unwanted connotations,
  these alternatives will have a place in what is to follow.
2 For an extended discussion of the linking of phrases, of *enchaînement*, see
  Jean-François Lyotard, *The Differend: Phrases in Dispute*, tr. Georges Van
  Den Abbeele (Minneapolis: University of Minnesota Press, 1988).
    Here it is also important to note possible linkages with parallel work being
  done in cultural studies and postcolonial studies. I have discussed some of the
  linkages between cultural studies, feminism, and deconstruction in my essay,
  "Doing Justice to Feminism," *Surfaces* II, 9 (1992). For insightful work which
  links deconstruction and feminism to postcolonial studies, see especially: Homi
  K. Bhabha, "DissemiNation: Time, Narrative, and the Margins of the Modern
  Nation," *Nation and Narration*, ed. Homi K. Bhabha (London and New York:
  Routledge, 1990); R. Radhakrishnan, "Ethnic Identity and Post-Structuralist
  Difference," *Cultural Critique*, 1987; Jenny Sharpe, *Allegories of Empire: The
  Figure of Woman in the Colonial Text* (Minneapolis: University of Minnesota
  Press, 1993); Gayatri Chakravorty Spivak, *In Other Worlds: Essays in Cultural
  Politics* (New York and London: Methuen, 1987); and *The Postcolonial Critic:
  Interviews, Strategies, Dialogues*, ed. Sarah Harasym (New York and London:
  Routledge, 1990).
3 I borrow this phrase from Robyn Wiegman, *Economies of Visibility: Race and
  Gender in United States Culture* (forthcoming, Duke University Press). For a
  discussion of deconstruction as interminable analysis, see Mark Krupnick,
  "Introduction," *Displacement: Derrida and After*, ed. Mark Krupnick
  (Bloomington: Indiana University Press, 1987), 14.
4 Modern lexicography defines words by usage (consensus), from at least Dr.
  Johnson. Prescriptive etymologists are a distinctly pre-modern phenomenon.
5 Alice A. Jardine, *Gynesis: Configurations of Woman and Modernity* (Ithaca:

Cornell University Press, 1985), 21n. I don't entirely agree with her, however, that feminism needs to recognize its connections "to larger theoretical issues." Accepting for the moment the way Jardine uses the term "theoretical," it strikes me that feminism is a larger theoretical issue, indeed is larger than a theoretical issue, in the first place. Perhaps a better way of putting this would be to suggest that feminism is indeed in conversation with theoretical issues other to itself.

6 It is also worth noting Elizabeth Meese's insistence on the variety of feminisms. As she puts it, "not all feminist figures shape up the same way or add up to the same sum" ((*Ex*)*tensions: Re-figuring Feminist Criticism* (Urbana: University of Illinois Press, 1990), 13).

7 Such is Mary Poovey's mistake when she concludes that "there are as many deconstructions as there are feminisms" ("Feminism and Deconstruction," *Feminist Studies* 14, 1 (Spring 1988), 51). I would certainly agree with her, however, that the problem of discussing the relationship between feminism and deconstruction must "Beg – or defer – the question of definition" (51).

8 Jonathan Culler, *On Deconstruction: Theory and Criticism after Structuralism* (Ithaca: Cornell University Press, 1982), 9.

9 Culler, *On Deconstruction*, 9.

10 "Deconstructionism" has been used in other contexts to make a similar point. Barbara Johnson usefully explains that "as soon as any radically innovative thought becomes an *ism*, its specific ground-breaking force diminishes, its historical notoriety increases, and its disciples tend to become more simplistic, more dogmatic, and ultimately more conservative, at which time its power becomes institutional rather than analytical" ("Nothing Fails Like Success," *A World of Difference* (Baltimore and London: Johns Hopkins University Press, 1987), 11). Derrida rephrases Johnson's remarks when he states that " 'deconstructionists' and 'deconstructionism' represent an effort to reappro-priate, tame, normalize this writing in order to reconstitute a new 'theory' – 'deconstructionism' with its method and its rules, its criteria of distinction between use and mention, the seriousness of its discipline and of its insti-tutions, etc." ("Some Statements and Truisms about Neologisms, Newisms, Positisms, Parasitisms, and Other Small Seismisms," tr. Anne Tomiche, *The States of "Theory": History, Art, and Critical Discourse*, ed. David Carroll (New York: Columbia University Press, 1990), 75–6).

Going back a bit further, Johnson's and Derrida's complaint about the "ism" dogging deconstruction sounds reminiscent of the Situationists' rhetoric. The *Internationale Situationiste*, No. 1, June 1958 (in *An Endless Adventure . . . An Endless Passion . . . An Endless Banquet: A Situationist Scrapbook*, ed. Iwona Blazwick (London: Verso, 1989) defines "situationism" as:

a meaningless term improperly derived from [situationist]. There is no such thing as situationism, which would mean a doctrine of interpretation of existing facts. The notion of situationism is obviously devised by antisitu-ationists. (22)

As a further note, the attendant danger of feminism may lie in the fact that it always is an "ism."

11 See, for instance, Jacques Derrida, "Letter to a Japanese Friend," tr. Andrew Benjamin, *Derrida and Différance*, ed. David Wood and Robert Bernasconi (Evanston, IL: Northwestern University Press, 1988); and "Some Statements and Truisms." I will come back to the force of Derrida's insistence on this point later in the introduction.

12 In putting my argument this way, I am not trying to protect a pure notion of "deconstruction" or "feminism," one which might be discovered, for instance, in the relationship forged between them.

13 Trinh T. Minh-ha, *Woman, Native, Other* (Bloomington: Indiana University Press, 1989), 42. For other commentaries on the role of "theory," see especially: Jacques Derrida, "Some Statements and Truisms"; and Jonathan Culler, "Criticism and Institutions: The American University," *Post-Structuralism and the Question of History*, ed. Derek Attridge, Geoff Bennington, and Robert Young (Cambridge: Cambridge University Press, 1987).

14 For a summary of the objections to feminism as philosophy and an excellent counter-argument see: Linda Singer, "Defusing the Canon: Feminist Rereading and Textual Politics," *The Question of the Other: Essays in Contemporary Continental Philosophy*, ed. Arleen B. Dallery and Charles E. Scott (Albany, NY: SUNY Press, 1989). Christopher Norris provides a convincing argument for deconstruction's crucial situation with regard to philosophy in "Philosophy as *Not* Just a 'Kind of Writing': Derrida and the Claim of Reason," *Redrawing the Lines: Analytical Philosophy, Deconstruction, and Literary Theory*, ed. Reed Way Dasenbrock (Minneapolis: University of Minnesota Press, 1989). Richard Rorty's objections to Norris's claims follow in his essay in the same volume, "Two Meanings of 'Logocentrism': A Reply to Norris."

15 Martin Heidegger, "The End of Philosophy and the Task of Thinking," *Basic Writings*, ed. David Farrell Krell (New York: Harper & Row, 1977), 376. It is important to note that for Heidegger "philosophy is metaphysics," where metaphysics is synonymous with Platonism (374).

16 This seems to be Rudolph Gasché's stumbling block in *The Tain of the Mirror* (Cambridge, MA: Harvard University Press, 1986). While Gasché has an admirable grasp of reflective philosophy and an appreciation of Derrida's work, he is curiously uninterested in how deconstruction's engagement with the tradition of reflective philosophy could cause him to write its history in other than the most traditional terms. Paradoxically, while deconstruction is Gasché's main interest, there is nothing particularly deconstructive about his own argument. By contrast, Derrida has continuously questioned the limits of philosophical discourse and examined what is meant by the name "philosophy." See especially: *"Privilège. Titre justificatif et remarques introductives, du droit à la philosophie* (Paris: Galilée, 1990), 36–41.

17 Jacques Derrida, "White Mythology," *Margins of Philosophy*, tr. Alan Bass (Chicago: University of Chicago Press, 1982), 244.

18 For an excellent discussion of Derrida's practice of putting terms under erasure, see: Gayatri Chakravorty Spivak, "Translator's Preface," in Jacques Derrida, *Of Grammatology*, tr. Gayatri Chakravorty Spivak (Baltimore and London: Johns Hopkins University Press, 1976), xiv-xviii.

19 Gayatri Chakravorty Spivak, "Feminism and Deconstruction, Again: Negotiating with Unacknowledged Masculinism," *Between Feminism and Psychoanalysis*, ed. Teresa Brennan (London and New York: Routledge, 1989), 206.

20 Derrida, "Letter to a Japanese Friend," 3. And, of course, not unlike Spivak's prose, Derrida's title carries with it its own Heideggerian echo. For the sake of reference, the full passage to which I am referring reads:

All the same, and in spite of appearances, deconstruction is neither an *analysis* nor a *critique* and its translation would have to take that into consideration. It is not an analysis in particular because the dismantling of a structure is not a regression toward a *simple element*, toward an *indissoluble origin*. These values, like that of analysis, are themselves philosophemes subject to deconstruction. No more is it a critique, in a general sense or in a Kantian sense. The instance of *krinein* or of *krisis* (decision, choice, judgment discernment) is itself, as is all the apparatus of transcendental critique, one of the essential "themes" or "objects" of deconstruction.

I would say the same about *method*. Deconstruction is not a method and cannot be transformed into one. Especially if the technical and procedural significations of the words are stressed.

21 Derrida, "Letter to a Japanese Friend," 4. Emphasis on "event" my own. Derrida later rephrases this remark in "Some Statements and Truisms," this time arguing for deconstruction as "the case":

Deconstruction is neither a theory nor a philosophy. It is neither a school nor a method. It is not even a discourse, nor an act, nor a practice. It is what happens, what is happening today in what they call society, politics, diplomacy, economics, historical reality, and so on and so forth. Deconstruction is the case. (85)

22 Spivak, "Feminism and Deconstruction, Again," 213.
23 There is also the problem, of course, that feminism and deconstruction do not give rise to a series of grammatical equivalents. Feminism does not, for example, turn out "feminismists" the way in which deconstruction has attendant "deconstructionists." Feminism is also always an "ism," as I mentioned earlier, and thus far has never become "femination." In Chapter 2, I will inquire further into the grammatical constraints that surround these terms.
24 If I sound a bit repetitive in my insistence on difference, it is because, as Domna Stanton so aptly points out, "the awareness that sameness permeates all efforts to speak difference, and further, that every alternative practice tends to erect itself as ultimate authority can instill the imperative of unceasing vigilance and self-interrogation" ("Difference on Trial: A Critique of the Maternal Metaphor in Cixous, Irigaray, and Kristeva," *The Thinking Muse: Feminism and Modern French Philosophy*, ed. Jeffner Allen and Iris Marion Young (Bloomington: Indiana University Press, 1989), 170).
25 See Luce Irigaray, "The 'Mechanics' of Fluids," *This Sex Which is Not One*, tr. Catherine Porter (Ithaca: Cornell University Press, 1985), 106–18.
26 A concern for this seemingly innocuous conjunction has been raised before. Shoshana Felman's introduction to *Literature and Psychoanalysis* begins by asking the question "What does the *and* really mean?" She goes on to explain, as I do here, that the coordinating function frequently becomes a subordinating one, where literature plays subordinated object to the subject of psychoanalysis – a master/slave relationship, to use Hegel's terms. Felman's volume is an attempt to deconstruct this hierarchy by considering "the relationship between psychoanalysis and literature *from the literary point of view*" (*Literature and Psychoanalysis: The Question of Reading – Otherwise*, ed. Shoshana Felman (Baltimore: Johns Hopkins University Press, 1982), 5–7).

Ruth Salvaggio has returned to Felman's argument in order to call attention to the force of the "and" in "Psychoanalysis and Deconstruction and Woman." More than a mere case of add ons, of more "ands," Salvaggio goes on to contend that "woman" is herself the disruptive third term, that *women* "are not the objects in [discourse], but the subjects who transform it." Thus, "women create intersubjective space" and "reinvent the 'and' " ("Psychoanalysis and Deconstruction and Woman," *Psychoanalysis and . . .* , ed. Richard Feldstein and Henry Sussman (New York: Routledge, 1990), 160). While I share Salvaggio's concern for the "and" in this context, I am less convinced that anything like "intersubjective space" is possible – hence my own emphasis on crossdisciplinarity, which tries to get away from a discourse of subjectivity, from the rule of the (reconfigured) subject.

27 Derrida, *Of Grammatology*, 162.
28 A few examples that I would like to call special attention to are: Hélène Cixous and Catherine Clément, *The Newly Born Woman*, tr. Betsy Wing (Minneapolis: University of Minnesota Press, 198); Jacques Derrida, *Spurs: Nietzsche's Styles/Éperons: les styles de Nietzsche*, tr. Barbara Harlow (Chicago: University of Chicago Press, 1978); and Trinh, *Woman, Native, Other*. Cixous begins her "Sorties" section with a proposition her essay sets out to undermine: "Thought has always worked through opposition" (*The Newly Born Woman*, 63); while in the final "Exchange" section, Cixous and Clément exchange remarks on mastery. Similarly, Derrida calls for the "transformation of the very value of hierarchy itself" ("*transformer la valeur même de hiérachie*") (*Spurs/Éperons*, 80–1).

Continuing this line of inquiry, Trinh Minh-ha asks: "Can knowledge circulate without a position of mastery? Can it be conveyed without the exercise of power?" Her response, like her questions, is double:

> No, because there is no end to understanding power relations which are rooted deep in the social nexus – not merely added to society nor easily locatable so that we can just radically do away with them. Yes, however, because in-between grounds always exist, and cracks and interstices are like gaps of fresh air that keep on being suppressed because they tend to render more visible the failures operating in every system. Perhaps mastery need not coincide with power. Then we would have to rethink mastery in terms of non-master, and we would have to rewrite women's relation to theory. (*Woman, Native, Other*, 41)

29 Derrida, *Spurs/Éperons*, 62–5. "*Et en vérité les femmes féministes contre lesquelles Nietzsche multiplie le sarcasme, ce sont les hommes. Le féminisme, c'est l'opération par laquelle la femme veut ressembler à l'homme, au philosophe dogmatique, revendiquant la vérité, la science, l'objectivité, c'est-à-dire avec toute l'illusion virile, l'effet de castration qui s'y attache. Le féminisme veut la castration – aussi de la femme. Perd le style.*" Translation modified and emphasis my own. It is, of course, important to note the play of genders here: feminism (nm), castration (nf), and style (nm).
30 Derrida, *Spurs/Éperons*, 92–3 (translation modified).
31 Jacques Derrida, "Deconstruction in America," *Critical Exchange* 17 (Winter 1985), 30.
32 Derrida, "Deconstruction in America," 30.
33 Jacques Derrida with Geoff Bennington, "On Colleges and Philosophy," *Postmodernism: ICA Documents*, ed. Lisa Appignanesi (London: Free Association Books, 1989).
34 Derrida, *Spurs/Éperons*, 96–7 (translation modified).
35 Derrida, *Spurs/Éperons*, 98–9 (translation modified).
36 Jacques Derrida, "Women in the Beehive: A seminar with Jacques Derrida," *Men in Feminism*, ed. Alice Jardine and Paul Smith (New York and London: Methuen, 1987), 196.
37 Denise Riley, *"Am I That Name?": Feminism and the Category of "Women" in History* (Minneapolis: University of Minnesota Press, 1988), 4; Jane Tompkins, "Me and My Shadow," *Gender and Theory: Dialogues on Feminist Criticism*, ed. Linda Kauffman (Oxford and New York: Basil Blackwell, 1989),

135; Nicole Ward Jouve, *White Woman Speaks with Forked Tongue: Criticism as Autobiography* (London and New York: Routledge, 1991), 7; Margaret Whitford, *Luce Irigaray: Philosophy in the Feminine* (London and New York: Routledge, 1991), 137; Tania Modleski, "Feminism and the Power of Interpretation: Some Critical Readings," *Feminist Studies/Critical Studies*, ed. Teresa de Lauretis (Bloomington: Indiana University Press, 1986), 130; Jane Marcus, "Still Practice, A/Wrested Alphabet: Toward a Feminist Aesthetic," *Feminist Issues in Literary Scholarship*, ed. Shari Benstock (Bloomington: Indiana University Press, 1987), 87. (Marcus directs her remark at "theory" in general, which for her includes deconstruction.)

My list is by no means intended to include all criticism ever directed at deconstruction by feminism. While this sample is meant to be representative, it will have undoubtedly excluded some voices and positions. For an excellent assessment and insightful interrogation of feminist dismissals of deconstruction, see Elizabeth Meese, *(Ex)tensions: Re-figuring Feminist Criticism*. Meese also is interested in what she calls the "alliance" of feminism and deconstruction and urges that negotiations between the two might be mutually beneficial.

38 Elaine Showalter, "Women's Time, Women's Space: Writing the History of Feminist Criticism," *Feminist Issues in Literary Scholarship*, 36.

39 Showalter, "Women's Time, Women's Space," 36, 42.

40 For all these rather dismissive accounts of deconstruction in the name of feminism, Bella Brodzki and Celeste Schenck still insist that feminism "had more to gain from the alliance" with deconstruction, than deconstruction had to gain from feminism ("Criticus Interruptus: Uncoupling Feminism and Deconstruction," *Feminism and Institutions: Dialogues on Feminist Theory*, ed. Linda Kauffman (Oxford and New York: Basil Blackwell, 1989), 196). Keeping Derrida's remarks in mind, this may sound plausible. I would still argue, however, that resistance to a relationship between feminism and deconstruction has found a good home on all sides of the debate.

41 Brodzki and Schenck, "Criticus Interruptus," 194–5. Their essay particularly takes on Bernard Duyfhuizen's "Deconstruction and Feminist Literary Theory II," collected in the same volume. But it also casts a wider net and includes an assessment of a variety of arguments about the relationship between feminism and deconstruction.

42 That gender determination cannot be taken for granted in this relationship becomes clearer by looking at how the terms themselves take a gender in French: *le féminisme* and *la déconstruction*. In what may seem like a counter-intuitive gender assignation to the English speaking reader, feminism is masculine, while deconstruction is feminine. The accidents of grammar show up the point I am trying to make about the ways in which feminism and deconstruction are not as easily separated on the grounds of gender as the "and" that stands between them have led some to believe.

43 It could be argued that the problem with my examples is that they are all women. While I could dismiss this objection as merely an unwarranted, essentialist intrusion, it is not without merit. On the one hand, as I will be arguing in Chapter 2, there is nothing essential about either gender or sexual difference. On the other hand, tell that to all the people who would not hesitate when asked to define themselves as either female or male. That an essentialist understanding of gender and sexual difference is alive and well is almost not a debatable point. Within the academy, arguments which could perhaps best be characterized by the infelicitous phrase "Men in Feminism," to borrow

from Alice Jardine and Paul Smith, are good indicators of why my list is the way it is.

44 Poovey, "Feminism and Deconstruction," 61.

45 Poovey, "Feminism and Deconstruction," 58–9. It is worth remarking that Poovey's argument is the mirror image of the "post-feminist" position, according to which feminism is a political tool that has, or soon will have, outlived its usefulness. Significantly, the deconstructive writers discussed in this book do not make "post-feminist" arguments of this sort. Thus, they avoid the problems of instrumental reasoning to which Poovey's "post-deconstructionist" argument succumbs.

46 Poovey, "Feminism and Deconstruction," 58.

47 Joan Wallach Scott, *Gender and the Politics of History* (New York: Columbia University Press, 1988), 41.

48 Poovey, "Feminism and Deconstruction," 61.

49 Poovey, "Feminism and Deconstruction," 62. At the beginning of her essay, Poovey believes that deconstruction calls feminism into question, whereas feminism must simply use deconstruction, take it at its word: "I want to try to explain both why deconstruction calls feminism into question and how feminism can use deconstruction" (51). But as the passage quoted in my text indicates, Poovey believes that feminism has more in store for deconstruction than she is at first willing to admit.

50 Johnson, "Gender Theory and the Yale School," *A World of Difference*, 32–40. It is important to note here that Johnson, while focusing on texts which have often been described as "deconstruction," limits her discussion to the male professors at Yale whose work was included in the volume *Deconstruction and Criticism*. Thus, her essay takes up Harold Bloom's work, which I would not consider deconstruction. For this reason, I have not included Johnson's remarks on Bloom.

51 Except, one presumes, when women provide the basis for metaphoric comparisons along the lines of "much reading is indeed like girl-watching, a simple expense of the spirit." Hartman's particularly sexist contribution to the deconstruction-is-not-feminism debate may prove more expensive than he once realized (*The Fate of Reading and Other Essays*, (Chicago: University of Chicago Press, 1975), 248).

52 Johnson, "Gender Theory and the Yale School," 34–8.

53 Johnson, "Deconstruction, Feminism, and Pedagogy," *A World of Difference*, 46.

54 Robert Scholes, "Reading like a Man," *Men in Feminism*, 205.

55 Scholes, "Reading Like a Man," 208.

56 Scholes does not consider this possibility, arguing instead that deconstruction denies difference and is thus both "androgynous" (212) and "genderless" (210).

57 Scholes, "Reading Like a Man," 213.

58 Scholes, "Reading Like a Man," 207.

59 This would be his reason for reviewing the implications of Jonathan Culler's "Reading as a Woman," the third chapter of *On Deconstruction*.

60 For a more extended discussion of this use of displacement, which, of course, owes a debt to Freud, see: Gayatri Chakravorty Spivak, "Displacement and the Discourse of Woman," and Mark Krupnick, "Introduction," both in *Displacement: Derrida and After*, 1–20, 169–95.

61 Krupnick, "Introduction," *Displacement: Derrida and After*, 16.

62 Jacques Derrida, " 'Eating Well,' or the Calculation of the Subject: An Inter-

view with Jacques Derrida," *Who Comes After the Subject?*, tr. Peter Connor
and Avital Ronell, ed. Eduardo Cadava, Peter Connor, and Jean-Luc Nancy
(New York and London: Routledge, 1991), 108.
63 Derrida, " 'Eating Well,' " *Who Comes After the Subject?*, 110.

2   QUESTIONS OF WOMEN

1 I will address the important distinction between indeterminacy and undecidability in Chapter 3.
2 A similar uncertainty surrounds the group "men." Given the extremely diverse
range of activities in which "men" have already engaged, this statement may
come as no surprise; given the certainty with which men have tended to be
defined by their activities, my statement might seem positively false. After all,
hasn't Western culture worked hard at defining precisely what men are and
what constitute proper manly activities? In recent years, feminism has engaged
in a different form of cultural work in order to demonstrate the ontological
and epistemological uncertainty of "men." By examining the unstable foundations upon which notions of masculinity have been constructed, feminism
has revealed that "men" are also yet to be determined. Some notable feminist
studies in this area include: Joseph A. Boone and Michael Cadden, *Engender-
ing Men: The Question of Male Feminist Criticism* (New York and London:
Routledge, 1990) and Kaja Silverman, *Male Subjectivity at the Margins* (New
York and London: Routledge, 1992).
3 For an informative discussion of the *mise en abyme* see: Andrew Benjamin,
Art, Mimesis, and the Avant-Garde (London and New York: Routledge, 1991),
13–17. The Quaker Oats box has also proven to be as much a rhetorical as a
commercial success when it comes to explaining the *mise en abyme*. (See, for
instance, Barbara Johnson's note to Jacques Derrida's "The Double Session,"
Dissemination (Chicago: University of Chicago Press, 1981), 265n.)
4 This is the point that Lacan explains so well in his seminar on vision ("The
Light and Line," *Four Fundamental Concepts of Psycho-Analysis*, ed. Jacques-
Alain Miller, tr. Alan Sheridan (New York: Norton, 1981):

> In the classical tale of Zeuxis and Parrhasios, Zeuxis has the advantage of
> having made grapes that attracted the birds. The stress is placed not on the
> fact that these grapes were in any way perfect grapes, but on the fact that
> even the eye of the birds was taken in by them. This is proved by the fact
> that his friend Parrhasios triumphs over him for having painted on the wall
> a veil so lifelike that Zeuxis, turning towards him said, *Well, and now show
> us what you have painted behind it.* By this he showed that what was at
> issue was certainly deceiving the eye (*tromper l'oeil*). A triumph of the
> gaze over the eye. (103)

The *mise en abyme* can usefully be understood as an elaborate *trompe l'oeil*.
In both cases, in the illusory search to find out what lies behind the veil (of
representation), the subject also becomes the *object* of the joke. What the
subject fails to recognize at first is that behind the veil is only another veil,
namely the canvas.
5 Jacques Derrida, "Sending: On Representation," *Social Research* 49, 2
(Summer 1982), 317.
6 Jacques Derrida, "Parergon," *The Truth in Painting*, tr. Geoff Bennington and
Ian McLeod (Chicago: University of Chicago Press, 1987), 34.
7 Derrida, "Sending: On Representation," 304.

8 Self-help manuals are such a growth industry that it would be impossible to give a comprehensive listing in this space. Specifically, I have in mind: Dr. Toni Grant, *Being a Woman: Fulfilling your Femininity and Finding Love* (New York: Random House, 1988); Hansen Shaevitz, *The Superwomen Syndrome* (New York: Warner Books, 1984); Megan Marshall, *The Cost of Loving: Women and the New Fear of Intimacy* (New York: G. P. Putnam's Sons, 1984). However, this is a small sampling in a time when self-help sections of popular bookstores are many times larger than philosophy or literary criticism. Given these circumstances, it seems appropriate that recently I found Michel Foucault's *The Care of the Self* (New York: Pantheon Books, 1986) shelved in the self-help section of a local bookstore.

9 bell hooks, *Feminist Theory: From Margin to Center* (Boston: South End Press, 1984), 46. hooks also provides an excellent analysis of what's wrong with the feminist rallying cry of "common oppression":

> The idea of "common oppression" was a false and corrupt platform disguising and mystifying the true nature of women's varied and complex social reality. Women are divided by sexist attitudes, racism, class privilege, and a host of other prejudices. Sustained woman bonding can occur only when these divisions are confronted and the necessary steps are taken to eliminate them. Divisions will not be eliminated by wishful thinking or romantic reverie about common oppression despite the value of highlighting experiences all women share. (44)

10 June Jordan, interview with Pratibha Parmar quoted in Pratibha Parmar, "Black Feminism: The Politics of Articulation," *Identity: Community, Culture, Difference*, ed. Jonathan Rutherford (London: Lawrence & Wishart, 1990), 112.

11 Judith Butler, *Gender Trouble* (New York and London: Routledge, 1990), 15.

12 Jacques Derrida, "Women in the Beehive: A Seminar with Jacques Derrida," *Men in Feminism*, ed. Alice Jardine and Paul Smith (New York and London: Methuen, 1987), 194.

13 Diana Fuss (*Essentially Speaking* (New York and London: Routledge, 1989), 14) criticizes Derrida in these terms:

> Derrida does not so much challenge that woman has an essence as insist that we can never "rigorously" or "properly" identify it. Woman's essence is simply "undecidable," a position which frequently inverts itself in deconstruction to the suggestion that it is the essence of woman to *be* the undecidable. To say that woman's essence is to be the undecidable is different from claiming that woman's essence is undecidable and different still from claiming that it is undecidable whether woman has an essence at all. Derrida's theory of essence moves between and among these contradictory positions, playing upon the undecidability and ambiguity which underwrites his own deconstructionist maneuvers.

In fact, Fuss has rather missed the point, and Derrida says something more interesting:

> Of course, saying that woman is on the side, so to speak, of undecidability and so on, has only the meaning of a strategical phase. In a given situation, which is ours, which is the European phallogocentric structure, the side of the woman is the side from which you start to dismantle the structure. So you can put undecidability and all of the other concepts which go with it on the side of femininity, writing and so on. But as soon as you have

reached the first stage of deconstruction, then the opposition between women and men stops being pertinent. Then you cannot say that woman is another name, or a good trope for writing, undecidability and so on. We need to find some way to progress strategically. Starting with deconstruction of phallogocentrism, and using the feminine force, so to speak, in this move and then – and this would be the second stage or level – to give up the opposition between men and women. At this second stage "woman" is clearly not the best trope to refer to all those things: undecidability and so on. The same could be said for undecidability itself! ("Women in the Beehive," *Men in Feminism*, 194)

14 Lyotard provides an extended examination of the differend in *The Differend: Phrases in Dispute*, tr. George Van Den Abbeele (Minneapolis: University of Minnesota Press, 1988). In general terms, Lyotard describes the differend as the case in which something "asks" to be put into phrases, and suffers from the wrong of not being able to be put into phrases right away (13). With regard to systems of justice, he offers this clarification:

> The plaintiff lodges his or her complaint before the tribunal, the accused argues in such a way to show the inanity of the accusation. Litigation takes place. I would like to call a differend [*différend*] the case where the plaintiff is divested of the means to argue and becomes for that reason a victim. If the addressor, the addressee, and the sense of the testimony are neutralized, everything takes place as if there were no damages. A case of differend between two parties takes place when the "regulation" of the conflict that opposes them is done in the idiom of one of the parties while the wrong suffered by the other is not signified in that idiom. (9)

The differend is not resolved by a retrial, where the same system is allowed supposedly to work better. The problem is not merely whether the existing system of justice works as it should. Rather, as Sarah Pelmas points out, it requires "a hearing we cannot yet imagine" where the plaintiff is no longer the voiceless victim ("Bearing Witness to the Differend: Clarence Thomas and Anita Hill," unpublished paper, 12).

15 Kimberlé Crenshaw, " 'Whose Story is it Anyway?': Feminist and Antiracist Appropriations of Anita Hill," *Race-ing Justice, En-gendering Power: Essays on Anita Hill, Clarence Thomas, and the Construction of Social Reality*, ed. Toni Morrison (New York: Pantheon, 1992), 411. Morrison's excellent collection, in which Crenshaw's essay appears, begins to do justice to what happened in and around the hearings. According to Morrison, "this volume is one of the several beginnings of these new conversations in which issues and arguments are taken as seriously as they are" (xxx).

16 Crenshaw, "Whose Story is it Anyway?," *Race-ing Justice, En-gendering Power*, 433.

17 In "Bearing Witness to the Differend," Pelmas offers an important analysis of this case which extends the parallel with Lyotard's notion of the differend.

18 Crenshaw, "Whose Story is it Anyway?," *Race-ing Justice, En-gendering Power*, 415.

19 I would suggest that this means that feminism is more than single issue politics, that it must do more than reiterate the question, "What about women?" Crenshaw provides an important example of what I'm talking about when she convincingly argues that "when feminism does not explicitly oppose racism, and when antiracism does not incorporate opposition to patriarchy, race and gender politics often end up being antagonistic to each other and both interests

lose" ("Whose Story is it Anyway?," *Race-ing Justice, En-gendering Power*, 405).

20 Pelmas, "Bearing Witness to the Differend," 13.

21 Joan Wallach Scott, *Gender and the Politics of History* (New York: Columbia University Press, 1988), 16.

22 Scott, *Gender and the Politics of History*, 16.

23 Scott, *Gender and the Politics of History*, 18–19. Scott also carefully outlines four important areas in which social history made its largest impact on women's history: 1. it provided "methodologies in quantification, in the use of details from everyday life, and in interdisciplinary borrowings from sociology, demography, and ethnography"; 2. "it conceptualized as historical phenomena family relationships, fertility, and sexuality"; 3. it "challenged the narrative line of political history ('white men make history') by taking as its subject large-scale social processes"; 4. it led to "the legitimization of a focus on groups customarily excluded from political history" (21).

24 Scott, *Gender and the Politics of History*, 22.

25 Christina Crosby, *The Ends of History: Victorians and "The Woman Question"* (London and New York: Routledge, 1991), 153–4. Crosby is especially indebted to Audre Lorde's essay collection, *Sister Outsider* (Trumansburg, NY: Crossing Press, 1984).

26 Crosby, *The Ends of History*, 154.

27 bell hooks, *Ain't I a Woman* (Boston: South End Press, 1981); Susan Cavin, *Lesbian Origins* (San Francisco: ism press, 1985); Esther Newton, *Mother Camp: Female Impersonators in America* (Chicago: University of Chicago Press, 1972); Barbara Christian, *Black Women Novelists: The Development of a Tradition* (Westport, CT: Greenwood Press, 1980).

28 Hélène Cixous makes a similar remark. According to her, "history is always in several places at once, there are always several histories in several places at once, there are always several histories underway; this is a high point in the history of women" (*The Newly Born Woman*, tr. Betsy Wing (Minneapolis: University of Minnesota Press, 1986), 160).

29 Scott, *Gender and the Politics of History*, 27. As I remarked in Chapter 1, Scott uses deconstruction as a tool with which to dismantle binary oppositions, especially as they concern issues of gender. Scott's remarks strike me as very useful, but they only take us so far. I will discuss this issue at greater length in the next section.

30 Denise Riley, *"Am I That Name?": Feminism and the Category of "Women" in History* (Minneapolis: University of Minnesota Press, 1988), 5.

31 Riley, *"Am I That Name?"*, 114.

32 Derrida offers a detailed articulation of the relationship between history, truth, and woman in *Spurs: Nietzsche's Styles/Éperons: les styles de Nietzsche*, tr. Barbara Harlow (Chicago: Aniversity of Chicago Press, 1978). Most significantly, he argues that:

> Truth has not always been woman. Woman is not always truth. Each has a history, forms a history – history itself perhaps, if the value of history has always appeared as such within the movement of truth – which philosophy cannot decode on its own, since it is itself part of that history. (86–7, translation modified)

33 Derrida, *Spurs/Éperons*, 50–1, translation modified. For a detailed outline of the way in which Derrida traces the figure of woman throughout Nietzsche's

writing, see: Alice A. Jardine, *Gynesis: Configurations of Woman and Modernity* (Ithaca: Cornell University Press, 1985).

34 Derrida discusses this point in detail in *Spurs/Éperons*, 106–7. For a further discussion of the way in which the figure of woman is used to assuage hermeneutical anxieties, see: Jacques Derrida and Christie McDonald, "Choreographies," *Diacritics* 12, 2 (Summer 1982), 69.

35 Ruth Salvaggio, 'Psychoanalysis and Deconstruction and Woman," *Psychoanalysis and ...* , ed. Richard Feldstein and Henry Sussman (New York and London: Routledge, 1990), 151.

36 Rosi Braidotti, *Patterns of Dissonance*, tr. Elizabeth Guild (New York: Routledge, 1991), 98–108.

37 Gayatri Spivak, "Displacement and the Discourse of Woman," *Displacement: Derrida and After*, ed. Mark Krupnick (Bloomington: Indiana University Press, 1987), 169–95. For a more sympathetic engagement on Spivak's part with Derrida's use of the figure of woman, see: "Love Me, Love My Ombre, Elle," *Diacritics* 14, 4 (Winter 1984), 19–36.

38 Drucilla Cornell, *Beyond Accommodation* (New York and London: Routledge, 1991), 85–6.

39 Derrida most clearly tries to spell out this historical predicament in "Choreographies":

> Perhaps woman does not have a history, not so much because of any notion of the "Eternal Feminine" but because all alone she can resist and step back from a certain history ... in which revolution, or at least the "concept" of revolution, is generally inscribed. That history is one of continuous progress, despite the revolutionary break – oriented in the case of the women's movement towards the reappropriation of woman's own essence, her own specific difference, oriented in short towards a notion of woman's "truth." (68)

40 Derrida, "Choreographies," 68.

41 In *The Ends of History*, Crosby tries to address this same problem by arguing that "reading 'women' as an effect rather than recognizing women as a substantive entity which waits to be discovered is radically historical, a radical remedy to history-as-truth" (155). I would agree with her insofar as she emphasizes the importance of the indeterminacy of women. However, I would argue that just because women are considered effects instead of entities does not guarantee that history is anything other than a new found narrative of the truth of effects.

42 A good example of what I am referring to here is Robert Scholes's essay, "Reading Like a Man," *Men in Feminism*. While I have expressed my reservations about his argument in Chapter 1, let me add that Scholes finds feminism ultimately at odds with deconstruction because feminism is based in a class concept (the class of "women"), while deconstruction exists to do away with those very same class concepts. Deconstruction, in Scholes's view, spells the end of women. For another critique of this aspect of Scholes's argument, see Fuss, *Essentially Speaking*.

43 Susan Faludi, *Backlash: The Undeclared War against American Women* (New York: Crown Publishers, 1991), 326.

44 Scott, *Gender and the Politics of History*, 41.

45 Elizabeth Weed, "Introduction: Terms of Reference," *Coming to Terms* (New York and London: Routledge, 1989), xxiv.

46 For detailed and thoughtful analyses of Freud's account of the subject of

women, see: Sarah Kofman, *The Enigma of Woman: Woman in Freud's Writings*, tr. Catherine Porter (Ithaca: Cornell University Press, 1985); Luce Irigaray, *Speculum of the Other Woman*, tr. Gilliam C. Gill. (Ithaca: Cornell University Press, 1985); and *This Sex Which is Not One*, tr. Catherine Porter (Ithaca: Cornell University Press, 1985).

47 Jacques Lacan, "The Agency of the Letter in the Unconscious," *Écrits: A Selection* (New York: Norton, 1977), 152.

48 Jane Gallop, *The Daughter's Seduction* (Ithaca: Cornell University Press, 1982), 11. Gallop also provides an excellent analysis of the same passage that I am discussing.

49 For detailed accounts and perceptive analyses of cases of "mistaken" identity, see: Holly Devor, *Gender Blending: Confronting the Limits of Duality* (Bloomington: Indiana University Press, 1989).

50 For an extended consideration of the relationship between sex/gender and division of labor see: Gayle Rubin, "The Traffic in Women: Notes on the 'Political Economy' of Sex," *Toward an Anthropology of Women*, ed. Rayna Rapp Reiter (New York: Monthly Review Press, 1975); and Luce Irigaray, "Women on the Market," *This Sex Which is Not One*.

51 Jacqueline Rose, "Introduction II," *Feminine Sexuality: Jacques Lacan and the école freudienne*, ed. Juliet Mitchell and Jacqueline Rose (New York: Norton, 1985), 42.

52 Scott, *Gender and the Politics of History*, 50. See also especially 28–50.

53 Teresa de Lauretis, *Technologies of Gender* (Bloomington: Indiana University Press, 1987), 4. Further references to this text will be cited parenthetically by page number.

54 This is not to be understood as the same thing as Derridean deconstruction. De Lauretis believes that Derrida is guilty of "displacing the question of gender onto an ahistorical, purely textual figure of femininity." According to her, "this kind of deconstruction of the subject is effectively a way to recontain women in femininity (Woman) and to reposition female subjectivity *in* the male subject, however that will be defined" (*Technologies of Gender*, 24).

55 Butler, *Gender Trouble*, 7.

56 Butler, "Immitation and Gender Insubordination," *Inside/Out: Lesbian Theories, Gay Theories*, ed. Diana Fuss (New York and London: Routledge, 1991), 28.

57 Paul de Man, *Allegories of Reading* (New Haven: Yale University Press, 1979), 249.

58 Suzanne J. Kessler, "The Medical Construction of Gender: Case Management of Intersexed Infants," *Signs* 16, 1, (1990). Further references to this text will be cited parenthetically by page number. I would like to thank Elizabeth Kuhlmann for calling my attention to Kessler's essay. A more well-known case is that of Herculine Barbin, now famous thanks to Foucault's presentation of it in *Herculine Barbin: Being the Recently Discovered Memoirs of a Nineteenth-Century Hermaphrodite*, tr. Richard McDougall (New York: Pantheon Books, 1980). See also: Anne Fausto-Sterling, *Myths of Gender: Biological Theories about Women and Men* (New York: Basic Books, 1985).

59 It is also worth noting Kessler's point that "after the infant's gender has been assigned, parents generally latch onto the assignment as the solution to the problem" (21). Just to make sure that family and friends also understand that the problem has been solved, physicians routinely advocate that the mother will allow some of "her women friends" to take a look at the baby's reconstructed genitals" (22). Seeing is believing, apparently.

60 Devor, *Gender Blending*, 11–12. I do not want to leave the impression, however, that gender stereotypes only dog a couple of isolated aspects of medical and biological science. To turn to another kind of example, it seems worth noting that the descriptions of reproductive organs, as well as the relationship between eggs and sperm, noticeably rely on a number of similar gender stereotypes. As Emily Martin thoroughly demonstrates in "The Egg and the Sperm: How Science has Constructed a Romance Based on Stereotypical Male-Female Roles," *Signs* 16, 3, (1991) 485–501, typically both scientific textbooks and journal articles represent sperm as valuable commodities which actively pursue and penetrate eggs. By contrast, eggs are described as passive receptacles which are both inefficiently produced and badly stored. That recent research indicates that this is far from an accurate description of events only further calls attention to the force of gender stereotypes within the medical and biological sciences.

61 Devor, *Gender Blending*, 43.

62 Devor, *Gender Blending*, 50.

63 Elizabeth Grosz, *Jacques Lacan: A Feminist Introduction* (London and New York: Routledge, 1990), 190.

64 Jacques Lacan, "God and the *Jouissance* of The Woman. A Love Letter," *Feminine Sexuality*, 144. Further references to this text will be cited parenthetically by page number.

65 Grosz also makes this claim and argues the case at some length in *Jacques Lacan: A Feminist Introduction*.

66 Irigaray, "Così Fan Tutti," *This Sex Which is Not One*, 90–1. In suggesting that Lacan would have more to learn from Saint Theresa's own writings, Irigaray seems to be stressing the value of women's own experience as recalled in autobiographical writings. This move is not without its own problems, as I will hope to make clear in the last section of this chapter.

67 See Irigaray, "Così Fan Tutti," *This Sex Which is Not One*, 96–7.

68 Derrida, "Le Facteur de la vérité," *The Post Card*, tr. Alan Bass (Chicago: University of Chicago Press, 1987), 441–2. For an excellent discussion of Derrida's engagement with Lacanian psychoanalysis, see: Cornell, *Beyond Accommodation*; and Barbara Johnson, *The Critical Difference* (Baltimore and London: Johns Hopkins University Press, 1980).

69 Monique Wittig, "The Mark of Gender," *The Poetics of Gender*, ed. Nancy K. Miller (New York: Columbia University Press, 1986), 64; "The Category of Sex," *Feminist Issues* 2, 2 (Spring 1982), 66.

70 Wittig, "The Mark of Gender," 67.

71 Butler, *Gender Trouble*, 20.

72 Derrida discusses this point, drawing a distinction between Hegel's and Heidegger's notion of Being. On the one hand, the Hegelian movement of the speculative dialectic neutralizes Being in order to ensure phallocentric mastery. On the other hand, Heidegger's *Dasein* is neutral (as opposed to neutralizing) in that it neither carries the marks of binary sexual opposition nor denies sexual difference. See: "Choreographies," 72, 74, and *"Différence sexuelle, différence ontologique (Geschlect I),"* *Heidegger et la question: de l'esprit et autres essais* (Paris: Flammarion, 1990).

73 Cornell, *Beyond Accommodation*, 182.

74 Cornell, *Beyond Accommodation*, 110.

75 Marjorie Garber provides an excellent analysis of transsexual and tranvestite gender constructions in "Spare Parts: The Surgical Construction of Gender,"

Vested Interests: Cross-Dressing and Cultural Anxiety (New York and London: Routledge, 1992). It is worth noting that Garber concludes:

> The transsexual body is not an absolute insignia of anything. Yet it makes the referent ("man" or "woman") seem knowable. Paradoxically it is to transsexuals and transvestites that we need to look if we want to understand what gender categories mean. For transsexuals and transvestites are *more* concerned with maleness and femaleness than persons who are neither transvestite nor transsexual. (110)

76 Devor, *Gender Blending*, viii.

77 Devor, *Gender Blending*, 154.

78 Jacques Derrida with Geoff Bennington, "On Colleges and Philosophy," *Postmodernism: ICA Documents*, ed. Lisa Appignanesi (London: Free Association Books, 1989), 227.

79 Derrida, "Restitutions," *The Truth in Painting*, 268.

80 Derrida, "Restitutions," *The Truth in Painting*, 306.

81 To demonstrate his point, Derrida even plays around with the symbolic significance of the shoes and goes on to ask: "could it be that, like a glove turned inside out, the shoe sometimes has the convex 'form' of the foot (penis) and sometimes the concave form enveloping the foot (vagina)?" ("Restitutions," *The Truth in Painting*, 267).

82 Derrida, "Choreographies," 76.

83 Irigaray, "Così Fan Tutti," *This Sex Which is Not One*, 95. Hélène Cixous also argues that one cannot talk about *a* female sexuality, any more than one can speak of a general or typical woman. Instead, she appeals to bisexuality as a notion that articulates a multiplicity of possible sites for desire and pleasure. According to Cixous, bisexuality "doesn't annul differences but stirs them up, pursues them, increases their number" ("Laugh of the Medusa," tr. Keith Cohen and Paula Cohen, *New French Feminisms*, ed. Elaine Marks and Isabelle de Courtivron (New York: Schocken Books, 1981), 254).

Cixous's use of the term "bisexuality" has led some feminists to conclude that she is doing nothing more than returning us to the binary oppositions of phallogocentric sexual difference, of male and female. That is certainly what Julia Kristeva maintains when she argues that bisexuality, no matter what qualifications accompany the term, always privileges "the totality of one of the sexes" and thus effaces difference ("Women's Time," *The Kristeva Reader*, ed. Toril Moi (New York: Columbia University Press, 1986), 209).

I would like to take both sides here. Kristeva correctly identifies both a problem with the use of the term "bisexuality" and the inevitable reduction that follows in Cixous's argument. However, Cixous is actually trying to increase rather than efface the possibility for sexual multiplicity. I want to hold on to this possibility of multiplicity and leave behind the term "bisexuality," which all too easily leads back to the reinscription of binary sexual difference.

84 For examples of this type of critique, see: Rosi Braidotti, *Patterns of Dissonance*; Margaret Whitford, *Luce Irigaray: Philosophy in the Feminine* (London and New York: Routledge, 1991); Nancy K. Miller, *Getting Personal: Feminist Occasions and Other Autobiographical Acts* (New York and London: Routledge, 1991). Miller reads Derrida's reference to the multiplication of sexual difference as somehow a "degendered dream" (78). She then goes on to argue that it is "the exclusive emphasis in deconstructive and feminist rhetorics on a radically decontextualized sexual difference that has papered over – with extremely serious consequences – both the institutional and political differ-

ences between men and women and the equally powerful social and cultural differences between women" (80). I hope to show in the chapters that follow that I think Miller is wrong on this count. I will argue that feminism and deconstruction do not "decontextualize" sexual difference but instead carefully consider the political roles institutions play. I will even go so far as to suggest that feminism and deconstruction together give rise to an ethical activism, addressing the very questions that concern Miller most.

85 Cornell, *Beyond Accommodation*, 19.

86 Cornell, *Beyond Accommodation*, 169.

87 Fredric Jameson, *The Political Unconscious* (Ithaca: Cornell University Press, 1981). See especially pp. 288ff, where Jameson clearly associates "utopian impulse" with "universal value" in his discussion of mass cultural texts.

88 For a feminist analysis of utopian literature, see Frances Bartkowski, *Feminist Utopias* (Lincoln, NB and London: University of Nebraska Press, 1989).

89 On this count, Cornell goes so far as to suggest that "woman 'is' only in language, which means that her 'reality' can never be separated from the metaphors and fictions in which she is presented" (*Beyond Accommodation*, 18).

90 Lacan, "God and the *Jouissance* of The Woman," *Feminine Sexuality*, 140.

91 Trinha T. Minh-ha, *Woman, Native, Other: Writing Postcoloniality and Feminism* (Bloomington: Indiana University Press, 1989), 100 (emphasis added).

92 Trinh, *Woman, Native, Other*, 103. For Trinh this process includes "a challenge to the notion of (sexual) identity as commonly defined in the West" (103).

93 See: Derrida, *Spurs*; "The Law of Genre"/"*La Loi du genre*," *Glyph* 7 (1980); "Living On/Border Lines," tr. James Hulbert, *Deconstruction and Criticism*, Harold Bloom et al. (New York: Seabury Press, 1979); and "The Double Session," *Dissemination*, tr. Barbara Johnson (Chicago: University of Chicago Press, 1981). If Derrida's attention to invagination and the hymen denaturalizes the body, it also, as Cornell argues in *Beyond Accommodation*, "resexualizes the supposedly neutral language of philosophy by using words which carry associations with the feminine body" (93).

94 Derrida, "The Double Session," *Dissemination*, 229, 241.

95 Derrida, "The Double Session," *Dissemination*, 265.

96 As Derrida demonstrates in "The Law of Genre," the figural work of invagination means that genres/genders are never pure but always mixed: "The law of the law of genre is precisely a principle of contamination, a law of impurity" (206). In her article "Feminism and Deconstruction: 'A Union forever Deferred,'" *Enclitic* 4, 2 (1980), Frances Bartkowski also examines the implications of Derrida's rhetoric of the body.

97 Irigaray, "This Sex Which is Not One," *This Sex Which is Not One*, 24.

98 Irigaray, "When Our Lips Speak Together," *This Sex Which is Not One*, 210.

99 See, for instance: Cornell, *Beyond Accommodation* and Fuss, *Essentially Speaking*.

100 See: Cixous and Clément, *The Newly Born Woman* and "The Laugh of the Medusa," *New French Feminisms*. Derrida makes a similar point in *Spurs*, when he remarks that "*Elle (s')écrit*" (56). The displacement of the subject and object in this neologistic verb is closer to the Greek middle voice and expresses the self-reflexive relationship between woman, writing, and the body. Spivak, however, cautions against making woman the name of writing. She urges us instead to "divide the name of woman so that we see ourselves as naming, not merely named" ("Feminism and Deconstruction, Again: Nego-

tiating with Unacknowledged Masculinism," *Between Feminism and Psycho-analysis*, ed. Teresa Brennan (London and New York: Routledge, 1989), 220.

101 Braidotti, *Patterns of Dissonance*, 123, 145. Other feminists have raised similar objections. Notably, de Lauretis argues that "if Nietzsche and Derrida can occupy and speak from the position of woman, it is because that position is vacant and, what is more, cannot be claimed by women" (*Technologies of Gender*, 32). Ruth Salvaggio finds Derrida to be engaged in a contest of "onemandownsmanship" with Lacan because "in a game where the object is to subvert mastery, everyone wants to be the woman" ("Psychoanalysis and Deconstruction and Woman," *Psychoanalysis and . . .* , 157).

102 Whitford, *Luce Irigaray: Philosophy in the Feminine*, 30, 132.

103 Spivak, "Displacement and the Discourse of Woman," *Displacement*, 188–90.

104 Johnson, "Introduction," *A World of Difference*, (Baltimore and London: Johns Hopkins University Press, 1987), 2–3.

105 This is in marked contrast to Scholes's attempt in "Reading Like a Man" to account for the incommensurability of deconstruction and feminism. Scholes's argument rests on a straightforward appeal to experience: "we are subjects constructed by our experience and truly carry traces of that experience in our minds and on our bodies" (218). This has lead him to claim that "one of the large issues at stake in the conjunction of feminism and deconstruction is precisely the question of what the experience of being a woman has to do with one's ability to read as a woman" (211). "Experience" may be a more problematical reference point than Scholes admits.

   Teresa de Lauretis has also interrogated the place experience holds in feminism. She concludes that feminism should not think of subjects construct-ing experience but of experience constructing subjectivity (*Alice Doesn't* (Bloomington: Indiana University Press, 1984), 159).

106 Paul de Man, "Autobiography as De-Facement," *The Rhetoric of Romanti-cism*, (New York: Columbia University Press, 1984), 70.

107 De Man, "Autobiography as De-Facement," 75–6.

108 Joan Scott, "Experience," *Feminists Theorize the Political*, ed. Judith Butler and Joan W. Scott (New York and London: Routledge, 1992), 30. Scott rightfully recognizes that there is nothing unmediated about experience. As she puts it, "experience is at once always already an interpretation *and* is in need of an interpretation" (37).

109 Present experience always escapes by becoming past event which, being under the rule of prosopopeia, is as much a product of that figure as the figure is a product of the referential event. See also Adorno, "After Ausch-witz," *Negative Dialectics*, tr. E. B. Ashton (New York: Continuum, 1973). For an extended meditation on the relationship between autobiography and memory in the context of de Man's work, see Derrida's *Memoires for Paul de Man*, tr. Cecile Lindsay, Jonathan Culler, and Eduardo Cadava, (New York: Columbia University Press, 1986).

110 Derrida poses the question, "What is experience?" on the next to last page of *Memoires of Paul de Man*, and significantly, he does not answer his own question (147). Derrida also offers a relevant discussion of experience in the opening section of *Of Grammatology*, tr. Gayatri Chakravorty Spivak (Baltimore and London: Johns Hopkins University Press, 1976), especially 60–2.

3   TOWARDS A GROUNDLESS SOLIDARITY

1 Barbara Johnson makes a similar point when she argues that "the profound intervention of feminism has indeed been not simply to enact a radical politics but to redefine the very nature of what is deemed political – to take politics down to what is *not* nearest to hand, and to bring it into the daily historical texture of the relations between the sexes" ("Is Writerliness Conservative?", *A World of Difference*, (Baltimore and London: Johns Hopkins University Press, 1987), 31).

2 It is important to note that I am not arguing, as would Diana Fuss, that politics is feminism's essence (*Essentially Speaking* (New York and London: Routledge, 1989), 37). Such an argument must necessarily assume that there is an essence to politics. However, the political is not an *a priori* condition. Fuss thinks that politics is the one term that feminism won't displace, but it seems to me that the force of feminism has been precisely its ability to displace and redefine what might count as politics. Even Fuss herself admits in a subsequent chapter that "we do not really know what politics is. . . . This uncertainty is embedded in the very noun 'politics,' which, unlike 'identity,' is irreducibly cast in the *plural*. That politics linguistically connote difference, in the way identity does not, immeasurably frustrates our attempts to locate and to anatomize the identity of politics" (105). What Fuss does not mention is that, while her observation holds true for English, it does not apply to a number of other languages in which political theory has been written.

3 See especially: John Rawls, *A Theory of Justice* (Cambridge, MA: Harvard University Press, 1971) and his own pluralist revision in *Political Liberalism* (New York: Columbia University Press, 1993); G. E. Moore, *Principia Ethica* (Cambridge: Cambridge University Press, 1959).

4 Jacques Derrida, "Deconstruction in America," *Critical Exchange* 17 (Winter 1985), 16.

5 Judith Butler, "Contingent Foundations: Feminism and the 'Question of Postmodernism,'" *Feminists Theorize the Political*, ed. Judith Butler and Joan W. Scott (New York and London: Routledge, 1992), 13.

6 Wendy Brown, "Feminist Hesitation, Postmodern Exposures," *differences* 3, 1 (Spring 1991), 71.

7 Nicole Ward Jouve, *White Woman Speaks with Forked Tongue* (London and New York: Routledge, 1991), 7. Significantly, some of Jouve's conclusions are reached by mistakenly opposing deconstruction to construction.

8 Margaret Whitford, *Luce Irigaray: Philosophy in the Feminine* (London and New York: Routledge, 1991), 123.

9 Or to return to Brown's argument: "feminist attachment to the subject is more critically bound to retaining women's experiences, feelings, and voices as sources and certifications of postfoundational political truth" ("Feminist Hesitations," 71).

10 In "Feminist Hesitations," Brown argues that feminism's fear of deconstructing the subject ultimately resides in its unwillingness to give up the "ground of specifically moral claims against domination" (75). Feminism, she contends, must get used to negotiating in the "domain of the sheerly political" (75). In short, "postmodernity unsettles feminism because it deprives us of the *moral* force that the subject, truth, and normativity coproduce in modernity" (78). For Brown, postmodern politics win out over modernist ethics. But I would argue that Brown's argument rests on a too neat separation of the political and the ethical. In the next chapter, I want to suggest that it is possible to

have an ethics without a subject, an ethics which is not reducible to moral philosophy.

11 Judith Butler provides an excellent discussion of this point in *Gender Trouble* (New York and London: Routledge, 1990).

12 Pratibha Parmar, "Black Feminism: The Politics of Articulation," *Identity: Community, Culture, and Difference*, ed. Jonathan Rutherford (London: Lawrence & Wishart, 1990), 107.

13 Within this same framework, feminist identity politics have frequently only been able to see one category of difference beyond "woman," making it possible to speak as a lesbian woman or a black woman but not as both.

14 Trinh Minh-ha, *Woman, Native, Other: Writing Postcoloniality and Feminism* (Bloomington: Indiana University Press, 1989), 104. Diana Fuss offers a good, basic explanation of the way identity functions in *Essentially Speaking*. While her emphasis on the role the unconscious plays in identity formation – an emphasis which echoes Jane Gallop's argument in *The Daughter's Seduction* (Ithaca: Cornell University Press, 1982) – is significant, Fuss's paradoxical claims like "all representations of identity [are] simultaneously possible and impossible" (102) are less useful.

15 Stuart Hall, "Cultural Identity and Diaspora," *Identity*, 222. Both Hall's and Trinh's understanding of the relationship between identity and difference owe a debt to Derrida, which they acknowledge.

16 Butler, "Contingent Foundations: Feminism and the Question of 'Postmodernism,' " *Feminists Theorize the Political*, 4.

17 Butler, *Gender Trouble*, 142.

18 Butler also raises this question in both *Gender Trouble* and "Contingent Foundations." Butler best summarizes her answer in "Contingent Foundations" when she writes that "any effort to give universal or specific content to the category of women, presuming that the guarantee of solidarity is required *in advance*, will necessarily produce factionalization, and that 'identity' as a point of departure can never hold as the solidifying ground of a feminist political movement" (15). My answer does differ insofar as I disagree with her claim in *Gender Trouble* that "the deconstruction of identity is not the deconstruction of politics; rather it establishes as political the very terms through which identity is articulated" (148). I want to make a more radical claim that the deconstruction of identity is also the deconstruction of politics – which does not mean the end of politics.

19 For a discussion of this point, see: "Introduction," Kathy E. Ferguson and Kirstie M. McClure, *differences* 3, 1 (Spring 1991), iii-vi.

20 Bill Readings, "The Deconstruction of Politics," *Reading de Man Reading*, ed. Lindsay Waters and Wlad Godzich (Minneapolis: University of Minnesota Press, 1989), 234. Readings goes on to discuss in some detail the deconstruction of the subject and its impact on political action.

21 Three particularly interesting texts that treat the complexity of rights-based politics are Alison M. Jaggar, "Sexual Difference and Sexual Equality," *Theoretical Perspectives on Sexual Difference* (New Haven: Yale University Press, 1990); Deborah L. Rhode, *Justice and Gender* (Cambridge, MA: Harvard University Press, 1989) and David L. Kirp, Mark G. Yudof, and Marlene Strong Franks, *Gender Justice* (Chicago: University of Chicago Press, 1986). Jaggar argues that "both the sex-blind and sex-responsive interpretations of equality seem to bear unacceptable threats to women's already vulnerable economic and social status" (145). In her extensive survey of the women's rights movement in the U.S., Rhode does not so much propose an alternative

to rights discourse as she argues for the importance of "reimagin[ing] its content and recogniz[ing] its limitations" (3). Kirp, Yudof, and Franks focus on public policy issues related to gender. They believe that gender justice means "enhancing choice for individuals, securing fair process rather than particular outcomes for the community" (12).

22 The way in which the abortion debate in the U.S. has turned around both the right to privacy and the right to equality has been discussed at great length, and it would be impossible to give a comprehensive list here. Some of the more relevant works include: Martha Minow, "Justice Engendered," *Harvard Law review* 101 (November 1987); Frances Olsen, "Unraveling Compromise," *Harvard Law Review* 103 (November 1989); Mary Poovey, "The Abortion Question and the Death of Man," *Feminists Theorize the Political*; Rosalind Pollack Petchesky, *Abortion and Women's Choice: The State, Sexuality, and Reproductive Freedom*, Revised Edition (Boston: Northeastern University Press, 1990).

23 In "The Abortion Question and the Death of Man," *Feminists Theorize the Political*, Poovey observes that "the abortion debate, like so many other rights based arguments, relies on "the language of rights [which] coincides with – indeed, is inextricable from – a set of assumptions about the nature of the individual who is possessed of those rights" (241). I would argue that Poovey's position is a deconstructive one, which is rather surprising in light of her earlier, more suspicious remarks about deconstruction's politics (see "Feminism and Deconstruction," *Feminist Studies* 14, 1 (Spring 1988)).

24 A variation on this same argument would appeal to a certain description of the *citizen* as more of a citizen than other descriptions. But although the terms are slightly altered, the ground upon which the argument rests is still humanistic.

25 Jean-François Lyotard, *The Differend: Phrases in Dispute*, tr. George Van Den Abbeele (Minneapolis: University of Minnesota Press, 1988).

26 Poovey, "The Abortion Question and the Death of Man," *Feminists Theorize the Political*, 240.

27 The case of Bowers v. Hardwick in Georgia (1986) is a good example of what I'm talking about. In this particular instance, the police stumbled in on two men engaged in "homosexual activity" in their own home. The two men were then charged and convicted of committing sodomy, with the understanding that "homosexual activity" was not protected under the Constitutional right to privacy. For an excellent discussion of this case, which also traces the various legal arguments which accumulated as the case wove its way through various appeals courts, see: Drucilla Cornell, "The Violence of the Masquerade: Law Dressed Up As Justice," *The Philosophy of the Limit* (New York and London: Routledge, 1992).

28 Cornell, "Gender, Sex, and Equivalent Rights," *Feminists Theorize the Political*, 293.

29 Cornell, "Gender, Sex, and Equivalent Rights," *Feminists Theorize the Political*, 281–2.

30 Interview with Homi Bhabha, "The Third Space," *Identity*, 216.

31 See Readings, "The Deconstruction of Politics," *Reading de Man Reading*. Readings argues that deconstruction opens the possibility of a rhetorical politics that is a radical displacement of the literal assurances of a political status quo.

32 Johnson takes a similar position when she argues that:

If undecidability is politically suspect, it is so not only to the left, but also to the right. Nothing could be more comforting to the established order than the requirement that everything be assigned a clear meaning or stand. ("Is Writerliness Conservative?," *A World of Difference*, 30–1)

33 Johnson, "Apostrophe, Animation, and Abortion," *A World of Difference*, 193–4.

34 Biddy Martin and Chandra Talpade Mohanty, "Feminist Politics: What's Home Got to Do with It?", *Feminist Studies/Critical Studies*, ed. Teresa de Lauretis (Bloomington: Indiana University Press, 1986), 194.

35 Leslie Wahl Rabine, "A Feminist Politics of Non-Identity," *Feminist Studies* 4, 1 (Spring 1988), 26.

36 Poovey, "Feminism and Deconstruction," *Feminist Studies*, 61. Poovey believes that "as it is typically practiced . . . deconstruction tends to work against . . . historically specific, political practices." She goes on to conclude that "it must be obvious to anyone familiar with deconstruction today that its politics, when they are visible, are most typically conservative" (60). Perhaps it is because this point is so obvious to Poovey that she fails to provide specific examples of deconstruction's conservative politics.

37 Jacques Derrida, "Afterword: Toward an Ethic of Discussion," *Limited Inc* (Evanston, IL: Northwestern University Press, 1988), 148.

38 Derrida, "Afterword: Toward an Ethic of Discussion," *Limited Inc*, 148.

39 Thus, for example, in the Third Critique, the indeterminate judgment of taste is the freest of all judgments for Kant, the judgment which is purely subjective (*Critique of Judgment*, tr. J. H. Bernard (New York: Hafner Press, 1951), § 35, 128–9.

40 Gayatri Chakravorty Spivak, "Revolutions That As Yet Have No Model: Derrida's *Limited Inc*," *Diacritics* 10, 4 (Winter 1980).

41 Spivak, "Revolutions That As Yet Have No Model," *Diacritics*, 49.

42 Jacques Derrida, "The Other Heading: Memories, Responses, and Responsibilities," *The Other Heading: Reflections on Today's Europe*, tr. Pascale-Anne Brault and Michael B. Naas (Bloomington: Indiana University Press, 1992), 78.

43 Here I think Derrida's argument is very close to Lyotard's in *The Postmodern Condition*, tr. Geoff Bennington and Brian Massumi (Minneapolis: University of Minnesota Press, 1984). Lyotard argues that the temporality of "the postmodern condition" is that of the future anterior: events take on significance in that they are understood as that which will have been (81).

44 Significantly, in "Autobiography as De-Facement," Paul de Man asks: "is it possible to remain . . . *within* an undecidable situation?" (*The Rhetoric of Romanticism*, (New York: Columbia University Press, 1984), 70). In what follows, de Man would seem to suggest that the answer is no, with the provision that we must keep re-asking this very question.

INSTITUTIONAL INTERRUPTIONS

1 I use the plural intentionally here, because I also am not trying to suggest that feminism and deconstruction are dependent upon any one institutional structure for support.

2 As I have pointed out earlier, the feminist line on institutions has primarily addressed the problem of exclusion, arguing that the exlusion of women should be redressed by the inclusion of women. This has taken a number of different forms and historically has operated at several levels. Most obviously, mainstream feminism has been on the side of affirmative action campaigns intended

to include women in institutions dominated by men – the academy, government, sports, to name a few. By contrast, separatist versions of feminism have sought to develop altogether alternative insitututions that include women but exclude men. In either instance, feminism has at different points been faced with the task of considering the political implications of the passage from outside to inside insitutional structures: what, in fact, constitutes inclusion? Do quotas effectively work to insure the inclusion of women within traditionally male institutions? In what respects and in what instances are separate institutions for women preferable? How can feminism address the unjust effects of "glass ceilings" which operate on the inside?

3 Jacques Derrida, *"Mochlos, l'œil de l'Université," Du droit à la philosophie* (Paris: Galilée, 1990), 424 (translation my own).

4 Allan Bloom, *The Closing of the American Mind* (New York: Simon & Schuster, 1987).

5 Jacques Derrida, "The Principle of Reason: The University in the Eyes of its Pupils," tr. Catherine Porter and Edward P. Morris, *Diacritics* 13, 3 (Fall 1983), 12.

6 Derrida, "The University in the Eyes of its Pupils," 13.

7 Corporate sponsorship of professorship takes various shapes. There are instances of direct corporate intervention – Coca-Cola's obvious sponsorship of Emory University, for instance – as well as more subtle efforts by family members to make sure that their "private" endowment includes the use of their surname, which is directly associated with a corporation – the Molson Chair, in the McGill University English Department is an example of this practice.

8 The politicization of the NEA and the NEH has been the subject of much debate in the U.S. academy. Problems at the NEA began to surface around the withdrawal of funding for art it labeled "obscene," including an exhibit of the late Robert Mapplethorpe's photography. There is also much information to support the claim that the NEH, especially under the direction of Lynne Cheney (whose husband was coincidently heading the Defense Department at the time), began almost exclusively to support conservative scholarship and scholars. For an attempt at an even-handed presentation of both sides of the NEH situation, see: Stephen Burd, "Chairman [sic] of Humanities Fund has Politicized Grants Process, Critics Charge," *The Chronicle of Higher Education* 38, 33 (April 22, 1992), 1, 32.

9 Thus, in "The University in the Eyes of its Pupils," Derrida will pose the multiply inflected question "today how can we not speak of the university?" in order to address the political and institutional conditions of "the work we do" as academics, as well as to initiate a reflection on "how one should not speak of the university" (3).

10 Derrida takes up the question of the relationship between politics and philosophy at an early point in his work. See his 1968 essay, "The Ends of Man," *Margins of Philosophy*, tr. Alan Bass (Chicago: University of Chicago Press, 1982).

11 As Samuel Weber puts it, a discipline is "an esoteric body of useful knowledge involving systematic theory and resting on general principles" (*Institution and Interpretation* (Minneapolis: University of Minnesota Press, 1987), 25).

12 It's worth noting that the university also administers itself by drawing disciplines together. Departments, as the representatives of the disciplines, tend to be grouped into various categories such as the College of Liberal Arts, the School of Business, and even larger conglomerations such as the College of

Arts and Sciences which, to add to the confusion, might distinguish itself from the School of Music (as if that were not an art) and the School of Engineering (as if that were not a science). While it would be possible to suggest that these larger groupings also represent disciplines, I would argue that they say more about university administrative policies and politics.

13 There are numerous discussions of the disciplinary structure of the university which go into much more detail than I have space for here. David Shumway provides a good overview of some of the work in this area and goes on to offer a useful analysis of the relationship between knowledge, disciplines, and professions. Shumway argues that after the eighteenth century a discipline became a way of thinking, a body of knowledge, which in some way limits discourse. However, disciplinary objects are not entirely fixed in that a discipline "allows the contained formation and reformation of discursive objects." But these objects are not always as natural as they appear, for as Shumway rightly observes "a discipline constitutes its own object[s]," which are not necessarily "founded on the natural things which they seem to represent." (David Shumway, "Discipline and the Genealogy of Knowledge," distributed in *The GRIP Report*, Vol. 9, available from the GRIP Project, Department of English, Carnegie Mellon University, Pittsburgh, PA 15213.)

14 Weber, *Institution and Interpretation*, 30. Weber is discussing Burton Bledstein, *The Culture of Professionalism* (New York: Norton, 1976).

15 Gerald Graff, *Professing Literature: An Institutional History* (Chicago: University of Chicago Press, 1987), 8–9.

16 Wlad Godzich, "Afterword: Religion, the State and Post(al) Modernism," in Samuel Weber, *Institution and Interpretation*, 157. Weber also argues that disciplines should be viewed as phobic resolutions of the anxiety produced by difference and uncertainty (*Institution and Interpretation*, 30).

17 My argument parallels a remark that Weber makes about deconstruction. Weber believes that a deconstructive pragmatics would "work from the 'inside' of the various disciplines, in order to demonstrate concretely, in each case, how the exclusion of limits from the field organizes the practice it makes possible, but in a way that diverges from the self-consciousness of the practitioners, as dictated by the ethos of professional competence" (*Institution and Interpretation*, 32).

18 Jacques Derrida, "Plato's Pharmacy," *Dissemination*, tr. Barbara Johnson (Chicago: University of Chicago Press, 1981).

19 See especially: Derrida, "Plato's Pharmacy," *Dissemination*, 97–8.

20 Derrida, "Plato's Pharmacy," *Dissemination*, 143.

21 Derrida, "Plato's Pharmacy," *Dissemination*, 70.

22 Derrida, "Plato's Pharmacy," *Dissemination*, 167.

23 Derrida, "Plato's Pharmacy," *Dissemination*, 104.

24 In this space, it would obviously be impossible to give an exhaustive list of feminist work on and in philosophy; I have referred to some of these texts throughout the course of my book. While numerous articles and books have appeared, it is significant that in the United States there now exists a journal (appropriately named *Hypatia*) devoted entirely to feminist philosophy.

25 Derrida uses this metaphor in "The Art of Memories," tr. Jonathan Culler, *Memoires for Paul de Man*, Revised Edition (New York: Columbia University Press, 1989). Discussing the "allegorical bent of deconstruction" in de Man's essay on Hegel's *Aesthetics*, Derrida makes the following observation:

> One first locates, in an architechtonics, in the art of the system, the "neglected corners" and the "*defective* cornerstone," that which, from the outset,

threatens the coherence and the internal order of the construction. But it is a cornerstone! It is required by the architecture which it nevertheless, in advance, deconstructs from within. It assures its cohesion while situating in advance, in a way that is both visible and invisible (that is, corner), the site that lends itself to a deconstruction to come. The best spot for efficiently inserting the deconstructive lever is a cornerstone. There may be other analogous places but this one derives its privilege from the fact that it is indispensible to the completeness of the edifice. A condition of erection, holding up the walls of an established edifice, it also can be said to maintain it, to contain it, and to be tantamount to the *generality* of the architechtonic system, "of the entire system" (72).

In giving this partial account of "Paul de Man's 'deconstructive' moves," Derrida is also quick to remind us that the architectural rhetoric should not be mistaken as another version of constructionism. "Rather, it [deconstruction] attacks the systematic (i.e., architechtonic) constructionist account of what is brought together, of assembly" (73).

26 It is worth noting, as does Gayatri Spivak, a certain tendency in the reception of Derrida's work: "the men who take to him take everything from him but his project of re-naming the operation of philosophy with the name of woman" (Gayatri Spivak, "Love Me, Love My Ombre, Elle," *Diacritics* 14, 4 (Winter 1984), 35). Two notable examples of the type of texts to which Spivak refers are: Jonathan Culler, *On Deconstruction* (Ithaca: Cornell University Press, 1982) and Christopher Norris, *Deconstruction and the Interests of Theory* (Norman, OK and London: University of Oklahoma Press, 1989).

27 Jane Gallop, *Reading Lacan* (Ithaca: Cornell University Press, 1985), 18. Gallop is making reference to Elaine Mark's article, "Breaking the Bread: Gestures toward Other Structures, Other Discourses," *Bulletin of the Midwest Modern Language Association*, 13 (Spring 1980).

28 Gallop, *Reading Lacan*, 18. Gallop concludes that the strength of "women's studies" lies in its "peculiar vantage point as neither quite subject nor object, but in a framework which sees that vantage as an advantage and not a shortcoming" (16). Both Gallop and Marks also echo Adrienne Rich's earlier remarks that women's studies does not broaden some "real" curriculum but rather challenges the very disciplinary foundations of the university. (Adrienne Rich, "Women's Studies – Renaissance or Revolution?", *Women's Studies* 3 (1976), 123–4.) Rich argues for the radical potential of women's studies, which she understands as "a pledge of resistance" (122).

29 Derrida, "The University in the Eyes of its Pupils," 17.

30 Likewise, not all versions of feminism will feel equally at home in all women's studies programs. For example, the focus on women's experience in some versions of women's studies would be seriously at odds with feminism that calls the entire notion of experience into question. Significantly, women's studies as a discipline does not proffer either a consensual acceptance or rejection of "experience." That is to say, women's studies can exist as a discipline without a consensual affirmation of female experience.

31 Derrida explores this point in "Women in the Beehive: A Seminar with Jacques Derrida," *Men in Feminism*, ed. Alice Jardine and Paul Smith (New York and London: Methuen, 1987), 191.

32 Gayatri Spivak, with Ellen Rooney, "In a Word. Interview," *differences* 1, 2 (Summer 1989), 144. Let me also say right away that I do not think that the problems with women's studies can be solved by changing the name to "Gender Studies." This name change would only sidestep the problems, not

answer them, and would go a long way in removing any institutional and political threat that "women's studies" might pose. As Joan Scott rightly argues, " 'gender' includes, but does not name woman," and so seems to pose no critical threat (Joan Scott, *Gender and the Politics of History* (New York: Columbia University Press, 1988), 31.

33 For a provocative critique of the pedagogy of women's studies, see: bell hooks, "Toward a Revolutionary Feminist Pedagogy,"*Talking Back, Thinking Feminist, Thinking Black* (Boston: Southend Press, 1989).

34 For more detailed discussions of these questions, see: Margaret L. Anderson, "Changing the Curriculum in Higher Education," *Signs* 12, 2 (1987); *Theories of Women's Studies*, ed. Gloria Bowles and Renate Duelli Klein (London: Routledge & Kegan Paul, 1983); Marilyn J. Boxer, "For and About Women: The Theory and Practice of Women's Studies in the United States," *Signs* 7, 3 (1982); Saskia Grotenhuis, "Women's Studies in the Netherlands: A Successful Institutionalization?", *Feminist Studies* 15, 3 (Fall 1989); Lynette McGrath, "An Ethical Justification of Women's Studies; or What's a Nice Girl Like You Doing in a Place Like This?", *Hypatia* 6, 2 (Summer 1991); Catherine R. Stimpson, "What Matter Mind: A Theory about the Practice of Women's Studies, *Women's Studies* 1 (1973); *Women's Studies and the Curriculum*, ed. Marianne Triplette (Winston-Salem, NC: Salem College, 1983). McGrath probably sums up the problem best when she argues that "in the bureaucratic, finite world of the university, as women's studies gains power it will also contribute to the exclusionary effects of all academic choices and of all efforts to valorize one set of materials, principles, persons, and points of view over another" (142).

35 Christina Crosby, "Dealing with Differences," *Feminists Theorize the Political*, ed. Judith Butler and Joan Scott (New York and London; Routledge, 1992), 131. Crosby finds that the problem U.S. women's studies has in dealing with difference lies in its methodology. According to Crosby, "much of U.S. women's studies is still bound to an empiricist historicism which is the flip side of the idealism scorned and disavowed by feminisms" (136).

36 Crosby, "Dealing with Differences," *Feminists Theorize the Political*, 142.

4   GROUNDLESS SOLIDARITY

1 Immanuel Kant, *Foundations of the Metaphysics of Morals* (1785), tr. Lewis White Beck (Indianapolis: Bobbs-Merrill Company, 1969), 59. To put this point slightly differently, for Kant morality is "the relation of actions to the autonomy of the will" (58).

2 John Rawls, *A Theory of Justice* (Cambridge, MA: Harvard University Press, 1971), 136. For a detailed discussion of Kant by Rawls, see "Kantian Construction in Moral Theory," *Journal of Philosophy* 77 (1980).

3 Paul de Man, *Allegories of Reading* (New Haven: Yale University Press, 1979), 206.

4 J. Hillis Miller, *The Ethics of Reading* (New York: Columbia University Press, 1987). According to Miller, de Man understands "ethical judgment and command" as "a necessary feature of human language" (46). Miller expands his own notion of ethics in *Versions of Pygmalion* (Cambridge, MA: Harvard University Press, 1990).

5 Miller takes this analysis farther, suggesting that "the difference between de Man and Kant (and it is quite a difference) is that Kant can have confidence in the ability of language and reason to formulate an understanding of a

nonlinguistic impossibility, whereas in de Man's case it is a matter of encountering the limits of the possibility of understanding the laws of language with language" (*The Ethics of Reading*, 56).

6 Miller, *The Ethics of Reading*, 49. Miller continues, adding the following clarification: "A statement can be true but not right or right but not true, but not both true and right at once" (49).

    There also is a significant difference between de Man's deconstructive ethics and Derrida's. For de Man, ethics is solely within language, and as such it is one discourse among others. As he puts it, "ethics (or, one should say, ethicity) is a discursive mode among others" (*Allegories of Reading*, 206). For Derrida, however, there is no one place for ethics, linguistic or otherwise, as his interest in Levinas would bear out. In what follows, it will become evident that I follow Derrida rather than de Man on this point.

7 For an excellent discussion of the violence at work when legal restrictions foreclose in advance what counts as rape, see: Judith Butler, "Contingent Foundations: Feminism and the Question of 'Postmodernism,'" *Feminists Theorize the Political*, ed. Judith Butler and Joan Scott (New York and London: Routledge, 1992) 18–19.

8 Jacques Derrida, "The Principle of Reason: The University in the Eyes of its Pupils," tr. Catherine Porter and Edward P. Morris, *Diacritics* 13, 3 (Fall 1983), 9. It would be possible to continue this foundationless argument by saying that if ethics is not grounded in the true, neither is the true grounded in the true. As Wittgenstein suggests, epistemologically there can be no certainty of certainty; if "the true is what is grounded, then the ground is not *true*, nor yet false" (*On Certainty*, ed. G. E. M. Anscombe and G. H. Wright, (New York: Harper Torchbooks, 1972), § 205).

9 Jacques Derrida, "Afterword: Toward an Ethic of Discussion," *Limited Inc*, (Evanston, IL: Northwestern University Press, 1988), 151.

10 Jean-Luc Nancy, "The Inoperative Community," tr. Peter Connor, *The Inoperative Community*, ed. Peter Connor, (Minneapolis: University of Minnesota Press, 1991), 15. Nancy goes so far as to suggest that "community is revealed in the death of others" (15). Drucilla Cornell also explores the deconstructive possibilities of community in *The Philosophy of the Limit* (New York and London: Routledge, 1992), 39–61.

11 Nancy, "Literary Communism," tr. Peter Connor, *The Inoperative Community*, 76.

12 Nancy, "The Inoperative Community," *The Inoperative Community*, 27. Importantly, unlike Derrida, Nancy clarifies the distinction between *Ungrund* and *Abgrund*.

13 Jacques Derrida, " 'Eating Well,' or the Calculation of the Subject: An Interview with Jacques Derrida," tr. Peter Connor and Avital Ronnel, ed. Eduardo Cadava, Peter Connor, and Jean-Luc Nancy (New York and London: Routledge, 1991), 110–11. It should be noted here that Derrida's work on ethics and his remarks about the Other are especially indebted to Levinas. The strong relationship between their work has been traced by: Robert Bernasconi, "The Trace of Levinas in Derrida," *Derrida and Différance*, ed. David Wood and Robert Bernasconi (Chicago: Northwestern University Press, 1988); Drucilla Cornell, *The Philosophy of the Limit*; Simon Critchley, *The Ethics of Deconstruction: Derrida and Levinas* (Oxford: Blackwell, 1992).

    Derrida's work is more distinct from Levinas's, however, than Derrida himself is sometimes willing to acknowledge (see, for instance, his remarks in *Altérités* (Paris: Osiris, 1986). The difference is especially important here, since

Levinas's ethics are blatantly patriarchal. Cornell takes him to task for his "sentimentalization of Woman" (*The Philosophy of the Limit*, 171, 85–90), and Gayatri Spivak is even less patient when she remarks that she finds it difficult to take Levinas's "prurient heterosexist, male-identified ethics seriously" ("French Feminism Revisited: Ethics and Politics," *Feminists Theorize the Political*, 77). Spivak does note Irigaray's attempts to undo "Levinas's sexism by degendering the active-passive division" (77). In this context, Irigaray's extended text on ethics is worth considering: *Éthique de la différence sexuelle* (Paris: Minuit, 1984). Derrida has also attempted, somewhat less successfully, to undo the sexist component of Levinas's ethics in *"En ce moment même dans cet ouvrage me voici," Psyche: inventions de l'autre* (Paris: Galilée, 1987).

14 Margolis, *Pragmatism Without Foundations* (Oxford: Basil Blackwell, 1986), 166.

15 Margolis, *Pragmatism Without Foundations*, 166.

16 Margolis, *Pragmatism Without Foundations*, 182.

17 Christie McDonald, "Changing the Facts of Life: The Case of Baby M," *Substance* 20, 1 (# 64, 1991).

18 McDonald, "Changing the Facts of Life: The Case of Baby M," 40.

19 McDonald, "Changing the Facts of Life: The Case of Baby M," 38.

20 McDonald, "Changing the Facts of Life: The Case of Baby M," 44.

21 Richard Rorty, *Contingency, Irony, and Solidarity* (Cambridge: Cambridge University Press, 1989), xvi.

22 Rorty, *Contingency, Irony, and Solidarity*, 191.

23 Rorty, *Contingency, Irony, and Solidarity*, 195.

24 Rorty, *Contingency, Irony, and Solidarity*, 198.

25 Rorty, *Contingency, Irony, and Solidarity*, 192.

26 Rorty, *Contingency, Irony, and Solidarity*, 198.

27 McDonald, "Changing the Facts of Life: The Case of Baby M," 39.

28 Drucilla Cornell, *Beyond Accommodation* (New York and London: Routledge, 1991).

29 William James, "What Pragmatism Means," *Pragmatism* (1907) (Indianapolis: Hackett Publishing Company, 1981), 26.

30 James, "What Pragmatism Means," *Pragmatism*, 26.

31 Lyotard's *The Differend: Phrases in Dispute* (tr. George Van Den Abbeele (Minneapolis: University of Minnesota Press, 1988)) phrases this question as the issue of "linkage."

32 See *Hume's Moral and Political Philosophy*, ed. Henry D. Aiken (New York: Hafner Press, 1975).

33 See Alasdair MacIntyre, *After Virtue* (Notre Dame: University of Notre Dame Press, 1981); Michael Sandel, *Liberalism and the Limits of Justice* (Cambridge: Cambridge University Press, 1982). MacIntyre also delivers a compelling critique of analytical philosophy's ahistoricism and convincingly argues for the necessity of interdisciplinary work in ethics. His insights into the limitations of emotivism are particularly relevant in this context. I am not, however, as won over by his arguments in favour of Aristotelian virtue.

34 Marilyn Friedman, "The Social Self and the Partiality Debates," *Feminist Ethics*, ed. Claudia Card (Lawrence: University Press of Kansas, 1991), 167.

35 Bernard Williams, *Moral Luck: Philosophical Debates, 1973–1980* (Cambridge: Cambridge University Press, 1981). Williams also uses a decidedly individualistic approach when he tries to come to terms with what he calls "how

things are in moral philosophy" (vii) in *Ethics and the Limits of Philosophy* (Cambridge, MA: Harvard University Press, 1985).

36 Friedman, "The Social Self and the Partiality Debate," *Feminist Ethics*, 167. As Friedman notes, "any resemblance between Williams's story of this hypothetical figure and the life of the painter Gauguin is not a coincidence" (167).

37 Friedman, "The Social Self and the Partiality Debate," *Feminist Ethics*, 167. While Friedman does a good job demonstrating the limitations of work like Williams's, she nonetheless concludes with a not very satisfying alternative: "global moral concern," which she characterizes as "partial but not parochial" (173). Having moved ethics away from patently anti-feminist approaches like Williams's, Friedman leads us to what I would characterize as a problematic ethics of empathy, which has not sufficiently concerned itself with working out the status of the self and the Other.

38 Carol Gilligan, *In A Different Voice* (Cambridge, MA: Harvard University Press, 1982).

39 Alison Jaggar, "Feminist Ethics: Projects, Problems, Prospects," *Feminist Ethics*, 83. Jaggar also cites what I would agree are the two other most prominent examples of ethics of care philosophy: Nel Noddings, *Caring: A Feminine Approach to Ethics and Moral Education* (Berkeley: University of California Press, 1984); Sarah Ruddick, *Maternal Thinking: Toward a Politics of Peace* (Boston: Beacon Press, 1989).

40 For an example of this type of objection, see Michele M. Moody-Adams, "Gender and the Complexity of Moral Voices," *Feminist Ethics*.

41 See Nel Noddings, *Caring: A Feminine Approach to Ethics and Moral Education* and "Ethics from the Standpoint of Women," *Theoretical Perspectives on Sexual Difference*, ed. Deborah L. Rhode (New Haven: Yale University Press, 1990). In the later essay, Noddings argues that "female experience, like male experience, can be reflected upon in a way that produces genuine moral insight and that failure to consider such experience and the virtues associated with it may condemn all of us to a state of moral dullness and incompleteness" (166).

42 Cornell, *Beyond Accommodation*.

43 John Rajchman, *Truth and Eros: Foucault, Lacan, and the Question of Ethics* (New York and London: Routledge, 1991), 143. As the full title of his book implies, Rajchman is not concerned with deconstruction. He concludes:

> The ethical thought of Foucault and Lacan is not meant to preclude, replace or "destroy" all others, but to raise this question. The "question of ethics" is always the question of what can be new in ethics, and so involves a "suspiciousness" about received values, as has always been the case.... Perhaps we need a kind of thinking that is not content to leave the question of who we are to moral theorists, but would introduce it into the heart of an ethical thought whose principle is that injustice is first and without end. (145, 147)

From this perspective, Rajchman does a good job arguing for the importance of Foucault's and Lacan's work on ethics; I only wish that he had expanded his argument to consider deconstruction, in particular Derrida's writings on ethics.

44 Laura Kipnis, "Reading Hustler," *Cultural Studies*, ed. Lawrence Grossberg, Cary Nelson, and Paula Treichler (New York and London: Routledge, 1992), 388–9.

45 Spivak argues for this interpretation of Irigaray's work in "French Feminism

Revisited," *Feminists Theorize the Political*, 75. She is specifically referring to a translated portion of Irigaray's *Éthique*, "Sexual Difference," tr. Seán Hand, *French Feminist Thought: A Reader*, ed. Toril Moi (Oxford: Basil Blackwell, 1987), 124. Stephen Heath goes on to explore the limitations of Irigaray's position in "The Ethics of Sexual Difference," *Discourse* 12, 2 (Spring-Summer 1990). It is also important to note that Irigaray is not the only "French feminist" to express a concern with ethics. Cixous remarks: "for me there is only ethics" ("An Exchange with Hélène Cixous," in Verena Andermatt Conley, *Hélène Cixous: Writing the Feminine* (Lincoln: University of Nebraska Press, 1984), 138). More specifically, Kristeva argues that the question of femininity is above all else ethical, which she stresses is not the same thing as a return to moral philosophy ("Talking About *Polylogue*," tr. Seán Hand, *French Feminist Thought*, 115–17).

46 See Levinas, *Totality and Infinity*, tr. Alphonso Lingis (Pittsburgh: Duquesne University Press, 1969), as well as Critchley's discussion of this problem in *The Ethics of Deconstruction*.

47 Derrida, "Afterword: Toward an Ethic of Discussion," *Limited Inc*, 116. Derrida makes similar statements in other essays. For instance, in "Force of Law: The Mystical Foundation of Authority" (tr. Mary Quaintance, *Cardozo Law Review* 11, 5–6 (July/August 1990), he argues:

> The undecidable remains caught, lodged, at least as ghost – but an essential ghost – in every decision, in every event of decision. Its ghostliness deconstructs from within any assurance of presence, any certitude or any supposed criteriology that would assure us of the justice of a decision, in truth of the very event of a decision. (965)

While in "Eating Well," he offers this position:

> I believe there is no responsibility, no ethico-political decision, that must not pass through the proofs of the incalculable or the undecidable. Otherwise everything would be reducible to calculation, program, causality, and, at best, "hypothetical imperative." (108)

48 Alice Jardine also argues for an "ethics of impossibility." In a move reminiscent of Lyotard and in accord with Derrida and Cornell, she asks us to consider the ethical significance of the *future anterior* ("Notes for an analysis," *Between Feminism and Psychoanalysis*, ed. Teresa Brennan (London and New York: Routledge, 1989), 83–2). Cornell puts this more straightforwardly when she says that "legal interpretation demands that we remember that future" (*The Philosophy of the Limit*, 111).

49 Cornell, *The Philosophy of the Limit*, 169.

50 Derrida, "Force of Law," 947.

51 This is the argument of David L. Kirp, Mark G. Yudof, and Marlene Strong Franks in *Gender Justice* (Chicago: University of Chicago Press, 1986), 126. As they explain it, the Parental Responsibility Act proposed to "limit parents to twenty-five hours a week of paid employment in order to make fathers and mothers equally responsible for child care," while the Neighborhood Playgroup Act covered, as might be suspected, "the recreational needs of children." Both acts are featured in the feminist document, *Woman in the Year 2000*, ed. Maggie Tripp (New York: Abor House, 1974). While overall Kirp, Yudof, and Franks have an important point to make about the value of process versus result-oriented public policy, I would not necessarily agree with their guiding principle that "justice means enhancing choice for individuals" (12).

52 Kirp, Yudof, and Franks, *Gender Justice*, 29.
53 Derrida, "Afterword," *Limited Inc*, 132–3.
54 Cornell, *Beyond Accommodation*, 20. Of course, legal naming has a variety of political effects, some of which are counter to the interests of feminism. Nonetheless, Cornell's emphasis is on the possibility of change, and she contends that without a consideration of deconstruction, feminism has been entrapped by its reduction of justice to calculated proportion and thus has failed to provide a way "to think of justice for women other than through our achieving equal measure to men" (114).
55 Derrida, "Force of Law," 939. This is something of an oversimplification. One could also obey laws because they were thought to be just. However, the point Derrida is trying to make is that laws are not generally obeyed because they represent justice but because of their authority, which may be detached altogether from justice.
56 Derrida, "Eating Well," 118. Earlier in the essay, in the context of a discussion of the subject as the principle of calculation, Derrida argues that "responsibility carries with it, and must do so, an essential excessiveness. It regulates itself neither on the principle of reason nor on any sort of accountancy" (108). Spivak puts the distinction Derrida draws in another perspective when she remarks that "the difference between undecidability and rights talk [is] the *différance* between justice and the Law" ("French Feminism Revisited," *Feminists Theorize the Political*, 65).
57 Derrida makes a rather odd move which I have chosen not to follow. He goes so far as to suggest:

> Deconstruction is justice ... 1. The deconstructibility of law (*droit*), of legality, legitimacy or legitimation (for example) makes deconstruction possible. 2. The undeconstructibility of justice also makes deconstruction possible, indeed is inseparable from it. 3. The result: deconstruction takes place in the interval that separates the undeconstructibility of justice from the deconstructibility of *droit* (authority, legitimacy, and so on). ("Force of Law," 945)

Derrida is, in effect, claiming that justice is the limit of deconstruction, the point at which deconstruction can go no further. But why would it follow that deconstruction must be justice? If justice remains unrepresentable, how could it be represented as deconstruction? And why is Derrida trying to *name* justice? I am not willing to concede that Derrida has answered these questions justly.
58 Cornell has taken Derrida's insistence on the distinction between law and justice, which is also Lyotard's insistence on the unrepresentability of justice, as crucial for feminism's understanding of its politics. As Cornell puts it:

> The possibility of the ethical lies in its impossibility; otherwise, the ethical would be reduced to the actual, to the totality of what is. This paradoxical formulation, in other words, is necessary if we are to respect the otherness of the Other. (*The Philosophy of the Limit*, 83)

According to Cornell, the work of Lyotard and Derrida proves important for ethical feminism precisely because it insists that "justice itself remain as unrepresentable as a full description of principle, either as system or theory" (*Beyond Accommodation*, 109).

Index

abortion 7, 23, 66, 68, 77–9, 82–4, 114, 139 n22
abyss 15, 23–5, 49–50, 62, 71, 99, 108–10, 115, 120
"academic" feminism 2, 91–3, 100
Acker, Kathy 65
anorexia and bulimia 62–3
autobiography 65–6, 134 n66

Baby M 112, 114
backlash 8, 44
Barthes, Roland 42
Bhabha, Homi 81
Bloom, Allan 86, 92
bodies: denaturalizing 61–4; materiality of 58–9; refiguration of 62–4
Braidotti, Rosi 39, 63
Brodzki, Bella and Celeste Schenck 19, 126 n40
Brown, Wendy 71, 138 n10
Butler, Judith 19, 32, 42, 49–50, 55–6, 70, 76–7, 139 n18

calculability 68, 111, 118
castration 16, 24, 54
Cavin, Susan 37
Cixous, Hélène 62–3, 65, 125 n28, 135 n83, 148 n45
Christian, Barbara 37
Clément, Catherine 125 n28
community 69, 109, 113
consensus 4, 25, 64, 67, 109, 144 n30
Cornell, Drucilla 19, 39, 42, 56, 58–9, 80–1, 114, 117–19, 146 n13, 149 n54, 150 n56
cosmetic surgery 62–3
Crenshaw, Kimberlé 34
Crosby, Christina 36–7, 102, 145 n35

crossdisciplines 11–13, 103; and interdisciplinarity 11–12
Culler, Jonathan 5–6, 127 n59

Dasein 5, 134 n72
de Beauvoir, Simone 42
deconstructionism 6–7, 10, 122 n10
definitions 4–6
de Lauretis, Teresa 48–50, 136 n101, 137 n105
de Man, Paul 21–2, 50–1, 65–6, 107, 141 n44, 143 n25, 145 nn5–6
Derrida, Jacques 12, 14, 15–18, 25–6, 29–30, 38–42, 57–8, 61–4, 70, 83–7, 90, 93, 98–101, 108–10, 118–19, 122 n10, 123 n16, 125 n28, 131 n28, 133 n54, 134 n72, 136 n100, 141 n43, 142 n9, 143 n25, 145 n6, 146 n13, 149 n47, 149 n55, 150 nn56–8
Descartes, R. 24
Devor, Holly 52–3, 56–8, 133 n49
difference 22–5, 31, 35, 84–5, 114–15, 118; among women 37, 49; and binary opposition 57, 135 n83; and hierarchy 87; and identity 103; obligation to 115, 117; racial difference 31, 34–5, 37; ratio of importance of differences 118; sex/gender difference 18, 21, 26, 48, 60–4, 117–18, 126 n43
differend 33–5, 79
disciplines 5–6; and location of feminism and deconstruction 9–13, 92–3; and structure of the university 95–104, 142 n12, 143 n17
displacement 24–5, 87, 115
duty 25–6, 85–8, 106

enchaînement 2, 13

ethical activism 88, 105–6, 117, 135 n84; and moral philosophy 117
ethical responsibility 85, 109–11, 113, 119
ethics 105–17, 145 n6, 146 n8, 148 n45; of care 107, 115–17; and epistemology 22, 107; and moral philosophy 87; and politics 69, 84–6, 89, 106, 138 n10; without subjects 106
ethnocentrism 113
experience 30, 58–61, 64–6, 71, 107, 134 n66, 137 n105, 137 n109, 144 n30

Faludi, Susan 44
Felman, Shoshana 124 n26
femininity as natural category 42–3
Freud, Sigmund 42, 45–6, 54
Friedman, Marilyn 115–16, 147 n37
Fuss, Diana 129 n13, 138 n2, 139 n14
future anterior 41, 149 n48

Gallup, Jane 47, 100–1, 139 n14, 144 n28
Gasché, Rudolph 123 n16
gender: as cultural construct 43–4; and distinction from sex 42–58; as performance or drag 49–50
Gilbert, Sandra 36
Gilligan, Carol 116–17
Godzich, Wlad 97
Graff, Gerald 96
Grosz, Elizabeth 53
groundless solidarity 25, 69, 84, 106, 109, 113–15, 120
Gubar, Susan 36

Hall, Stuart 75–6
Hartmann, Geoffrey 21
Hegel, Georg 75, 86, 134 n72
Heidegger, Martin 10, 57–8, 134 n72
"her-story" 35–42; criticisms of 36–8; as methodology 36
Hill, Anita 34–5
Hirsch, E. D. 86
history 9, 35–42; feminist challenge to male subject 36; as revelation of identity 36–7; tenses of 40–2
humanism 55, 113
Hobbes, Thomas 76
hooks, bell 31, 37
Hume, David 115
hymen 61, 136 n93

identity 44, 71, 109; as normative ideal 71–3; and relation to differences 74; and thematic criticism 7
identity politics 8, 68–77, 80–1, 101, 107, 138 n13; and erasure of difference 72–4; and pragmatic aspect for feminism 72; and representation of identity categories 74–5
indeterminacy 28, 31, 45, 59, 105–6
institutions 11, 64, 89–104, 135 n84
intersubjectivity 123 n26
invagination 61, 63–4, 136 n93
Irigaray, Luce 14, 42, 54, 58, 62–3, 118, 146 n13, 148 n45

Jagger, Alison 116
James, William 112, 114–15
Jameson, Fredric 59
Jardine, Alice 4, 7, 122 n5, 149 n8
Johnson, Barbara 19, 21–2, 64, 82, 122 n10, 140 n32
Jordan, June 31
jouissance 53
Jouve, Nicole Ward 18, 71
judgment 25–6, 44, 87–8, 95, 103–4, 105–9, 115–20
justice 15, 22, 25, 31, 35, 87, 106, 108, 114–20, 149 n47, 150 n57; and calculation 111, 118, 149 n54; contractural theory of 106; social justice v. just society 105; as unrepresentable 118–20

Kant, Immanuel 24, 44–5, 75, 83–4, 87–8, 106–7, 145 n5
Kessler, Suzanne 51–3
Kipnis, Laura 117
Kirp, David, Mark Yudof, and Marlene Strong Franks 149 n51
Kristeva, Julia 42, 135 n83, 148 n45
Krupnick, Mark 25

Lacan, Jacques 39, 42, 46–9, 53–5, 61, 136 n101
law 70, 73, 76, 119, 149 n47, 150 n57
legislation 119
lesbianism 55, 60–1, 73, 138 n13
Levinas, Emmanual 118, 145 n5, 146 n13
Locke, John 76
Lorde, Audre 37, 65

Lyotard, Jean-François 33, 79, 85, 107, 122 n2, 141 n43, 150 n58

McDonald, Christie 112–14
MacIntyre, Alisdair 116, 147 n33
Marcus, Jane 18
Margolis, Joseph 111–12
Marks, Elaine 100–1, 144 n28
Martin, Biddy 82–3
Martin, Emily 134 n60
materialism 61
medical science 51–3, 56, 112, 114, 133 n60
Meese, Elizabeth 122 n6
Miller, J. Hillis 21, 107, 145 n5
mise en abyme 25, 27–30, 32, 71
modernism 9, 24, 120; modernist subject and feminist identity politics 70–6
Modleski, Tania 18
Mohanty, Chandra Talpade 82–3
Moore, G. E. 69
moral philosophy 115–17; and ethics of care 116–17; gender bias in 115–16
Moseley-Braun, Carol 35
movements 8–9; and identity politics 8

Nancy, Jean-Luc 109–10
nature 45, 50–3; injustice of appeals to 79–80
negotiation 81–2, 106
Newton, Esther 37
Nietzsche, Friedrich 15
Noddings, Nel 116–17

obligation 24–5, 32, 40, 42, 86–8, 107–11, 113–20
Oedipal interaction 47, 99
oppression 25; and feminist appeals to common oppression 31, 73–4; hierarchy of 73–5
Other: responsibility to 86, 109–11, 114, 150 n58

Paine, Thomas 77
pairings of deconstruction and feminism 1–4, 13–14, 121 n1, 126 n40; and grammatical subordination 13–14; as heterosexual couple 3, 18–19, 126 n42
Parmar, Pratibha 73, 76
pedagogy 21–4, 85, 101
Pelmas, Sarah 35, 130 n14

phallocentrism 16, 53, 55
pharmakon 99–100, 102
philosophy 9–11, 59, 92, 98–100, 103, 123 n16
Plato 58, 76, 99
political action 18, 31, 67; without subjects 71–2, 76
politics 9; and deconstruction as evasion of 18, 67; of institutions 103–4; of knowledge 89–90, 95; and philosophy 94; of undecidability 67, 81–8, 90, 106, 140 n32
Poovey, Mary 19–21, 80, 83, 122 n7, 127 n45, 140 n23
post-feminism 8, 120, 127 n45
pragmatism 106, 111–15
pro-choice movement 114–15
psychoanalysis 45–8, 53–5; and feminist critiques 53

Rabine, Leslie Wahl 83
Rajchman, John 117, 148 n43
rape 66, 108, 119
Rawls, John 69, 76, 106–7
Readings, Bill 77, 81
representation 1–3, 27–30, 35–6, 40, 65–6
responsibility 85–8, 103–4, 109–11, 119–20, 150 n56
Rich, Adrienne 144 n28
rights-based politics 77–81, 140 n23, 150 n56; and conjugal rights 79–80; and equal rights 78; and equivalent rights 80–1; strategic appeal to 80
Riley, Denise 18, 38
Rorty, Richard 112–14
Rose, Jacqueline 17, 48, 53
Rousseau, Jean-Jacques 59, 76, 86

Saint Augustine 59, 117
Saint Teresa 53–4
Salvaggio, Ruth 39, 124 n26, 136 n101
Sandel, Michael 116
Saussure, Ferdinand de 46
Schapiro, Meyer 57–8
Scholes, Robert 22–4, 132 n42, 137 n105
Scott, Joan 19, 20, 36, 44, 48–9, 66, 144 n32
Sellers, Wilfrid 113
sex: and common sense 27; and distinction from gender 42–58; as natural category 42–3

sex/gender difference: and binary logic
    63; and complementarity 57–8; and
    visibility 61; and visual certainty 23,
    47, 52–4, 57–8, 61
Showalter, Elaine 18, 36
Shumway, David 142 n13
sodomy laws 80, 140 n27
solidarity 69, 105, 108–9, 113–15, 120
Spivak, Gayatri Chakravorty 12, 19, 39,
    63–4, 84–5, 87, 101, 118, 136 n100,
    144 n26, 145 n13, 148 n45, 150 n56
Stanton, Domna 124 n24
subjectivity 29, 64, 69–81, 105–6, 110;
    and agency 106; as common interest
    of feminism and deconstruction
    69–70; deconstruction of the subject
    70–1; and identity politics 72–7; and
    the modern state 70; and political
    identity 71, 76–7; some feminists'
    response to deconstruction of the
    subject 71–2, 138 n10
surrogate motherhood 112, 114

technology 112–14
theory 5–6; and distinction from
    practice 6, 8, 12, 59, 93, 102;

feminism and deconstruction as 6–8;
    as tool box 19
Thomas, Clarence 34
Tompkins, Jane 18
Trinh, Minh-ha 8, 61, 75–6, 125 n8

undecidability 32, 105, 141 n44; and
    Derrida's distinction from
    indeterminacy 83–4; and feminist
    response 82–3, 129 n13; and political
    action 32, 67, 82
utopia 58–9

Weber, Samuel 96, 143 n17
Weed, Elizabeth 45
Weigman, Robyn 3
Whitford, Margaret 18, 63
Williams, Bernard 116, 147 n37
Wittgenstein, Ludwig 146 n8
Wittig, Monique 55, 57
Woman 7, 32, 49; as political identity
    72–7; as Truth 17, 38, 54, 131 n32
women's studies 12, 17, 100–3; and
    gender studies 144 n32; and multi-
    disciplinary studies 11; and relation
    to feminism 101, 144 n30